FEDERAL JURISDICTION

ADVISORY BOARD
AMERICAN CASEBOOK SERIES
HORNBOOK SERIES AND BASIC LEGAL TEXTS
NUTSHELL SERIES AND BLACK LETTER SERIES

CURTIS J. BERGER
Professor of Law
Columbia University School of Law

JESSE H. CHOPER
Dean and Professor of Law
University of California, Berkeley

DAVID P. CURRIE
Professor of Law
University of Chicago

DAVID G. EPSTEIN
Professor of Law
University of Texas

ERNEST GELLHORN
Dean and Professor of Law
Case Western Reserve University, Franklin T. Backus Law School

YALE KAMISAR
Professor of Law
University of Michigan

WAYNE R. LaFAVE
Professor of Law
University of Illinois

RICHARD C. MAXWELL
Professor of Law
Duke University

ARTHUR R. MILLER
Professor of Law
Harvard University

JAMES J. WHITE
Professor of Law
University of Michigan

CHARLES ALAN WRIGHT
Professor of Law
University of Texas

FEDERAL JURISDICTION

MARTIN H. REDISH
Professor of Law, Northwestern University

BLACK LETTER SERIES

WEST PUBLISHING CO.
ST. PAUL, MINN.
1985

COPYRIGHT © 1985 By WEST PUBLISHING CO.
50 West Kellogg Boulevard
P.O. Box 64526
St. Paul, Minnesota 55164–0526

All rights reserved
Printed in the United States of America

Library of Congress Cataloging in Publication Data

Redish, Martin H.
    Federal jurisdiction.

    (Black letter series)
    1. Judicial power—United States—Outlines, syllabi, etc. 2. Jurisdiction—United States—Outlines, syllabi, etc. I. Title.
KF8700.Z9R34 1985   347.73′202   85–5395
                            347.30712

ISBN 0–314–89681–3

Redish Fed.Juris. BLS

PUBLISHER'S PREFACE

This "Black Letter" is designed to help a law student recognize and understand the basic principles and issues of law covered in a law school course. It can be used both as a study aid when preparing for classes and as a review of the subject matter when studying for an examination.

Each "Black Letter" is written by experienced law school teachers who are recognized national authorities in the subject covered.

The law is succinctly stated by the author of this "Black Letter." In addition, the exceptions to the rules are stated in the text. The rules and exceptions have purposely been condensed to facilitate quick review and easy recollection. For an in-depth study of a point of law, citations to major student texts are given. In addition, a **Text Correlation Chart** provides a convenient means of relating material contained in the Black Letter to appropriate sections of the casebook the student is using in his or her law school course.

If the subject covered by this text is a code or code-related course, the code section or rule is set forth and discussed wherever applicable.

FORMAT

The format of this "Black Letter" is specially designed for review. (1) **Text.** First, it is recommended that the entire text be studied, and, if deemed necessary, supplemented by the student texts cited. (2) **Black Letter Rules.** Second, in refining your review, study the "Black Letter" rules of law set out in the text in bold italic type. (3) **Capsule Summary.** The Capsule Summary is an abbreviated review of the subject matter which can be used both before and after studying the main body of the text. The headings in the Capsule Summary follow the main text of the "Black Letter." (4) **Table of Contents.** The Table of Contents is in outline form to help you organize the details of the subject and the Summary of Contents gives you a final overview of the materials. (5) **Practice Examination.** The Practice Examination in Appendix B gives you the opportunity of testing yourself with the type of question asked on an exam, and comparing your answer with a model answer.

In addition, a number of other features are included to help you understand the subject matter and prepare for examinations:

Short Questions and Answers: This feature is designed to help you spot and recognize issues in the examination. We feel that issue recognition is a major ingredient in successfully writing an examination.

Perspective: In this feature, the authors discuss their approach to the topic, the approach used in preparing the materials, and any tips on studying for and writing examinations.

Analysis: This feature, at the beginning of each section, is designed to give a quick summary of a particular section to help you recall the subject matter and to help you determine which areas need the most extensive review.

Examples: This feature is designed to illustrate, through fact situations, the law just stated. This, we believe, should help you analytically approach a question on the examination.

Glossary: This feature is designed to refamiliarize you with the meaning of a particular legal term. We believe that the recognition of words of art used in an examination helps you to better analyze the question. In addition, when writing an examination you should know the precise definition of a word of art you intend to use.

We believe that the materials in this "Black Letter" will facilitate your study of a law school course and assure success in writing examinations not only for the course but for the bar examination. We wish you success.

THE PUBLISHER

SUMMARY OF CONTENTS

	Page
CAPSULE SUMMARY OF FEDERAL JURISDICTION	1
PERSPECTIVE	21

PART ONE: THE FEDERAL COURTS AND THE POLITICAL BRANCHES OF THE FEDERAL GOVERNMENT

1. Problems of Judicial Review ... 25
2. Congressional Power to Regulate Federal Jurisdiction ... 37
3. Legislative Courts ... 47

PART TWO: THE STRUCTURE OF FEDERAL COURT JURISDICTION

4. Federal Question Jurisdiction ... 55
5. Diversity Jurisdiction ... 61
6. Pendent and Ancillary Jurisdiction ... 71
7. Jurisdictional Amount ... 81
8. Supreme Court Jurisdiction ... 89

PART THREE: FEDERAL COURTS, FEDERALISM AND THE STATES

		Page
9.	State Courts and Federal Power	105
10.	State Sovereign Immunity and the Eleventh Amendment	115
11.	Abstention	125
12.	The Anti-injunction Statute	133
13.	"Our Federalism"	139
14.	Removal Jurisdiction	149
15.	Civil Rights Removal Jurisdiction	157
16.	Habeas Corpus	163
17.	The Law to Be Applied in the Federal Courts: The Erie Doctrine	171
18.	Federal Common Law	183

APPENDICES

App.		
A.	Answers to Review Questions	193
B.	Model Examination	201
C.	Glossary	207
D.	Text Correlation Chart	215
E.	Table of Cases	217

TABLE OF CONTENTS

	Page
CAPSULE SUMMARY OF FEDERAL JURISDICTION	1
PERSPECTIVE	21

PART ONE: THE FEDERAL COURTS AND THE POLITICAL BRANCHES OF THE FEDERAL GOVERNMENT

1. **Problems of Judicial Review** — 25
   - I. Standing — 26
     - A. Sources and Purposes of the Standing Requirement — 26
     - B. Taxpayer Standing — 27
     - C. The "Interest-Injury" Requirements and the Ideological Plaintiff — 28
     - D. Third-Party Standing — 29
   - II. Ripeness — 30
     - A. Concept and Purpose — 30
     - B. Development of the Legal Doctrine — 30
   - III. Mootness — 31
     - A. Concept and Purpose — 31
     - B. Mootness in Class Actions — 32
   - IV. Political Question Doctrine — 32
     - A. Concept and Purposes — 32
     - B. Categories of Cases to Which the Political Question Doctrine Has Been Applied — 33
     - C. Areas in Which Application of the Political Question Doctrine Has Been Denied — 35

2. Congressional Power to Regulate Federal Jurisdiction 37
  I. Introduction to the Problem 38
     A. Distinction Between Congressional Power to Regulate Lower Federal Court Jurisdiction and Supreme Court Jurisdiction 38
     B. Relevance of "External" Constitutional Limitations 38
  II. Congressional Power to Regulate Lower Federal Court Jurisdiction 39
     A. The Traditional Theory of Broad Congressional Power 39
     B. Alternative Constructions of Article III 40
  III. Congressional Power to Control Supreme Court Appellate Jurisdiction 40
     A. Ex parte McCardle and the Theory of Broad Congressional Power 40
     B. The "Essential Functions" Thesis 41
     C. The Limitation-as-to-Fact Theory 41
  IV. Limitations on Congressional Power Deriving From Other Parts of the Constitution 42
     A. Equal Protection 42
     B. Due Process 42
     C. Separation of Powers 43
  V. Congressional Power to Vest Article III Federal Courts With Non-article III Power 43
     A. Characteristics of an Article III Court 43
     B. The Concept of "Non-article III Powers" 43
  VI. The "Constitutional Fact" Doctrine 44
     A. The Crowell Decision 44
     B. Current Status 44

3. Legislative Courts 47
  I. Legislative Courts: Definition and Characteristics 48
     A. The Concept of Legislative Courts 48
     B. Examples of Legislative Courts 48
  II. Constitutional Limits on the Authority of Legislative Courts 48
     A. Reconciling Legislative Courts With Article III 48
     B. The "Inherently Judicial" Concept 49
     C. "Adjuncts" to Article III Courts 50

PART TWO: THE STRUCTURE OF FEDERAL COURT JURISDICTION

4. Federal Question Jurisdiction 55
  I. Introduction: The Constitutional-Statutory Dichotomy 56
     A. The Nature of the Dichotomy 56
     B. Consequences of the Dichotomy 56
  II. The Constitutional Power 56
     A. The Osborn Decision 56
     B. Protective Jurisdiction 57
  III. The Statutory Scope 58
     A. Introduction 58
     B. The Statutory Structure 58
     C. The Scope of Statutory Federal Question Jurisdiction 58
     D. The "Well-Pleaded Complaint" Rule 59

SUMMARY OF CONTENTS

5. Diversity Jurisdiction 61
    I. Introduction: The Scope and Policies of the Diversity Jurisdiction 62
        A. The Current Statutory Structure 62
        B. The Purposes and Policies of Diversity Jurisdiction 62
        C. The "Complete Diversity" Requirement 62
    II. The Meaning of Citizenship 64
        A. The Concept of Domicile 64
        B. The Determination of Domicile 64
    III. The Citizenship of Corporations and Associations 64
        A. Corporations 64
        B. Associations 66
        C. Trusts 66
    IV. Judge-Made Exceptions to the Diversity Jurisdiction 67
        A. Types of Exceptions Fashioned 67
        B. Rationale of the Exceptions 68
    V. Manufactured Diversity 68
        A. The Statutory Structure and History 68
        B. Application of § 1359 69

6. Pendent and Ancillary Jurisdiction 71
    I. Introduction: The Scope of the Subject 72
        A. Definitional Matters: The Distinctions and Similarities Between Pendent and Ancillary Jurisdiction 72
        B. The Hybrid of "Pendent Party" Jurisdiction 73
        C. The Constitutional Issue 73
        D. The Purposes and Risks of Pendent and Ancillary Jurisdiction 73
    II. Pendent Jurisdiction 73
        A. Pendent Power: Development of the "Same Operative Facts" Test 73
        B. The "Power"—"Discretion" Dichotomy 76
    III. Ancillary Jurisdiction 76
        A. Historical Development 76
        B. The Scope and Limits of Ancillary Jurisdiction 77
    IV. Pendent Party Jurisdiction 78
        A. The Aldinger Case 78
        B. Post-Aldinger Developments and Implications 79

7. Jurisdictional Amount 81
    I. Introduction: Rationale and Scope of the Jurisdictional Amount Requirement 82
        A. The Need for a Jurisdictional Amount Requirement 82
        B. The Applicability of the Jurisdictional Amount Requirement 82
    II. Measurement of the Jurisdictional Amount 83
        A. The "Legal Certainty" Test 83
        B. The "Good Faith" Requirement 84
        C. The "Viewpoint" Issue 85
    III. Aggregation of Claims 86
        A. Traditional Aggregation Rules 86
        B. Aggregation Rules and Class Actions 86
        C. Implications of Snyder and Zahn for the Viewpoint Rules 88

8. Supreme Court Jurisdiction 89
    I. Original Jurisdiction of the Supreme Court 90
        A. Types of Actions Covered 90
        B. Relation Between the Supreme Court's Original and Appellate Jurisdictions 90

II.	Appellate Jurisdiction of the Supreme Court	92
	A. The Appeal-Certiorari Distinction	92
	B. The Final Judgment Rule	94
	C. The "Independent and Adequate State Ground" Doctrine	96
	D. Supreme Court Review of State Court Findings of Fact	100

PART THREE: FEDERAL COURTS, FEDERALISM AND THE STATES

9. State Courts and Federal Power — 105

I.	Introduction	106
	A. Scope of the Inquiry	106
	B. The Role of State Courts in the Federal System	106
II.	State Court Power to Adjudicate Federal Law	107
	A. The Concepts of Concurrent and Exclusive Jurisdiction	107
	B. The Concept of "Implied Exclusivity" and the Claflin Presumption of Concurrent Jurisdiction	107
	C. State Court Adjudication of Issues Falling Within Exclusive Federal Jurisdiction	108
III.	State Court Power to Control Federal Officers	109
	A. The Power to Issue Writs of Habeas Corpus: The Doctrine of Tarble's Case	109
	B. Mandamus and Injunctions	110
	C. Relevance of Federal Officer Removal	110
IV.	State Court Obligation to Adjudicate Federal Claims	111
	A. The Traditional Rule	111
	B. The "Valid Excuse" Doctrine	111
	C. State Court Obligation to Employ Federal Procedures in Adjudicating Federal Claims	112

10. State Sovereign Immunity and the Eleventh Amendment — 115

I.	Introduction: The Concept of Sovereign Immunity and the Passage of the Eleventh Amendment	116
	A. The Concept of Sovereign Immunity	116
	B. The Chisholm Decision and the Passage of the Eleventh Amendment	116
II.	Construction of the Eleventh Amendment	117
	A. The Extension of the Eleventh Amendment to Suits by In-State Residents	117
	B. Alternative Theories of Construction	117
III.	Reconciling the Eleventh Amendment With the Fourteenth Amendment	119
	A. Statement of the Problem	119
	B. The Doctrine of Ex parte Young	120
IV.	Constructive Waiver of the Eleventh Amendment Defense	122
	A. The Traditional Waiver Rule	122
	B. The Concept of Constructive Waiver	122
V.	The Issue of Congressional Intent	123
	A. Congressional Intent and the Constructive Waiver Doctrine	123
	B. Congressional Intent and Section 5 of the Fourteenth Amendment	124

11. Abstention — 125

I.	Introduction	126
	A. The Concept of Judge-Made Abstention	126
	B. The Forms of Judge-Made Abstention	126

II. Pullman Abstention ... 126
A. The Pullman Case ... 126
B. Purposes of Pullman Abstention ... 127
C. Harms of Pullman Abstention ... 127
D. The Confines of Pullman Abstention ... 128
III. Thibodaux Abstention ... 128
A. The Thibodaux Case ... 128
B. The Rationale of Thibodaux Abstention ... 129
C. The Confusion Caused by Mashuda ... 129
IV. Burford Abstention ... 129
A. The Burford Decision ... 129
B. The Rationale of Burford Abstention ... 130
V. Colorado River Abstention ... 130
A. The Colorado River Case ... 130
B. The Colorado River Criteria ... 130
C. The Will Case ... 130
VI. Procedural Aspects of Abstention ... 131
A. The England Doctrine ... 131
B. Certification ... 131

12. The Anti-Injunction Statute ... 133
I. Introduction ... 134
A. The Statutory Provision ... 134
B. History and Policy ... 134
II. The Scope of the Exceptions ... 135
A. The "Relitigation" Exception ... 135
B. The "Expressly Authorized" Exception ... 135
C. The "In Aid of Jurisdiction" Exception ... 136
III. Other Statutory Restrictions on Federal Injunctions Against State Activities ... 137
A. The Tax Injunction Act of 1937 ... 137
B. The Johnson Act of 1934 ... 137
IV. Injunction of Federal Judicial Proceedings ... 138
A. Injunction by a Federal Court ... 138
B. Injunction by a State Court ... 138

13. "Our Federalism" ... 139
I. Introduction ... 140
A. The Concept of "Our Federalism" ... 140
B. Relationship to the Anti-injunction Statute ... 140
C. The Contours of "Our Federalism" ... 140
II. Historical Development ... 141
A. Pre-Younger v. Harris ... 141
B. The Dombrowski Decision ... 141
III. Younger v. Harris and the Modern Development of "Our Federalism" ... 142
A. The Younger Decision ... 142
B. The Rationale of "Our Federalism" ... 142
C. Exceptions to "Our Federalism" ... 143
IV. Timing of Federal Intervention ... 143
A. The Distinction Between Future and Ongoing Prosecutions ... 143
B. Limitations on the Steffel Doctrine ... 144
C. Post-Trial Intervention ... 145

V.	Applicability to Civil Proceedings	145
	A. Background	145
	B. Post-Younger Developments	145
VI.	Applicability to Non-judicial State Action	146
	A. State Executive Actions	146
	B. State Administrative Actions	146

14. Removal Jurisdiction ... 149

I.	Introduction: The Concept and Structure of Removal	150
	A. The Concept of Removal	150
	B. Types of Removal Jurisdiction	150
	C. The "Derivative Jurisdiction" Limitation	151
II.	Removal and Original Jurisdiction Contrasted	151
	A. Federal Question Jurisdiction	151
	B. Diversity	153
	C. Counterclaims	154
III.	Procedure on Removal	155
	A. The Statutory Framework	155
	B. Injunction of State Proceedings	155
	C. Remand	156

15. Civil Rights Removal Jurisdiction ... 157

I.	Introduction: The Structure and History of Civil Rights Removal—An Overview	158
	A. Current Status and Structure	158
	B. Historical Development	158
II.	The Distinction Between State Statutes and State Practice: The Strauder-Rives Doctrine	159
	A. The Strauder Decision	159
	B. The Rives Decision	159
III.	Modern Case Law	160
	A. Background	160
	B. The Rachel Decision	160
	C. The Peacock Decision	161
IV.	The Meaning of "Equal Civil Rights"	162
	A. The History of "Equal Civil Rights" Language	162
	B. Interpretation	162

16. Habeas Corpus ... 163

I.	Introduction: The Origins of the Writ	164
	A. The Concept of Habeas Corpus	164
	B. History of the Writ	164
II.	Current Statutory Structure	164
	A. The Basic Statute	164
	B. Habeas Corpus for State Prisoners	165
	C. Exhaustion of State Remedies	165
	D. Review of State Court Findings	166
	E. Habeas Corpus and the Exclusionary Rule	167
	F. Habeas Corpus for Federal Prisoners	167
III.	Habeas Corpus, Waiver and the Adequate State Ground	168
	A. Applicability of the Adequate State Ground Doctrine to Habeas Corpus	168
	B. The Doctrine of Fay v. Noia and Subsequent Developments	168

SUMMARY OF CONTENTS

17. The Law to Be Applied in the Federal Courts: The Erie Doctrine 171
  I. The History and Meaning of the Rules of Decision Act 172
    A. Historical Development 172
    B. The Erie Decision and the Rules of Decision Act 172
  II. Post-Erie Developments 173
    A. The York Decision and the "Outcome Determination" Test 173
    B. The Byrd Decision and the Balancing of State and Federal Interests 174
  III. The Hanna Decision: Recognition of the Statutory and Constitutional Origins of the Erie Doctrine 176
    A. The Facts of Hanna 176
    B. Hanna's Three-Part Structural Analysis 176
    C. The Constitutional Test 176
    D. The Rules of Decision Act: Development of the Modified Outcome Determination Test 177
    E. The Rules Enabling Act 178
    F. Post-Hanna Developments 179
  IV. Specific Applications of the Erie Doctrine 180
    A. Choice of Law 180
    B. Interpleader 181
  V. Determining the Applicable State Law 181
    A. Statement of the Problem 181
    B. The General Approach to the Issue of Uncertain State Law 181

18. Federal Common Law 183
  I. Introduction: The Sources of and Justification for Federal Common Law 184
    A. Federal Common Law and the Erie Doctrine 184
    B. Federal Common Law and the Rules of Decision Act 184
    C. The Reach of Federal Common Law 184
  II. The Areas of Federal Common Law 185
    A. Description of Categories 185
    B. Federal "Proprietary" Interests 185
    C. International Relations 187
    D. Admiralty 187
    E. Interstate Disputes 189
    F. Interstate Pollution 189
    G. Enforcement of Constitutional Rights 189

APPENDICES

App.
A. Answers to Review Questions 193
B. Model Examination 201
C. Glossary 207
D. Text Correlation Chart 215
E. Table of Cases 217

CAPSULE SUMMARY

PART ONE: RELATIONS BETWEEN THE FEDERAL COURTS AND THE POLITICAL BRANCHES OF THE FEDERAL GOVERNMENT

1. PROBLEMS OF JUDICIAL REVIEW

A. Introduction: The Federal Courts and Judicial Review

1. Long accepted tradition, if not explicit constitutional language, vests in the judiciary the power to review federal governmental action to determine whether it comports with the requirements of the Constitution.

2. However, there exists potential danger to a democratic society if an unrepresentative judiciary may too easily void the decisions of the representative branches of government. For this reason, both constitutional and nonconstitutional principles of judicial restraint have imposed limitations on the power of the judiciary to exercise its review function. This section considers several of the most important of these limitations.

B. Standing

1. The concept of standing requires that a litigant have a direct, concrete interest in the outcome of the case.

2. To a certain extent, the principle derives from the constitutional requirement of case or controversy, but it also is designed to achieve important policy goals. Unless a plaintiff has actually suffered injury, it is generally thought that there will be no assurance that that plaintiff will take a sufficiently strong interest in the case, and therefore he may not litigate the case to the fullest.

C. Ripeness
1. Under the "ripeness" doctrine, federal courts are not permitted to adjudicate cases which are premature, when it is not yet clear that any injury will be incurred by the plaintiff.

2. The doctrine assures that legal issues will not be resolved in the abstract, and prevents the conduct of litigation that may ultimately prove to be unnecessary.

D. Mootness
1. Under the "mootness" doctrine, federal courts may not adjudicate cases which, because of changed circumstances, can no longer have an impact upon the interests of the litigants.

2. In such instances, the court's decision would amount to nothing more than an advisory opinion, prohibited by the constitutional requirement of case or controversy.

3. However, the Supreme Court has recognized a limited exception for cases presenting issues "capable of repetition, yet evading review."

E. Political Question Doctrine
1. This doctrine assumes that certain issues of constitutional law are beyond the authority of the federal judiciary to resolve.

2. It has been suggested that the doctrine is designed to avoid dangerous confrontations between the judiciary and the political branches over issues which the courts are incapable of deciding, either because of a lack of judicially manageable standards, a lack of important information necessary to resolve a dispute, or the presence of a matter of great political sensitivity, such as certain matters of foreign policy.

2. CONGRESSIONAL POWER TO REGULATE FEDERAL JURISDICTION

A. Lower Federal Court Jurisdiction
1. Under Article III of the Constitution, the judicial power is "vested in one supreme court, and in such inferior courts as the Congress may from time to time ordain and establish." It has been traditionally assumed that since Congress did not have to create lower federal courts in the first place,

it may abolish them completely, and it can therefore take the lesser step of curbing their jurisdiction.

2. Congress may exercise such power, it is widely thought, because it may choose to employ the state courts as initial interpreters and enforcers of federal law.

3. Some have criticized this traditional logic, and have urged alternative analyses, but for the most part, the traditional view is still accepted.

B. Supreme Court Jurisdiction

1. Unlike the lower federal courts, the Supreme Court's existence is mandated by the Constitution. However, the Court's appellate jurisdiction—by far the most important aspect of its power—is given "with such exceptions, and under such regulations as the Congress shall make." The traditional interpretation of this language is that Congress may remove categories of cases from the Supreme Court's appellate jurisdiction.

2. Some have questioned this conclusion, arguing that Congress may not interfere with the performance of the Supreme Court's "essential functions", though there exists no specific textual basis in the Constitution for this theory.

3. Though there exists some relevant case law interpreting this provision, it is ambiguous. The Supreme Court has never provided a definitive construction. However, the Court has held that while Congress may have the power to revoke the Court's appellate jurisdiction, it may not vest the jurisdiction while asking the Court to act in an unconstitutional manner.

3. LEGISLATIVE COURTS

A. The Concept of the Legislative Court

1. Legislative courts are judicial bodies, established by Congress, whose judges lack the life tenure and salary protections given to judges of Article III federal courts.

2. Hence, judges of these courts may be given limited terms of office or have their salaries reduced.

3. Today, the best known examples of legislative courts are the territorial courts and the Tax Court.

B. Constitutional Limits on the Use of Legislative Courts

1. Congress may not vest the federal judicial power exclusively in legislative courts, lest it easily circumvent the salary and tenure requirements of Article III.

2. The Supreme Court has held that matters that are "inherently judicial"—*i.e.*, suits traditionally adjudicated by the courts—may not be heard by legislative courts.

3. However, Congress may vest in legislative courts the power to adjudicate cases asserting "public" rights, *i.e.*, those rights created by Congress, to be exercised against the federal government.

PART TWO: THE STRUCTURE OF FEDERAL COURT JURISDICTION

4. FEDERAL QUESTION JURISDICTION

A. The Constitutional Power

1. Article III, section 2 of the Constitution extends the federal judicial power to all cases "arising under this Constitution, the Laws of the United States, and treaties made, or which shall be made, under their authority." In the early years of the nation, the Supreme Court construed this provision very broadly, to include any case in which a federal issue might arise.

2. However, the constitutional "arising under" provision does not itself automatically vest power to adjudicate in the federal courts. Rather, it merely marks the outer limit of congressional power to vest jurisdiction in the federal courts. Thus, even if today the Supreme Court were to give the "arising under" provision of the Constitution such a broad construction (an extremely doubtful result), the federal courts could not adjudicate cases falling within this broad authority unless and until Congress chose to vest that jurisdiction, something which to date Congress has not done.

B. The Statutory Power

1. Under 28 U.S.C.A. § 1331, Congress has vested jurisdiction in the federal courts to adjudicate civil actions "arising under the Constitution, laws, or treaties of the United States." This general federal question statute has its origins in legislation first enacted in 1875.

2. Though the language is similar to that of the constitutional provision, the Supreme Court has held that the scope of the statutory provision is considerably narrower than that of its constitutional counterpart.

3. Though various formulations of the standard for determining the presence of federal question jurisdiction have been devised, the generally

accepted test is whether the complaint establishes that the right to relief depends upon the construction or application of the Constitution or laws of the United States. For purposes of the statutory provision, it is not enough that a question of federal law is merely lurking in the background.

C. The Well-Pleaded Complaint Rule

1. The Supreme Court, interpreting the statutory (not the constitutional) "arising under" provision, has held that a case does not arise under federal law unless the issue of federal law appears on the face of the plaintiff's well-pleaded complaint.

2. The plaintiff may not anticipate a federal defense that the defendant will raise in order to establish federal question jurisdiction.

3. Hence, even if the entire case will ultimately turn on an issue of federal law, it will not fall within the federal district court's federal question jurisdiction unless it is the plaintiff's properly-drawn complaint that raises the federal issue.

4. The Supreme Court has held that the use of the declaratory judgment mechanism may not circumvent the well-pleaded complaint principles.

5. DIVERSITY JURISDICTION

A. The Concept and Purpose of Diversity Jurisdiction

1. Article III, section 2 of the Constitution extends the federal judicial power to suits between citizens of different states. The current statute in which Congress vests the diversity jurisdiction in the federal courts is 28 U.S.C.A. § 1332.

2. The diversity grant applies to suits which arise under state law. Thus, although no issue of federal law will likely be present, the generally assumed purpose of the diversity jurisdiction is to avoid possible prejudice to out-of-state citizens that could result from adjudication in state court.

3. Today, many question the validity of the assumption that state courts are likely to be prejudiced against out-of-state citizens, and argue that the diversity jurisdiction is not worth its cost to the federal courts. However, numerous attempts to have the jurisdiction modified or repealed in Congress have failed.

B. The "Complete Diversity" Requirement

1. The Supreme Court early held that the diversity jurisdiction extends only to suits where the diversity of citizenship is "complete", *i.e., all* plaintiffs are citizens of different states from *all* defendants.

2. More recently, the Court made clear that the complete diversity requirement represents merely a construction of the existing diversity statute, rather than of the constitutional provision, so the requirement may be repealed by Congress. The present interpleader statute is an instance in which Congress has abandoned the requirement of complete diversity in favor of merely "minimal" diversity, *i.e.*, at least one plaintiff is a citizen of a different state from at least one defendant. However, the complete diversity requirement continues as an implied term of the general diversity statute.

C. Judge-Made Exceptions
1. The Supreme Court has recognized exceptions to the diversity jurisdiction for state cases involving probate or domestic relations.

2. The historical origins of these exceptions are questionable, and while both areas may be deemed to be of substantial state concern, it is difficult to distinguish them from many other substantive matters which remain within the diversity jurisdiction.

D. Manufactured Diversity
1. 28 U.S.C.A. § 1359 denies jurisdiction in cases in which a party "has been improperly or collusively made or joined to invoke the jurisdiction" of the federal courts.

2. The statute's purpose is to prevent litigants who desire access to what they deem the more advantageous federal forum from creating diversity jurisdiction by assigning claims to out-of-state residents or appointing executors and guardians from out of state, solely for the purpose of creating diversity.

6. PENDENT AND ANCILLARY JURISDICTION

A. Pendent and Ancillary Jurisdiction Contrasted
1. Both pendent and ancillary jurisdiction extend the federal court's jurisdiction to situations in which the statutory jurisdictional requirements are not met.

2. For either form of jurisdiction to apply, the claim must be factually related to a claim that does fall within the federal court's jurisdiction. For pendent jurisdiction the two claims must derive from a common nucleus of operative fact. For ancillary jurisdiction, the two claims must arise from the same transaction or occurrence.

3. The fundamental difference between pendent and ancillary jurisdiction is that pendent is employed when a single plaintiff appends his additional claim onto a claim properly in federal court against a single

defendant, while ancillary applies when either a third party or the defendant appends a claim, not properly in federal court standing alone, onto the plaintiff's properly brought federal action.

4. Even if pendent *power* exists, a federal court must consider whether in its *discretion* pendent jurisdiction should be allowed.

B. The "Pendent Party" Concept
1. "Pendent party" jurisdiction represents a hybrid between pendent and ancillary jurisdiction. It usually applies to cases in which a single plaintiff attempts to join an additional opposing litigant or litigants to a proper federal suit, when there exists no independent basis for jurisdiction over the additional litigants.

2. The Supreme Court has held that this form of jurisdiction may not apply to attempts by a federal civil rights plaintiff to join a municipality under state tort law, primarily because to do so would undermine the congressional decision not to subject municipalities to liability for violations of 42 U.S.C.A. § 1983, a civil rights statute. It is unclear whether pendent party jurisdiction will be allowed in many other situations.

3. Where federal jurisdiction is exclusive, the Supreme Court has indicated that pendent party jurisdiction may be appropriate.

7. JURISDICTIONAL AMOUNT

A. The Concept of Jurisdictional Amount
1. Congress has chosen to impose a minimum jurisdictional amount requirement in certain jurisdictional statutes, in order to reserve the time and resources of the federal courts for cases that are deemed to be of sufficient magnitude and importance.

2. Originally, the jurisdictional amount requirement was inserted in both the general federal question and diversity jurisdictional statutes. However, Congress has repealed the requirement in federal question cases. Currently, 28 U.S.C.A. § 1332, the general diversity jurisdiction statute, requires that the matter in controversy exceed $10,000, exclusive of interests and costs.

B. Measurement of Jurisdictional Amount
1. The Supreme Court has held that for the jurisdictional amount requirement to be met, the claim in excess of the minimum must be made in good faith. Dismissal for failure to meet the minimum is justified only if it appears to a legal certainty that the claim is really for less than the jurisdictional amount.

2. Courts have differed over whether the jurisdictional amount in controversy is to be determined solely by examining the amount the plaintiff stands to gain, or by also considering the amount the defendant may lose. Especially in a case in which only equitable relief is sought, those two figures are not necessarily identical. The majority of decisions consider only the plaintiff's viewpoint, though if the goal of the requirement is to extend federal jurisdiction only to significant cases, it would seem to make no difference whether it is plaintiff or defendant who stands to gain or lose in excess of the minimum.

3. A single plaintiff is allowed to aggregate the amounts of all of his separate claims against a single defendant, whether or not those claims arise out of the same transaction or occurrence.

4. However, claims by or against multiple parties can be aggregated only when the claims would be deemed "joint", rather than "several", according to common law standards. The Supreme Court has held that these rules apply to modern class actions, despite the fact that in 1966 Rule 23 of the Federal Rules of Civil Procedure, governing class actions, was amended to do away with the joint-several distinction. The Court held that the use of these rules to determine matter in controversy represented a construction of the statutory jurisdictional amount requirement, not of Rule 23. As a result of the Court's decision, members of a class may not aggregate their claims to equal $10,000. The Court subsequently held that each member of a class action to which the jurisdictional amount requirement is applicable must meet the minimum; thus, absent class members with claims less than the minimum are not allowed to append their claims onto a named class member whose individual claim does exceed the minimum, unless their rights are deemed "joint".

8. SUPREME COURT JURISDICTION

A. Original Jurisdiction

1. Article III, section 2 of the Constitution extends the Supreme Court's original jurisdiction to "cases affecting ambassadors, other public ministers and consuls, and those in which a state shall be a party. . . ."

2. Though the Court's original jurisdiction extends only to these categories of cases, lower federal courts are also constitutionally permitted to assert jurisdiction over such cases, and the Supreme Court may also assert appellate jurisdiction over them.

B. Appellate Jurisdiction

1. By far the greatest portion of the Court's business concerns cases falling within its appellate jurisdiction, which extends to all the remaining categories of cases included in the federal judicial power, as described in Article III, section 2.

2. The Supreme Court exercises its appellate jurisdiction through one of two statutorily described procedures: appeal or certiorari. Each device applies to certain situations described in the statutes. As a technical matter, the Court's appeal jurisdiction is mandatory, while its certiorari jurisdiction is discretionary. However, as a practical matter, the Court treats its appeal jurisdiction as a matter of its discretion. This is so, even though the Court's dismissal of an appeal, even in a summary manner, is technically a decision on the merits of the case. The same is not true of a denial of certiorari.

C. The Final Judgment Rule

1. Under the applicable statute, the Supreme Court may review only "final judgments" rendered by the state's highest court. The rule is designed to foster interests of efficiency and federalism.

2. However, the Court has recognized a number of judge-made exceptions to the finality rule, and in recent years has construed the concept in a manner that significantly expands the term's meaning.

D. The "Independent and Adequate State Ground" Doctrine

1. The Supreme Court will not review a state court decision, even if a federal issue has been raised, if the state decision is supported by an independent and adequate state law ground.

2. The doctrine is designed in part to avoid the issuance of an advisory opinion by the Supreme Court, since if the decision would have the same result, regardless of the resolution of the federal issue, because of legitimate state law considerations, the Supreme Court's decision of the federal issue would have no impact upon the litigants. The rule is also designed to further the interests of federalism, by avoiding unnecessary Supreme Court interference with the enforcement of valid state laws.

3. However, the Supreme Court retains the authority to decide whether the state law ground is, in fact, adequate.

PART THREE: FEDERAL COURTS, FEDERALISM AND THE STATES

9. STATE COURTS AND FEDERAL POWER

A. State Court Power to Adjudicate Federal Law

1. When Congress enacts a federal statute creating a cause of action, it may vest jurisdiction to enforce that statute exclusively in the federal courts, or it may vest jurisdiction concurrently in the state or federal courts. Though Congress rarely chooses to do so, theoretically it may vest exclusive original jurisdiction in the state courts.

2. If Congress explicitly describes the allocation of jurisdiction in the statute, there is little difficulty in executing that allocation.

3. If—as is common—Congress is silent on the issue of the state courts' authority to interpret and enforce the law, the Supreme Court has established a presumption in favor of concurrent jurisdiction, that can be rebutted only in narrow (though largely undefined) circumstances.

4. While Congress has explicitly rendered federal jurisdiction exclusive in a number of situations, such as patent and copyright jurisdiction, the number of instances of implied exclusive jurisdiction is small. The leading example of such exclusivity are suits under the federal antitrust laws.

B. State Court Power to Control Federal Officers

1. The Supreme Court has held that state courts may not issue writs of habeas corpus or mandamus to federal officers. While the Supreme Court has never definitively resolved the issue, most lower courts to consider the matter have extended this principle to bar state court injunctions against federal officers. The legal basis for this conclusion is unclear, and it has been criticized by those who point to the apparent understanding of the Constitution's framers that state courts were the equal of the federal courts. Nevertheless, the rule remains good law.

2. The rule does not extend, however, to suits for damages or criminal prosecutions of federal officers, who generally have the option of removing such suits to federal court under the federal officer removal statute.

3. It is unclear whether the ban on state court relief against federal officers would stand if Congress has prohibited the federal courts from issuing such relief. In precluding state court habeas corpus, however, the Supreme Court did note the availability of such relief in the federal courts.

C. State Court Obligation to Adjudicate Federal Suits

1. Under the Supremacy Clause, state courts are obligated to enforce federal law, even when it conflicts with state law.

2. The Supreme Court has held that in most instances, state courts may not decline to adjudicate federal claims.

3. In certain instances, the Court has accepted as a "valid excuse" particular grounds for a state court's unwillingness to adjudicate federal suits. These include the limited nature of the state court's jurisdiction, and the applicability of the doctrine of *forum non conveniens*.

4. However, a state court may not refuse to adjudicate a federal claim simply because the claim is federal, or because the state court disagrees with the federal law to be enforced, or because the federal law is inconsistent with state law.

10. STATE SOVEREIGN IMMUNITY AND THE ELEVENTH AMENDMENT

A. The Concept of Common Law Sovereign Immunity

1. The principle of sovereign immunity, precluding suit against the government, derives from the precept, developed in England, that the King can do no wrong.

2. Though the Constitution's framers no where formally endorsed the doctrine, it is clear that they were aware of its existence at common law, and did not intend to undermine it.

3. However, in *Chisholm v. Georgia*, 2 U.S. (2 Dall.) 419 (1793), the Supreme Court interpreted a clause of Article III, section 2, (which describes the federal "judicial power"), as effectively repealing state sovereign immunity and vesting jurisdiction over suits brought by out-of-state residents against states.

4. This was apparently a misreading of the framers' intent, and shortly after the decision the Eleventh Amendment was adopted, in order to overrule *Chisholm*.

B. The Scope of the Eleventh Amendment

1. The Eleventh Amendment provides that "The judicial power of the United States shall not be construed to extend to any suit in law or equity, commenced or prosecuted against one of the United States by citizens of another state, or by citizens or subjects of any foreign state."

2. Though the amendment's language does not bar federal suits against states brought by in-state residents, the Supreme Court has held that the bar extends to such suits as well (though there is a dispute among the current Justices as to whether this decision merely recognized a common law form of sovereign immunity for such suits, or actually intended to extend

the amendment's constitutional bar to them. If it was the former, then Congress could repeal the immunity through legislative action).

C. The Waiver Principle
1. Historically, the sovereign could waive its immunity against suit, and the same principle applies to state sovereign immunity, of both the common law and constitutional varieties.

2. In the rare instance in which the state expressly waives its immunity, no problems result. However, the Supreme Court has on occasion recognized a doctrine of *implied* waiver, under which a state may be held to have waived its immunity indirectly, through its actions. For example, if Congress expressly conditions receipt of a benefit to the state on the state's waiver of its immunity, acceptance of the benefit by the state might be construed as a waiver.

3. The Supreme Court's decisions are often unclear as to whether the waiver concept applies only in cases such as the example described above, or can be applied more broadly, so that a state's ratification of the Constitution could be construed as a waiver of its common law sovereign immunity, to the extent of Congress' power to legislate pursuant to Article I, section 8 of the Constitution.

4. More recently, however, a majority of the Court has expressed doubt about the validity of the implied waiver concept, so it is possible that the doctrine will no longer be applied.

D. Effect of the Fourteenth Amendment
1. Section 5 of the Fourteenth Amendment provides that Congress may enforce the Amendment's protections by means of appropriate legislation.

2. The Supreme Court has held that this provision supercedes the Eleventh Amendment's limits on the federal judicial power, allowing Congress to enact legislation subjecting the states to suit in federal court as a means of enforcing the Fourteenth Amendment.

11. ABSTENTION

A. *Pullman* Abstention
1. In *Railroad Commission of Texas v. Pullman*, 312 U.S. 496 (1941), the Supreme Court established the doctrine that when a federal court is faced with a constitutional challenge to a state law whose meaning is ambiguous, and one of the conceivable constructions would render the law constitutional while another would render it unconstitutional, the court will abstain so that the state courts can be given an opportunity to provide a definitive construction.

2. If the federal court abstains, a litigant may reserve the right to return to federal court for a decision on the constitutional issue, once the state court has construed the state law.

3. The primary justification for *Pullman* abstention is that it may avoid unnecessary federal judicial review of the constitutionality of state law.

4. The doctrine has been criticized, however, because it has often resulted in substantial delays in the resolution of constitutional challenges to state law.

B. *Burford* and *Thibodaux* Abstention

1. In *Louisiana Power & Light Co. v. City of Thibodaux*, 360 U.S. 25 (1959), and *Burford v. Sun Oil Co.*, 319 U.S. 315 (1943), the Supreme Court recognized two forms of seldomly-invoked abstention: in *Burford*, for complex state administrative schemes involving important state functions for which a network of state judicial review is provided, and in *Thibodaux* for some ill-defined category of areas of great state concern, involving the exercise of the state's "sovereign prerogative."

2. Unlike Pullman abstention, these forms of the doctrine are not limited to constitutional challenges. Also unlike *Pullman*, once the federal court abstains, the case does not return to federal court.

C. *Colorado River* Abstention

1. The Supreme Court has recognized the authority of a federal court in certain instances to stay itself in favor of a parallel state proceeding.

2. However, the Court has imposed severe restrictions on the availability of this form of abstention, in light of the interest in allowing a plaintiff access to federal court to enforce federal rights.

12. THE ANTI-INJUNCTION STATUTE

A. The Statutory Structure

1. The Anti-Injunction Statute currently provides that "[a] court of the United States may not grant an injunction to stay proceedings in a State court except as expressly authorized by Act of Congress, or where necessary in aid of its jurisdiction, or to protect or effectuate its judgments."

2. Though the Supreme Court has indicated that the three exceptions are the exclusive means of avoiding the statute's bar, the Court has recognized an additional exception for suits by the United States or one of its agencies.

B. History of the Statute
1. The statute derives from the Judiciary Act of 1789.

2. For most of its history, the statute was framed in absolute terms, although the Court recognized several judge-made exceptions.

3. The present version was adopted in 1948, as part of the general revision of the Judicial Code.

4. The statute is designed primarily to avoid undue federal judicial interference with the operation of the state courts.

13. "OUR FEDERALISM"

A. The Basic Concept
1. The doctrine known as "Our Federalism" is a judge-made principle that severely restricts federal judicial authority to interfere with certain types of state judicial proceedings, in cases in which the bar of the Anti-Injunction statute is inapplicable.

2. The doctrine has generally been applied to limit federal judicial interference in state criminal proceedings for the purpose of protecting federal civil rights (recognized as an "expressly authorized" exception to the Anti-Injunction Statute).

3. It is associated most closely with the Supreme Court's decision in *Younger v. Harris*, 401 U.S. 37 (1971), and its companion cases.

B. The Outer Reaches of the Doctrine
1. The Supreme Court has in most cases included within its bar declaratory, as well as injunctive relief.

2. In addition, the Court has extended its ban of federal interference in state criminal proceedings to include certain state civil proceedings brought by the state to enforce important state policies.

3. The doctrine does not apply to *prospective*, as opposed to ongoing state proceedings. However, the bar will apply, even if the federal action was filed prior to the filing of the state proceeding, if by the time the state proceeding is filed there have been no proceedings of substance on the merits in the federal proceeding.

C. Policies Behind the Doctrine
1. To a great extent, the doctrine is designed to avoid interference in the functioning of the state judicial process, and to avoid insulting state

judiciaries by questioning their competence or good faith as enforcers of federal rights.

2. In addition, to a lesser extent the doctrine is intended to prevent undue federal judicial interference with state legislative and executive policies.

14. REMOVAL JURISDICTION

A. Concept and Structure

1. While normally a plaintiff has the option of choosing the forum (within jurisdictional limits), Congress in certain instances has allowed the defendant in a state court action to choose the federal forum by removing the case to federal court.

2. Removal is allowed only when the case could have been brought originally in federal court.

3. When removal is allowed, then, in most cases both plaintiff and defendant have the option of selecting the federal forum. (In some cases, Congress has denied defendant the option of removal, such as in the Federal Employers' Liability Act).

B. Types of Removal

1. Removal is provided for in both federal question and diversity cases.

2. In addition, Congress has provided for federal officer removal and civil rights removal. The latter category has been interpreted narrowly [see the following section].

15. CIVIL RIGHTS REMOVAL JURISDICTION

A. Statutory Structure

1. The Civil Rights Removal Statute, 28 U.S.C.A. § 1443, provides in part that a civil action or criminal prosecution commenced in state court may be removed to federal court, when the action has been brought against a person "who is denied or cannot enforce in the courts of such state a right under any law providing for the equal civil rights of citizens of the United States. . . ."

2. The present law derives from the Civil Rights Act of 1866. Originally, removal could take place either before or after state trial, but that practice was altered to allow removal only prior to state trial. This creates a potential problem of federalism, because it requires the federal court on removal to predict whether the defendant would be denied his civil

rights in state court. In part for this reason, the statute has received an extremely narrow construction.

B. Judicial Interpretation
1. The Supreme Court has allowed civil rights removal when a state statute establishes a judicial procedure that violates federal civil rights.

2. However, if the same invalid practice results from judicial custom, rather than statute, the Court denies removal.

3. The Court has allowed removal under the statute when the federal civil right asserted by the state court defendant is the right to public accommodations guaranteed by the 1964 Civil Rights Act, because as interpreted the public accommodations provision is violated by the very institution of the state prosecution of protected conduct, rather than only by a conviction.

16. HABEAS CORPUS

A. Statutory Structure
1. The writ of habeas corpus, a means for judicially testing the validity of an individual's confinement under government authority, is provided for in 28 U.S.C.A. § 2241. Under separate statutes, habeas corpus in federal court is made available both to state and federal prisoners.

2. 28 U.S.C.A. § 2254(b), concerning habeas corpus for state prisoners, requires exhaustion of available state remedies prior to federal judicial consideration.

B. Habeas Corpus and the Exclusionary Rule
1. The Supreme Court has held that a state prisoner afforded the opportunity in state court for full and fair consideration of a claim that evidence had been illegally seized and therefore should have been excluded from trial, could not have the issue reviewed by a federal court on habeas corpus.

2. The Court has refused to apply this principle, however, to a claim of racial discrimination in the selection of the grand jury that issued the indictment.

C. The Adequate State Ground Doctrine
1. Traditionally, the Supreme Court applied the adequate state ground doctrine to habeas corpus relief, so that a federal court would not consider a federal challenge on habeas if the petitioner had failed to follow valid state procedures in the course of his exhaustion of his state remedies.

2. In *Fay v. Noia*, 372 U.S. 391 (1963), however, the Court held that the adequate state ground doctrine did not apply to habeas corpus, unless the petitioner had made a conscious choice to by-pass his state judicial remedies.

3. *Noia* was effectively abandoned in *Wainwright v. Sykes*, 433 U.S. 72 (1977), where the Court held that a state defendant's failure to raise a contemporaneous objection to the admission of certain evidence, though not as a result of a deliberate by-pass, precluded habeas review.

17. THE LAW TO BE APPLIED IN THE FEDERAL COURTS: THE *ERIE* DOCTRINE

A. The Rule of *Swift v. Tyson*

1. The Rules of Decision Act, presently codified in 28 U.S.C.A. § 1652, provides: "The laws of the several states, except where the Constitution or treaties of the United States or Acts of Congress otherwise require or provide, shall be regarded as rules of decision in civil actions in the courts of the United States, in cases where they apply." The original version of the statute appeared in section 34 of the Judiciary Act of 1789.

2. In *Swift v. Tyson*, 41 U.S. (16 Pet.) 1 (1842), Justice Story held that while state statutes constituted "rules of decision" which the Act required the federal courts to follow, state judicial decisions were, for the most part, not "laws" but merely *evidence* of what the law was, and therefore need not be observed under the Act. As a result of *Swift*, the federal courts developed a "general federal common law", even though the jurisdictional basis was merely diversity of citizenship.

B. The *Erie* Decision

1. In *Erie Railroad Co. v. Tompkins*, 304 U.S. 64 (1938), the Supreme Court, pointing to historical, social, philosophical and constitutional difficulties, overruled *Swift*.

2. The Court in *Erie* held that a federal court sitting in a case in which there existed no applicable substantive federal statutory or constitutional law must apply relevant state substantive laws.

C. *Post-Erie* Developments

1. The Court held in *Guaranty Trust Co. of New York v. York*, 326 U.S. 99 (1945), that a federal court sitting in diversity must apply relevant state law when failure to do so would produce different results in state and federal court. This test is generally referred to as the "outcome determination" test.

2. The Court seemed to abandon (or at least substantially modify) the "outcome determination" test in *Byrd v. Blue Ridge Rural Electric*

Cooperative, Inc., 356 U.S. 525 (1958), where it appeared to replace it with a test that, for legal issues that were in some sense procedural, balanced the comparative importance of the use of the state rule to achieve substantive state goals with that of the use of the federal standard to the federal system. This balancing of interests approach was widely considered to be too imprecise to provide substantial guidance to future courts attempting to employ it.

3. In *Hanna v. Plumer*, 380 U.S. 460 (1965), the Court implicitly rejected the *Byrd* balancing test, and replaced it with an approach that recognizes three conceivable inquiries under *Erie:* a constitutional test, a standard under the Rules of Decision Act when no other federal statute was applicable, and the test of the federal statute if another statute was applicable (such as the Rules Enabling Act if a Federal Rule of Civil Procedure was relevant).

4. For cases controlled by the Rules of Decision Act (*i.e.* when no other federal statute was applicable), the Court held that state law must be followed when use of a separate federal standard would so affect the outcome of the case that it would influence the plaintiff's choice of forum in a diversity case between state and federal court (one of the important concerns expressed in *Erie* about *Swift* or would lead to inequitable administration of the law).

18. FEDERAL COMMON LAW

A. Federal Common Law and the *Erie* Doctrine

1. While the Supreme Court held in *Erie* that there exists no general federal common law, the Court has long recognized certain narrow areas in which the federal courts are authorized to create their own body of federal common law, superceding relevant state law.

2. It is arguable that federal common law conflicts with the commands of the Rules of Decision Act, which dictates that state law controls in the absence of relevant federal statute, constitutional provision or treaty.

3. Though the Court has never directly considered this question, it has noted that the creation of federal common law is designed to fill "gaps" left in federal statutory schemes, implying that the use of federal common law is indirectly authorized by an act of Congress.

B. The Reach of Federal Common Law

1. The Supreme Court has developed federal common law in the following areas: federal "proprietary" interests; international relations; admiralty; interstate disputes; interstate pollution, and enforcement of constitutional rights.

2. The Court has concluded that federal common law controls all cases, not specifically covered by federal statute, in which the actions of the government have their origin in the Constitution or federal statutes. While this category is potentially very broad, the Court has also indicated that if there exists no strong interest in having a separate federal standard, the federal court should adopt the relevant state law as federal common law. In most such cases in which no federal statutory or constitutional provision is applicable, then, as a practical matter state law will be applied, even though the federal government is a party to the case.

*

PERSPECTIVE

APPROACH TO FEDERAL JURISDICTION

The study of federal jurisdiction is basically the study of the federal courts—their internal structure and operation, their relationship to the other branches of the federal government and their interaction with the judicial and political segments of the state governments. The subject constitutes a unique blend of highly technical and detailed statutory analysis with the study of broad theoretical issues of federalism and separation of powers. It is this combination of very different modes of thought that makes the study of federal jurisdiction so fascinating.

To gain the most from the course, the student should recognize the importance of both approaches, and not emphasize one over the other in analyzing the material. For example, the student must be able simultaneously to comprehend the highly theoretical issues surrounding the controversy over congressional power to regulate the jurisdiction of the federal courts, and the technicalities of removal jurisdiction. Whatever area of the course is being studied, however, the student should always attempt to relate the practical legal doctrines to the policies behind the development of the federal judiciary and its role as part of a dynamic federal system, in which the often competing interests of state and federal governments must be reconciled.

The student will find available a number of resources to aid in understanding the complexities of the subject. One is a book which I authored several years ago, entitled *Federal Jurisdiction: Tensions in the Allocation of Judicial Power* (1980). In addition, there is the excellent book by Professor Charles Alan Wright, *The Law of Federal Courts* (4th ed. 1983). Finally, Professor David Currie has authored *Federal Jurisdiction in a Nutshell* (2d ed. 1981).

APPROACH TO EXAMINATIONS

In deciding how to prepare for an examination in federal jurisdiction, a great deal may depend on whether the test will include short answers, or instead will consist exclusively of essay questions. If the examination contains numerous short answer questions, it is likely that the professor is interested in the student's knowledge and understanding of specific legal doctrines and statutory structure. A student preparing for such an examination should emphasize the details of the various jurisdictional statutes and judge-made principles, and should consider closely the specific elements of each. Obviously, if the examination is open-book, less emphasis will have to be placed on memorization. However, given the limited time generally available during an examination a student should be very hesitant to rely too heavily on access to the book. In any event, it is unlikely that a test emphasizing short answer questions will be open-book.

If the examination is predominately or exclusively of the essay variety, the student should be prepared to deal with some of the many unresolved policy issues in the field. As in most law school exam questions of this variety, it is likely that there is no one set answer, and it is important both to explain why you have reached your conclusion and why you have rejected opposing arguments. But while it is important to include broad policy analysis in such questions, it is also important to demonstrate familiarity with detailed statutes and doctrines that are applicable. Particularly in an essay question, the two modes of analysis are not mutually exclusive.

PART ONE

THE FEDERAL COURTS AND THE POLITICAL BRANCHES OF THE FEDERAL GOVERNMENT

Analysis

1. *Problems of Judicial Review*
2. *Congressional Power to Regulate Federal Jurisdiction*
3. *Legislative Courts*

1

PROBLEMS OF JUDICIAL REVIEW

Analysis

I. Standing
    A. Sources and Purposes of the Standing Requirement
    B. Taxpayer Standing
    C. The "Interest-Injury" Requirements and the Ideological Plaintiff
    D. Third-Party Standing

II. Ripeness
    A. Concept and Purpose
    B. Development of the Legal Doctrine

III. Mootness
    A. Concept and Purpose
    B. Mootness in Class Actions

IV. Political Question Doctrine
    A. Concept and Purposes
    B. Categories of Cases to Which the Political Question Doctrine Has Been Applied
    C. Areas in Which Application of the Political Question Doctrine Has Been Denied

I. STANDING

A. SOURCES AND PURPOSES OF THE STANDING REQUIREMENT

    1. *The Supreme Court has for many years established that a party may not litigate a case in the federal courts unless he has "standing" to bring the suit.*

    2. *Though, as will be seen later, the exact contours of the standing requirement have fluctuated over the years, basically the concept implies the need for a litigant to have some direct, concrete interest in the outcome of the case: i.e., that the conduct of which the plaintiff complains has caused him real injury.*

    3. To an undefined extent, the standing requirement is of a constitutional magnitude, deriving from the "case or controversy" requirement of Article III of the Constitution.

    a. The Constitution prohibits the federal courts from issuing advisory opinions—*i.e.*, decision on matters that are not part of a live controversy, and will have no impact on litigants. If a plaintiff has not been injured, it has been suggested that no live controversy exists.

    b. It is also thought that unless a plaintiff has actually suffered injury, there can be no assurance that he will take a sufficiently strong interest in the case to litigate it to its fullest. If this result occurs, the courts will be deciding important legal issues without the benefit of complete assistance from the parties.

    c. Some commentators have responded, however, that many institutional litigants possessing solely an ideological interest in the case are as likely to provide a vigorous litigation as are many individual litigants.

    4. Though to a certain extent the standing requirement has constitutional stature, the Supreme Court has implied that it is also in part a judicially-created prudential doctrine, that may be overruled by Congress.

Example: Tenants of an apartment complex filed complaints with the Secretary of Housing and Urban Development pursuant to the Civil Rights Act of 1968, claiming that their landlord discriminated against nonwhites and that as a result the tenants lost social and economic benefits. The Supreme Court held they had standing, because they fell within the statutory definition of "person aggrieved." Concurring Justice White stated that he would have difficulty finding a case or controversy absent the direct authorization of the Civil Rights Act of 1968. *Trafficante v. Metropolitan Life Insurance Co.*, 409 U.S. 205 (1972).

B. TAXPAYER STANDING

1. One subset of the standing problem concerns the extent to which taxpayers may sue to challenge the constitutionality of governmental spending programs.

2. The Supreme Court held in *Frothingham v. Mellon,* 262 U.S. 447 (1923), that federal taxpayers lacked standing to challenge the constitutionality of federal expenditures, because of the enormous invitation to litigation such a practice would allow. To have standing, the Court held, a party "must be able to show not only that the statute is invalid but that he has sustained or is immediately in danger of sustaining some direct injury as the result of its enforcement, and not merely that he suffers in some indefinite way in common with people generally."

3. However, in the subsequent decision of *Flast v. Cohen,* 392 U.S. 83 (1968), the Supreme Court held that federal taxpayers had standing if "they can demonstrate the necessary stake as taxpayers in the outcome of the litigation to satisfy Article III requirements." Such a status could be established (a) only in suits challenging statutes enacted pursuant to Congress' power under the taxing and spending clause of Article I, section 8 of the Constitution and (b) only if the taxpayer can establish a "nexus between that status and the precise nature of the constitutional infringement alleged."

   a. The Court purported to distinguish *Frothingham* because the taxpayer there had failed to allege that Congress had breached a specific limitation upon its taxing and spending power.

   b. However, commentators have questioned whether the two decisions really are distinguishable.

   c. Two concurring Justices in *Flast* expressed the view that taxpayer standing should be allowed only in cases challenging laws under the First Amendment's establishment-of-religion clause.

4. In *Valley Forge Christian College v. Americans United for Separation of Church and State Inc.,* 454 U.S. 464 (1982), the Supreme Court held that taxpayer standing was not allowed when the challenge was not to a congressional action, but to a decision by an executive department to transfer a parcel of federal property, and when that property transfer was not an exercise of authority conferred by the taxing and spending clause of Article I, section 8.

5. Since *Frothingham,* however, the Supreme Court has recognized that *local* (as opposed to *federal*) taxpayers have standing to challenge local legislative action.

C. THE "INTEREST-INJURY" REQUIREMENTS AND THE IDEOLOGICAL PLAINTIFF

1. *In non-taxpayer cases, the Supreme Court follows an analogous standard to determine whether litigants have standing: The plaintiff must have suffered an injury in fact and must come within the "zone of interests" protected by the relevant statute. In addition, the plaintiff must establish that obtaining legal redress would actually improve his position.*

Examples: To have standing, prospective tenants attempting to challenge restrictive zoning ordinances have to allege more than that the ordinances had prevented builders from constructing low-income housing. In addition, they must allege facts that demonstrate that but for the restrictive zoning practices, there exists a probability that they would have been able to purchase or lease in the area. *Warth v. Seldin*, 422 U.S. 490 (1975).

Low-income individuals and organizations sue federal officials, alleging that a revenue ruling announcing a policy of extending favorable tax treatment to hospitals not serving indigents improperly encouraged hospitals to deny services to indigents and constituted a misinterpretation of the Internal Revenue Code. Standing is absent, because "it does not follow from the allegation . . . that the denial of access to hospital services in fact results from petitioners' new Ruling, or that a court-ordered return by petitioners to their previous policy would result in these respondents' receiving the hospital services they desire." *Simon v. Eastern Kentucky Welfare Rights Organization*, 426 U.S. 26 (1976).

An arguably inconsistent decision is *Duke Power Co. v. Carolina Environmental Study Group, Inc.*, 438 U.S. 59 (1978). There plaintiffs, organizations and individuals who were located within close proximity to planned nuclear power facilities, sued the power company and others, challenging the constitutionality of the provisions of the Price-Anderson Act, limiting private liability in the event of a nuclear accident. The Supreme Court found that the plaintiffs had standing, noting that operation of the power plants had immediate harmful effects (such as the increase of thermal pollution of the lakes) and caused plaintiffs injury in fact, even though no accident had occurred. The Supreme Court accepted the lower court finding that, but for the protections of the Price-Anderson Act, the power plants would not have been built. However, once the plants had been built, the question still remained whether winning the case would remedy the harms plaintiffs were presently suffering.

2. Because of its "injury-in-fact" prerequisite, the Supreme Court has refused to find standing on the basis of an assertion of a strong interest in the case, absent an allegation of injury in fact. This result effectively excludes so-called "ideological plaintiffs" from having standing, at least solely on the basis of their ideological or social concern. However, the Court has recognized that the "injury-in-fact" requirement may be met by non-economic harm, such as harm to purely aesthetic interests. *Sierra Club v. Morton*, 405 U.S. 727 (1972); *United States v. SCRAP*, 412 U.S. 669 (1973). As a practical matter, ideologically-motivated organizations rarely have difficulty in obtaining a plaintiff who meets the Court's minimal "injury-in-fact" requirement.

D. THIRD-PARTY STANDING

1. *Traditionally, the Supreme Court applies the rule that "one to whom application of a statute is constitutional will not be heard to attack the statute on the ground that impliedly it might also be taken as applying to other persons or other situations in which its application might be unconstitutional."* *United States v. Raines*, 362 U.S. 17 (1960).

a. In other words, generally individuals do not have standing to assert the rights of others.

b. In most applications, this principle does not derive from Article III's "case or controversy" requirement, because individuals attempting to assert the rights of others may have a very real interest in the success of the claim that others' rights have been violated.

Example: A defendant is prosecuted for violating a law that he claims is so broad that it could be applied unconstitutionally to others, even though a more narrow statute could be drafted that would constitutionally penalize the particular defendant. If the defendant is allowed to have the law declared unconstitutional because it could be unconstitutionally applied to others, he will gain a direct benefit.

c. Instead, the traditional third-party standing rule, at least in the context of a constitutional challenge, derives largely from prudential precepts about the judiciary's limited role: Courts in a democratic society should not seek out statutes for constitutional perusal unless and until the statute has been directly applied in an unconstitutional manner.

2. However, the Supreme Court has recognized a limited exception to the traditional rule when the constitutional challenge is premised on the First Amendment right of free expression. This exception is contained in what is known as the "overbreadth" doctrine.

a. The rationale for this exception is that free speech rights are of paramount importance, and that there exists a danger that if a law violative of the First Amendment remains in force individuals may be "chilled" from expressing their views, thereby effectively insulating the law from constitutional challenge.

b. In recent years, the Supreme Court has narrowed this exception to the traditional rule, labelling it "strong medicine." Thus, the Court will not allow one to whom a law may be constitutionally applied challenge the law as overbroad unless the overbreadth is "substantial," meaning that the law must be unconstitutional in the large majority of its applications. *Broadrick v. Oklahoma*, 413 U.S. 601 (1973); *New York v. Ferber*, 458 U.S. 747 (1982).

II. RIPENESS

A. CONCEPT AND PURPOSE

1. *The "ripeness" requirement posits that the federal courts may not adjudicate cases in which it is speculative whether the plaintiff will actually suffer injury, rendering the case premature.*

2. To a certain extent, the requirement flows from Article III's "case or controversy" requirement, because if a dispute has not ripened, no real controversy, with a well-developed factual setting, yet exists.

3. The ripeness requirement thus assists the courts by assuring that legal issues will be resolved in specific factual contexts and prevents litigation that may ultimately prove to be unnecessary because no injury is ever inflicted.

B. DEVELOPMENT OF THE LEGAL DOCTRINE

1. While the Supreme Court has traditionally demonstrated great reluctance to adjudicate cases when harm to the plaintiff is not certain, at other times, especially when the Court perceives the likelihood of undue hardship from delay, the Court has allowed adjudication, even though no harm has yet been inflicted.

Examples: A Union challenges the constitutionality of a federal statute declaring unlawful specified political activities of federal employees. The plaintiffs have not yet violated the act's provisions, and have not been charged under its terms. The Supreme Court held that the case was not ripe, because it was purely speculative whether any harm would result to plaintiffs. *United Public Workers of America v. Mitchell*, 330 U.S. 75 (1947). The problem with the Court's analysis is that presumably the only alternative means to challenge the law would be to risk criminal penalties by actually violating the law.

Teachers bring a constitutional challenge to a provision of a New York statute regulating the employment as teachers of those advocating overthrow of the government by force and violence, though the plaintiffs do not allege that they had engaged in the proscribed conduct or that they had any intention to do so. The Supreme Court decided the case on its merits, without raising the ripeness issue. *Adler v. Board of Education*, 342 U.S. 485 (1952).

A pregnant woman attempted to challenge a statute prohibiting abortions. The Supreme Court found the case ripe for adjudication. *Roe v. Wade*, 410 U.S. 113 (1973).

III. MOOTNESS

A. CONCEPT AND PURPOSE

1. *The mootness doctrine posits that cases which, because of changed circumstances, no longer can have an impact upon the interests of the litigants may not be adjudicated in the federal courts.*

Example: Plaintiff challenges the constitutionality of a state law school's admissions process. He is successful in the trial court and that court grants his request to have him admitted to the entering law school class. By the time the case reaches the United States Supreme Court for review, the plaintiff is approaching completion of his final year in law school. The Supreme Court holds the case to be moot, because its decision will not affect the plaintiff's interests. *DeFunis v. Odegaard*, 416 U.S. 312 (1974).

2. The doctrine is thought to derive from Article III's "case or controversy" requirement, because if the result in the case can have no impact upon the litigants it amounts to an impermissible advisory opinion.

3. Despite the doctrine's assumed constitutional base, the Supreme Court has recognized an exception for cases presenting issues "capable of repetition, yet evading review." *Southern Pacific Terminal Co. v. Interstate Commerce Commission*, 219 U.S. 498 (1911). However, if moot cases are not "cases or controversies" for purposes of Article III, it is questionable whether adjudication of cases falling within this exception is constitutional.

Example: Plaintiff, a pregnant woman, challenges the constitutionality of a state law prohibiting her from getting an abortion. By the time the case reaches the Supreme Court she is no longer pregnant. The Supreme Court agrees to adjudicate the case, because it falls within the exception for cases that will evade review; the limited time period of pregnancy will effectively preclude any similar case from reaching the Supreme Court for review. *Roe v. Wade*, 410 U.S. 113 (1973).

4. The Supreme Court has held that the mootness doctrine does not apply, even though the defendant has refrained from the conduct sought to be stopped by the plaintiff, when "[t]he defendant is free to return to his old ways" and there exists a strong public interest in resolving the legal issue. *United States v. W.T. Grant Co.*, 345 U.S. 629 (1953).

   a. However, this exception will not apply when there is no reasonable expectation that the challenged activity will continue. *County of Los Angeles v. Davis*, 440 U.S. 625 (1979).

B. MOOTNESS IN CLASS ACTIONS

1. The Supreme Court has held that a certified class action in which the representative plaintiff no longer has an interest in the outcome will not be deemed moot when because of the passage of time "no single challenger will remain subject to [the law's] restrictions necessary to see such a lawsuit to its conclusion." *Sosna v. Iowa*, 419 U.S. 393 (1975).

2. While in *Sosna* the class action had been certified before the representative plaintiff's claim was mooted, the Court has held that "[a]lthough one might argue that *Sosna* contains at least an implication that the critical factor for Art. III purposes is the timing of class certification, other cases, applying a 'relation back' approach, clearly demonstrate that timing is not crucial." *United States Parole Commission v. Geraghty*, 445 U.S. 388 (1980).

IV. POLITICAL QUESTION DOCTRINE

A. CONCEPT AND PURPOSES

1. *The "political question doctrine" postulates that there exist certain issues of constitutional law which are beyond the authority and competence of the federal judiciary to resolve.*

2. The doctrine is designed to avoid troubling confrontations between the federal judiciary and the coordinate branches of the federal government. The doctrine has been held to have no applicability to clashes between the federal judiciary and branches of state governments.

3. In *Baker v. Carr*, 369 U.S. 186 (1962), the Supreme Court noted six separate factors, the presence of any one of which will trigger the doctrine's applicability:

a. a textual commitment of a matter to another branch of the federal government.

Example: The Supreme Court has held that claims made under the provision of Article IV, section 4 of the Constitution that "[t]he United States shall guarantee to every State in this Union a Republican form of Government" present a political question, in part because by its terms the provision may be deemed to commit enforcement to the other branches of the federal government. *Luther v. Borden*, 48 U.S. (7 How.) 1 (1849).

b. "a lack of judicially discoverable and manageable standards" for resolving the legal issue.

Example: The "Republican form of government" clause is characterized as an example of such a provision.

c. "the impossibility of deciding without an initial policy determination of a kind clearly for nonjudicial discretion. . . ."

d. The danger of "expressing lack of the respect due coordinate branches of government . . . ."

e. "an unusual need for unquestioning adherence to a political decision already made. . . ."

Example: The Court has invoked the political question doctrine to avoid deciding questions about the validity of the amendment process.

f. "the potentiality of embarrassment from multifarious pronouncements by various departments on one question."

B. CATEGORIES OF CASES TO WHICH THE POLITICAL QUESTION DOCTRINE HAS BEEN APPLIED

1. *Republican form of government clause*

a. In *Luther v. Borden, supra,* the Supreme Court refused to decide which of two competing factions constituted the legitimate government of Rhode Island, invoking the political question doctrine.

b. In *Texas v. White*, 74 U.S. (7 Wall.) 700 (1868), the Court held that only Congress had authority to reestablish and recognize governments in the states that had seceded during the Civil War.

2. *Foreign affairs*

a. In *Goldwater v. Carter*, 444 U.S. 996 (1979), the Supreme Court ordered dismissed a complaint by several members of Congress challenging the legality of the President's unilateral notice of termination of the nation's mutual defense treaty with the Republic of China, because neither two-thirds of the Senate nor a majority of both houses of Congress had approved.

b. Justice Rehnquist, speaking for four Justices in *Goldwater*, concurred separately, arguing that the case was non-justiciable because it involved the authority of the President to conduct foreign affairs.

c. In *Baker v. Carr, supra,* the Court held that issues of foreign affairs frequently turn on standards that defy judicial application, or involve the exercise of a discretion demonstrably committed to the executive or legislator. However, the Court added that "it is error to suppose that every case or controversy which touches foreign relations lies beyond judicial cognizance."

3. *Validity of enactments*

4. *Dates of duration of hostilities*

5. *Regulation of political parties*

a. While in a number of cases the Supreme Court has demonstrated a willingness to review the constitutionality of the actions of political parties, in *Cousins v. Wigoda*, 419 U.S. 477 (1975), the Court expressly left unresolved the question "whether or to what extent national political parties and their nominating conventions are regulable by, or only by, Congress."

6. *Judicial Review of the training and weaponry of the National Guard*

a. In *Gilligan v. Morgan*, 413 U.S. 1 (1973), the Supreme Court held that constitutional challenges to the training and weaponry of the Ohio National Guard are non-justiciable.

b. The Court found a conflict with a coordinate branch of the *federal* government, because Article I, section 8, clause 16 of the Constitution vests in Congress the power "[t]o provide for organizing, arming, and disciplining the Militia, and for governing such part of them as may be employed in the service of the United States, reserving to the States respectively the appointment of the officers, and the authority of training the Militia according to the discipline *prescribed by Congress.*" (Emphasis added by the Court).

C. AREAS IN WHICH APPLICATION OF THE POLITICAL QUESTION DOCTRINE HAS BEEN DENIED

1. *The constitutionality under the equal protection clause of state representational apportionment.*

   a. The Court rejected the applicability of the doctrine to such cases in *Baker v. Carr, supra.*

   b. Justice Frankfurter, dissenting in *Baker,* argued that such apportionment cases were in reality "republican form of government" cases, and therefore should be deemed non-justiciable.

2. *Exclusion of a member of Congress by one of the houses of Congress.*

   a. *Powell v. McCormack,* 395 U.S. 486 (1969).

*

2

CONGRESSIONAL POWER TO REGULATE FEDERAL JURISDICTION

Analysis

I. Introduction to the Problem
   A. Distinction Between Congressional Power to Regulate Lower Federal Court Jurisdiction and Supreme Court Jurisdiction
   B. Relevance of "External" Constitutional Limitations
II. Congressional Power to Regulate Lower Federal Court Jurisdiction
   A. The Traditional Theory of Broad Congressional Power
   B. Alternative Constructions of Article III
III. Congressional Power to Control Supreme Court Appellate Jurisdiction
   A. Ex parte McCardle and the Theory of Broad Congressional Power
   B. The "Essential Functions" Thesis
   C. The Limitation-as-to-Fact Theory
IV. Limitations on Congressional Power Deriving From Other Parts of the Constitution
   A. Equal Protection
   B. Due Process
   C. Separation of Powers

- V. *Congressional Power to Vest Article III Federal Courts With Non-article III Power*
  - A. *Characteristics of an Article III Court*
  - B. *The Concept of "Non-article III Powers"*
- VI. *The "Constitutional Fact" Doctrine*
  - A. *The* Crowell *Decision*
  - B. *Current Status*

I. INTRODUCTION TO THE PROBLEM

A. DISTINCTION BETWEEN CONGRESSIONAL POWER TO REGULATE LOWER FEDERAL COURT JURISDICTION AND SUPREME COURT JURISDICTION

1. In understanding the scope of congressional power to limit or regulate federal jurisdiction, it is first necessary to understand the differences between control of the jurisdiction of the lower federal courts and that of the Supreme Court. The primary difference flows from Article III of the Constitution (the judicial article). That provision expressly mandates the creation of the Supreme Court; however, it expressly vests in the hands of Congress at least the original decision whether or not to create lower federal courts. As will be seen, all assumptions about congressional power to control lower federal court jurisdiction flow from this fact.

2. Since the Supreme Court's existence is required, of course no similar conclusions may be drawn about Congress' power over that court's jurisdiction. However, the Supreme Court's appellate jurisdiction—by far the greatest portion of its authority—is given "both as to law and fact, with such exceptions, and under such regulations as the Congress shall make." In debating congressional power to control Supreme Court appellate jurisdiction, it is this language that is relevant.

B. RELEVANCE OF "EXTERNAL" CONSTITUTIONAL LIMITATIONS

1. In addition to considering the meaning of the language of Article III, those who debate congressional power over federal jurisdiction also point to other provisions of the Constitution which might conceivably limit congressional power.

2. In particular, these include the Due Process Clause of the Fifth Amendment, the "equal protection" component that has been read into that clause, and the largely implicit constitutional doctrine of Separation of Powers.

II. CONGRESSIONAL POWER TO REGULATE LOWER FEDERAL COURT JURISDICTION

A. THE TRADITIONAL THEORY OF BROAD CONGRESSIONAL POWER

1. Article III provides that "the judicial power of the United States shall be vested in one supreme court, and in such inferior courts as the Congress may from time to time ordain and establish." By its terms, the provision appears to have vested in Congress the original decision whether or not to establish lower federal courts. This language is fortified by the generally accepted historical analysis, which posits an initial deadlock between the framers who believed the Constitution should mandate the creation of lower federal courts and those who believed the Constitution should prohibit their creation and instead rely exclusively on the state courts as original forums for the adjudication of federal law, with supervision by the Supreme Court. Out of this deadlock grew the "Madisonian Compromise", under which Congress was given the choice of whether or not to establish lower federal courts.

2. Though Congress immediately established lower federal courts in the Judiciary Act of 1789, it has been—and, to a great extent, continues to be—assumed that since Congress need not have created lower federal courts, it may abolish them, and that since it has the power to abolish them completely, it may instead choose to take the lesser step of "abolishing" them as to certain cases, *i.e.*, to limit their jurisdiction, without actually abolishing them.

3. This logical principle that "the greater includes the lesser" has explained the Supreme Court's long-held conclusion that Congress has broad power to limit the jurisdiction of the lower federal courts. *See, e.g., Sheldon v. Sill*, 49 U.S. (8 How.) 441 (1850); *Lockerty v. Phillips*, 319 U.S. 182 (1943).

4. Because the framers vested discretion in Congress to choose not to create lower federal courts, it was apparently their assumption that Congress could choose instead to rely on state courts as the primary adjudicators of federal law and enforcers of federal rights. This conclusion is underscored by Article VI, clause 2, of the Constitution (the Supremacy Clause), which obligates the state courts to obey and enforce federal law as "the supreme law of the land . . . any thing in the Constitution or laws of any state to the contrary notwithstanding." Thus, although Congress created lower federal courts in 1789, it was not until 1875 that it enacted a long-lasting general "federal question" statute; until that time, Congress to a great

extent relied on the state judiciary as original forums for adjudication of federal law.

B. ALTERNATIVE CONSTRUCTIONS OF ARTICLE III

1. *Justice Story's Theory:* In the early 1800's, Justice Joseph Story argued that Congress lacked any authority to regulate lower court jurisdiction, because Article III states that the federal judicial power "shall be vested" in the Supreme Court and the lower federal courts. He construed this to require that the federal judicial power be exercised *somewhere* in the federal judiciary. Since the Supreme Court has only appellate jurisdiction in many areas, Story reasoned that if no lower court existed there would be no original forum from which an appeal to the Supreme Court could be taken. However, even if one were to accept Story's construction of "shall be vested" (and its validity is by no means clear), Story's theory disregards the possible use of the state courts as an original forum, and it has not been widely accepted.

2. *The "Changing Circumstances" Theory:* Several modern commentators have argued that changing circumstances today render the original plan of the framers unworkable. This is because at the time of the drafting of the Constitution the framers could rely on the availability of the Supreme Court to unify federal law and to police state courts, the current Supreme Court workload makes this assumption today incorrect. This theory has never been tested in the courts, and the likelihood of its widespread acceptance is questionable.

III. CONGRESSIONAL POWER TO CONTROL SUPREME COURT APPELLATE JURISDICTION

A. *EX PARTE MCCARDLE* AND THE THEORY OF BROAD CONGRESSIONAL POWER

1. In *Ex parte McCardle,* 74 U.S. (7 Wall.) 506 (1868), the Supreme Court refused to decide an appeal from a lower court's denial of a writ of habeas corpus challenging the constitutionality of one congressional program of post-Civil War Reconstruction, because after oral argument Congress had repealed the statute giving the Court appellate jurisdiction.

2. While the decision contains broad language recognizing broad congressional authority under the Exceptions Clause to limit the Court's appellate jurisdiction, the availability of an alternative avenue of Supreme Court review in that case limits the decision's precedential force. The

Supreme Court has thus never definitively answered the questions about the complete scope of Congress' authority under the Exceptions Clause.

B. THE "ESSENTIAL FUNCTIONS" THESIS

1. Several commentators have argued that Congress may not make exceptions to the Supreme Court's appellate jurisdiction that will destroy the essential role of the Supreme Court in the constitutional plan. The asserted functions of the Court deemed to be "essential" are to provide a uniform interpretation of federal law and to police state court interpretation and enforcement of federal law.

2. While there exists neither a linguistic nor firm historical basis upon which to support this theory, its advocates find it implicit in our constitutional structure. The theory has never been tested in the courts.

C. THE LIMITATION-AS-TO-FACT THEORY

1. Several commentators have focused on the phrase immediately preceding the Exceptions Clause. Article III, section 2 states that the Supreme Court shall have appellate jurisdiction, "both as to law and fact", with such exceptions and regulations as Congress shall make. It has been argued that Congress' authority under the Exceptions Clause was therefore intended to be limited to the power to limit Supreme Court review of factual determinations.

2. But while evidence does exist to support the contention that the framers were concerned with Supreme Court review of lower court findings of fact, the language of the clause does not lend itself to such a limited interpretation, and that the framers did not intend so narrow a scope is evidenced by the broader limits of the Supreme Court's appellate jurisdiction enacted in the Judiciary Act of 1789. *McCardle* at least implicitly rejected this theory, since the limitation on the Court's appellate jurisdiction upheld there was not confined to review of factual findings.

IV. LIMITATIONS ON CONGRESSIONAL POWER DERIVING FROM OTHER PARTS OF THE CONSTITUTION

A. EQUAL PROTECTION

1. While the fifth amendment contains no express equal protection provision, the Supreme Court has construed the amendment's Due Process Clause to include such a requirement. Thus, it is clear that Congress could not employ its Article III power to prohibit racial or religious minorities from gaining access to the federal courts.

2. In fact, it has been argued by some commentators that the equal protection component extends further, to prevent Congress from limiting access to the federal courts for specific fundamental rights, because such a limitation would discriminate on the basis of a fundamental right.

B. DUE PROCESS

1. The Supreme Court has held that the Due Process Clause requires that neither liberty nor property may be taken absent some form of hearing before an independent adjudicator. It has even been suggested that due process may require an independent *judicial* forum, though the status and contours of this requirement have not been fully defined. *See, e.g., Battaglia v. General Motors Corp.*, 169 F.2d 254 (2d Cir.1948), *cert. denied*, 335 U.S. 887.

2. However, it is unlikely that this constitutional requirement imposes significant limits on Congress' power to close off either the jurisdiction of the lower federal courts or the appellate jurisdiction of the Supreme Court. As to the former, while due process may prevent Congress from denying access to *any* judicial form for the adjudication of a constitutional right (*see Battaglia, supra*) traditionally Congress has been able to satisfy the due process requirement by allowing the *state* courts to serve as the ultimate protector of constitutional rights. This is because under the framers' assumptions in the "Madisonian Compromise" and under the Supremacy Clause, state courts are both empowered and obligated to vindicate federal rights.

3. Due Process is not violated by a limitation of the Supreme Court's appellate jurisdiction, because due process has never been construed to require any level of appellate review.

C. SEPARATION OF POWERS

1. While Congress may well retain broad power to limit the jurisdiction of the federal courts, the implied constitutional doctrine of separation of powers has been construed to confine that power. For example, the Supreme Court has held that Congress may not employ its power under the Exceptions Clause to demand that the Supreme Court act in an unconstitutional manner.

2. This is so, even if it were accepted that Congress could instead remove the Court's appellate jurisdiction completely. *United States v. Klein*, 80 U.S. (13 Wall.) 128 (1871). The same is probably true for Congress' power over lower federal court jurisdiction. *Cf. Yakus v. United States*, 321 U.S. 414 (1944) (Rutledge, J., dissenting).

V. CONGRESSIONAL POWER TO VEST ARTICLE III FEDERAL COURTS WITH NON-ARTICLE III POWER

A. CHARACTERISTICS OF AN ARTICLE III COURT

1. *Article III courts are the federal courts whose judges possess the protections of life tenure and salary provided in Article III, section 1 of the Constitution.*

2. The federal District Courts, Courts of Appeals and Supreme Court are all Article III federal courts.

B. THE CONCEPT OF "NON-ARTICLE III POWERS"

1. Traditionally, the Article III federal courts hear cases falling within the categories listed in Article III, section 2, to which the federal "judicial power" is extended. On occasion, Congress has attempted to have Article III federal courts hear cases that fall nowhere within the categories listed in Article III, section 2.

2. The *Tidewater* Decision

a. In *National Mutual Insurance Co. v. Tidewater Transfer Co., Inc.*, 337 U.S. 582 (1949), the Supreme Court upheld legislation vesting the Article III federal courts with jurisdiction over suits between citizens of a state and those of the District of Columbia. The Court had many years earlier held that the District was not a "state" for purposes of the diversity of citizenship jurisdiction as described in the "judicial power" of Article III, section 2. Since no issue of federal law was involved, the case did not come within any of the categories listed in the Constitution. Three Justices concluded that Congress had authority to vest the federal courts with jurisdiction over non-Article III cases, by means of its legislative powers under Article I.

  b. Concerned about both federalism and separation-of-powers factors, six Justices rejected such authority. However, two of those Justices concurred in upholding the jurisdictional statute, on the ground that the District should properly be deemed a "state" for diversity purposes.

VI. THE "CONSTITUTIONAL FACT" DOCTRINE

A. THE *CROWELL* DECISION

1. In *Crowell v. Benson*, 285 U.S. 22 (1932), the Supreme Court held that Congress could not constitutionally take away from the judiciary final authority to find, *de novo*, those facts that determine the constitutionality of the governmental action or legislation in question.

2. The Court was not entirely clear as to the basis of its decision. In part, it was separation of powers, but it also appeared to include a due process element.

3. Justice Brandeis dissented, arguing that since Congress could choose to close off the federal courts and instead have these findings made in state court, it could also be able to have them finally determined in non-judicial federal agencies. He concluded that the only time judicial review of factual findings was required was when personal liberty was at stake and the Due Process Clause required it.

B. CURRENT STATUS

1. *Crowell* was for many years attacked by commentators, and it has often been contended that the doctrine is dead. However, the decision has never been overruled (though it has been modified in that a *de novo* judicial hearing is not required).

2. *Crowell* itself concerned property rights that, as a matter of substantive constitutional law, have received diminished protection since the time of that decision. To the extent personal liberty is at stake, it is likely that the *Crowell* doctrine will continue to play a role.

*

3

LEGISLATIVE COURTS

Analysis

I. Legislative Courts: Definition and Characteristics
   A. The Concept of Legislative Courts
   B. Examples of Legislative Courts
II. Constitutional Limits on the Authority of Legislative Courts
   A. Reconciling Legislative Courts With Article III
   B. The "Inherently Judicial" Concept
   C. "Adjuncts" to Article III Courts

I. LEGISLATIVE COURTS: DEFINITION AND CHARACTERISTICS

A. THE CONCEPT OF LEGISLATIVE COURTS

1. *"Legislative" courts, also referred to as "Article I" courts, are federally-created judicial bodies whose judges lack the life tenure and salary protections given to judges of the Article III federal courts.* Thus, the judges of legislative courts may be given limited terms, have their salaries reduced, or may be removed from office. These courts are often called "Article I" courts, because they are usually created pursuant to one of Congress' enumerated powers under Article I of the Constitution, combined with the Necessary and Proper Clause.

2. Unlike the Article III federal courts, legislative courts are not bound by the "case or controversy" requirement of Article III, and thus are capable of issuing advisory opinions.

B. EXAMPLES OF LEGISLATIVE COURTS

1. Current examples of legislative courts are the territorial courts, the military courts, the local courts in the District of Columbia and the Tax Court.

2. Originally, the Supreme Court held that the Court of Claims and Court of Customs were legislative courts. However, in 1962 the Court held both the Court of Claims and the Court of Customs and Patent Appeals to be Article III courts. More recently, Congress has replaced these courts with the United States Court of Appeals for the Federal Circuit and a trial forum known as the United States Claims Court. The new court, which is composed of the twelve judgeships of the previous courts, remains an Article III court.

II. CONSTITUTIONAL LIMITS ON THE AUTHORITY OF LEGISLATIVE COURTS

A. RECONCILING LEGISLATIVE COURTS WITH ARTICLE III

1. By the use of legislative courts, Congress effectively circumvents the salary and tenure protections for judges provided in Article III. If there were no limit on the types of cases which legislative courts could be given, the constitutional protections of salary and tenure would become meaningless.

2. While it is conceivable that the salary and tenure protections could be given an absolute construction, effectively barring the use of federal courts whose judges lacked these protections as adjudicators of cases falling within the "judicial power" of Article III, since Chief Justice Marshall's decision in *American Insurance Co. v. Canter*, 26 U.S. (1 Pet.) 511 (1828),

holding the territorial courts to be legislative courts, the existence of at least some of these non-Article III courts has been established.

3. While the Supreme Court held in *Williams v. United States*, 289 U.S. 553 (1933), that a legislative court could exercise absolutely none of the federal "judicial power" as described in Article III, section 2, the decision was overruled in *Glidden Co. v. Zdanok*, 370 U.S. 530 (1962), and it is now accepted that legislative courts may exercise at least a portion of the federal judicial power.

B. THE "INHERENTLY JUDICIAL" CONCEPT

1. The Court has established that some cases are "inherently judicial" and cannot be heard by legislative courts.

2. Under *Crowell v. Benson*, 285 U.S. 22 (1932), it appears that constitutional issues must be decided by a court independent of the political branches of the federal government, whether an Article III federal court or a state court (whose judges' salary and tenure are not subject to federal regulation).

3. In *Palmore v. United States*, 411 U.S. 389 (1973), the Supreme Court held that Congress could create legislative courts, even when they may exercise authority to deny personal liberty, in the District of Columbia. While the decision is ambiguous, it is at least in large part premised on the unique relationship between Congress and the District, and is arguably limited to this context.

4. The Supreme Court has also recognized that the military courts may take away personal liberty, even though their judges lack the salary and tenure protections of Article III.

5. In *Northern Pipeline Construction Co. v. Marathon Pipe Line Co.*, 458 U.S. 50 (1982), the Supreme Court held that "private" rights—suits between private individuals on a state law claim—were inherently judicial and therefore could not be adjudicated by the Bankruptcy Courts, which did not have Article III status. The opinion of Justice Brennan made clear that "public rights"—rights given to individuals by the federal government, to be exercised against that government,—could be adjudicated by legislative courts.

a. The reason why public rights may be adjudicated by legislative courts, according to the plurality in *Northern Pipeline*, is that since Congress need not have created the right in the first place, it logically may place conditions on its method of enforcement.

b. In dissent, Justice White argued that the test should be based on a balancing process, weighing the interest in salary and tenure protections against the governmental interest in maintaining flexibility.

C. "ADJUNCTS" TO ARTICLE III COURTS

1. In addition to legislative courts, there are a number of other federal non-Article institutions that are involved in the adjudicatory process. The primary ones are administrative agencies and magistrates.

2. These institutions are permitted to adjudicate even "inherently judicial" matters, because they are deemed to function merely as "adjuncts", or assistants, to the Article III federal courts.

3. In such situations, it is thought that the "judicial power" remains in the Article III court.

4. In response to *Northern Pipeline*, Congress has transformed the Bankruptcy Courts into adjuncts to the Article III District Courts.

REVIEW QUESTIONS (PART I)

1. T or F   A private individual hears that the parents of a deformed infant in conspiracy with the doctors of a county hospital are not feeding the infant properly. The individual files suit in federal court to protect the federal civil rights of the infant. The private individual has standing to bring the suit.

2. T or F   A state files a prosecution against one of two individuals distributing political leaflets at a shopping center, and threatens the second individual with prosecution if she continues or returns. The second individual files suit in federal court, seeking a declaratory judgment that her future prosecution would violate her constitutional rights, and an injunction against prosecution. The second individual's case is not yet ripe for adjudication.

3. T or F   Blacks file suit in federal court, challenging the constitutionality of the operation of a major political party's primary in their state, on the grounds that blacks are improperly excluded from participation. The defendants contend that the federal court may not adjudicate the dispute because of the political question doctrine. The federal court is correct in deciding that the political question doctrine does not preclude it from adjudicating the suit.

4. T or F   Because Congress retains power under Article III to regulate the jurisdiction of the lower federal courts, it may prohibit certain racial and religious groups from gaining access to those courts.

5. T or F   Because the Supreme Court's existence is mandated by Article III of the Constitution while that of the lower federal courts is not, Congress possesses no power to control Supreme Court jurisdiction.

6. T or F   Though Congress retains power to regulate the jurisdiction of the federal courts, it cannot order them to convict an individual without allowing them to inquire into the constitutionality of the law under which the prosecution has been brought.

7. T or F   In light of the Supreme Court's decision that Congress may not establish separate bankruptcy courts whose judges lack the salary and tenure protections of Article III, it logically follows that federal administrative agencies are similarly unconstitutional.

8. T or F   A soldier about to be shipped to Grenada sues in federal court, claiming that the military involvement in Grenada is unconstitutional because it does not follow a declaration of war by Congress, and seeking an injunction against his transfer. The federal court will refuse to hear the suit, because of the political question doctrine.

9. T or F   Under accepted principles of standing, an organization with a special interest in an area of social concern may bring an action to challenge governmental interference in that particular area.

10. T or F   Application of the mootness doctrine is influenced by the degree of public interest in having the particular legal issue resolved.

11. T or F   Though Congress is authorized to circumvent the Article III federal courts by creating legislative courts, issues of constitutional interpretation must be finally resolved by an Article III court.

12. T or F   The decision in *Ex parte McCardle* definitively upholds plenary congressional authority to limit the Supreme Court's appellate jurisdiction.

13. T or F   A Congressional exclusion of Supreme Court appellate jurisdiction in constitutional cases violates the Fifth Amendment's Due Process Clause.

14. T or F Congress may require Article III federal courts to adjudicate cases falling outside the scope of the judicial power, described in Article III, section 2 of the Constitution.

15. T or F Congress may not require Article III federal courts to issue advisory opinions.

Write an essay in response to the following question:

You are a legal assistant to a United States Senator who is unhappy with the Supreme Court's decision holding prayer in public schools unconstitutional. He would like to learn your views on the constitutionality of various pieces of legislation which he is considering proposing:

(1) A statute requiring the federal courts to hold that prayer in public schools is constitutional.

(2) A statute prohibiting any federal court from adjudicating cases concerning the constitutionality of prayer in the public schools.

(3) A statute prohibiting any court, state or federal, from adjudicating cases concerning the constitutionality of prayer in the public schools.

(4) A statute similar to proposal 3, except that in addition the law would create a new federal legislative court to adjudicate finally all such cases, in lieu of the existing federal or state courts.

Prepare a memorandum in response to the Senator's request.

PART TWO

THE STRUCTURE OF FEDERAL COURT JURISDICTION

Analysis

4. Federal Question Jurisdiction
5. Diversity Jurisdiction
6. Pendent and Ancillary Jurisdiction
7. Jurisdictional Amount
8. Supreme Court Jurisdiction

4

FEDERAL QUESTION JURISDICTION

Analysis

I. Introduction: The Constitutional-Statutory Dichotomy
   A. The Nature of the Dichotomy
   B. Consequences of the Dichotomy
II. The Constitutional Power
   A. The *Osborn* Decision
   B. Protective Jurisdiction
III. The Statutory Scope
   A. Introduction
   B. The Statutory Structure
   C. The Scope of Statutory Federal Question Jurisdiction
   D. The "Well-Pleaded Complaint" Rule

I. INTRODUCTION: THE CONSTITUTIONAL–STATUTORY DICHOTOMY

A. THE NATURE OF THE DICHOTOMY

1. *The issue of federal question jurisdiction is in reality two separate legal issues: (a) interpretation of Congress' power to vest the federal courts with federal question jurisdiction under the "arising under" clause of Article III, section 2 of the Constitution, and (b) interpretation of existing statutory grants of authority to the federal courts to hear federal question cases.*

2. As will be seen, the constitutional and statutory provisions have been interpreted in very different ways.

B. CONSEQUENCES OF THE DICHOTOMY

1. The important point to keep in mind in considering these two issues is that *the constitutional provision determines how far Congress can go in vesting federal question jurisdiction in the federal courts, while the statutory provision determines how far Congress actually has gone.*

II. THE CONSTITUTIONAL POWER

A. THE *OSBORN* DECISION

1. Article III, section 2 of the Constitution extends the federal judicial power to all cases "arising under this Constitution, the Laws of the United States, and treaties made, or which shall be made, under their authority."

2. In *Osborn v. Bank of the United States*, 22 U.S. (9 Wheat.) 738 (1824), Chief Justice Marshall appeared to give this "arising under" clause an extremely broad construction.

   a. Marshall held that when any issue of federal law *might* appear in the case, the case can be deemed to "arise under" federal law for purposes of Article III, allowing the federal court to decide all issues of state law involved, even if the federal issue never actually appears in the case.

   b. Though *Osborn* has never been overruled, its broad language has been heavily criticized in dictum by modern Justices.

3. It has been suggested by commentators that *Osborn* was never intended to be read so broadly, despite its broad language. Rather, the argument proceeds, *Osborn* should be limited to cases involving a federal instrumentality, (such as the Bank of the United States, involved in that case), because it is in such cases that a strong federal interest is present, even if only state law is involved. However, Marshall's opinion appears to be broader than this narrow construction.

B. PROTECTIVE JURISDICTION

1. *Protective jurisdiction is the term used to describe two distinct theories to justify, under the "arising under" provision of Article III, the vesting of authority in the federal courts to hear cases involving solely issues of state law.*

2. Since Congress has never attempted to vest such authority in the federal courts, the legal validity of these theories has never been determined. However, both theories are severely criticized in the dissenting opinion of Justice Frankfurter in *Textile Workers Union v. Lincoln Mills*, 353 U.S. 448, 476 (1957).

3. The "Greater-Includes-the-Lesser" Theory

   a. One version of the theory, associated with Professor Herbert Wechsler, suggests that if Congress has constitutional authority to legislate substantively in an area, it can logically take the lesser step of not enacting substantive law but instead vesting jurisdiction in the federal courts to apply relevant state law.

   b. The theory can be criticized, because it is not necessarily true that the jurisdictional grant is somehow a "lesser" step than legislating substantively; rather, they may instead be viewed as conceptually distinct.

   c. This theory also disregards the fact that the need for the expertise of the federal courts—one of the primary justifications for the invocation of federal question jurisdiction—is absent when only state law issues are involved.

4. The "Articulated-and-Active-Federal-Policy" Theory

   a. The other version of protective jurisdiction, developed by Professor Paul Mishkin, suggests that when Congress has a preexisting active and articulated policy in an area, Congress may protect its program from being undermined by state court adjudication by allowing the federal courts to adjudicate even pure state law issues in areas related to the federal program.

   b. As an illustration, Professor Mishkin points to the cases upholding provisions of the bankruptcy law vesting jurisdiction in the federal courts to adjudicate non-diverse suits under state law when the bankrupt is a party. He also views *Osborn* an illustration of his approach.

III. THE STATUTORY SCOPE

A. INTRODUCTION

 1. Today, many deem the adjudication and protection of federal rights to be the primary function of the federal courts.

   a. Despite this fact, it was not until 1875 that Congress enacted a permanent general federal question statute.

 2. The current version of the general federal question statute is 28 U.S.C.A. § 1331, which provides that "[t]he district courts shall have original jurisdiction of all civil actions arising under the Constitution, laws, or treaties of the United States." The wording is strikingly similar to the language of the "arising under" clause of Article III, section 2.

 3. In addition, there exists historical evidence that the statute's primary drafter intended the statute to have a scope identical to that given the constitutional provision.

 4. Despite these facts, the statutory provision has uniformly received a construction much narrower than that given the constitutional provision. It is assumed that, at least without stronger evidence, Congress would not wish to burden the federal courts with so many cases having only a tangential relation to federal interests.

B. THE STATUTORY STRUCTURE

 1. While Section 1331 is the general federal question statute, a number of other jurisdictional statutes represent more specific exercises of the "arising under" jurisdiction. One is 28 U.S.C.A. § 1338(a) which provides the federal courts with jurisdiction over cases arising under acts of Congress relating to patents, plant variety protection, copyrights and trademarks.

 2. Federal jurisdiction under section 1338(a) is expressly made exclusive. Thus, a finding that a federal court has jurisdiction over a case under section 1338(a) automatically means the state courts lack jurisdiction over the same case. Some have argued that this fact should lead to the scope of this jurisdiction receiving an interpretation narrower than that given to section 1331, but on the whole the statutes have been construed identically.

C. THE SCOPE OF STATUTORY FEDERAL QUESTION JURISDICTION

 1. The "Cause of Action" Test.

   a. In *American Well Works Co. v. Layne and Bowler Co.*, 241 U.S. 257 (1916), Justice Holmes adopted a narrow test for determining whether a case "arises under" federal law for purposes of the federal question statute: A case arises under the law that creates the cause of action. Thus, if state law creates the cause of action, the case cannot "arise under" federal law, even if the substance of the case will substantially concern issues of federal law.

b. The test has been criticized, because it tends to place form over substance: if the bulk of the case will ultimately turn on matters of federal law, the need for the expertise of the federal courts is as great as when the cause of action is itself federal.

c. Today, the test has been largely superceded as a means of determining what cases do not "arise under" federal law, but it is generally true that a case that meets the Holmes test will be held to fall within federal question jurisdiction.

d. However, even if Congress creates the cause of action, if Congress directs that the substance of the law to be applied is state-created, cases under the cause of action may not be deemed to fall within the federal question statute. *See Shoshone Mining Co. v. Rutter*, 177 U.S. 505 (1900).

2. Expansion of the "arising under" jurisdiction.

a. Cases subsequent to *American Well* significantly expanded the statutory scope of federal question jurisdiction. *Today, the most widely used test is that a case falls within the federal question statute if the plaintiff's complaint establishes that the right to relief depends upon the construction or application of the Constitution or laws of the United States.* *Smith v. Kansas City Title & Trust Co.*, 255 U.S. 180 (1921). Thus, a case may "arise under" federal law, even if the cause of action is state-created.

b. However, if the question of federal law is merely "lurking in the background", federal question jurisdiction will not be found. *Gully v. First National Bank in Meridian*, 299 U.S. 109 (1936).

3. The "substantiality" requirement.

a. The Supreme Court has held that an essential element of federal question jurisdiction is that the federal issue not be "frivolous" or "insubstantial".

b. The Court has acknowledged, however, that in some senses this question in reality goes to the substantive merits of the claim, rather than to the question of jurisdiction.

D. THE "WELL-PLEADED COMPLAINT" RULE
   1. Origins of the rule.

a. In *Louisville & Nashville Railroad v. Mottley Co.*, 211 U.S. 149 (1908), *the Supreme Court held that a case does not arise under federal law for purposes of the federal question statute unless the issue of federal law appears on the face of plaintiff's well-pleaded complaint.*

b. Thus, even if the case will ultimately turn on issues of federal law, the case does not fall within federal question jurisdiction if the issue of federal law was raised initially in the defense.

c. The plaintiff is not allowed to anticipate the federal defense by inserting and responding to it in the complaint.

d. The rule's justification is to avoid expenditure of federal judicial effort on cases that ultimately contain no federal issue.

e. However, this justification does not explain the inability of either party to remove to federal court a state case in which a federal issue is raised initially in the defendant's answer.

2. Declaratory judgments.

a. *A plaintiff may not circumvent the well-pleaded complaint rule by means of the declaratory judgment device.*

b. If, absent the declaratory judgment procedure, a plaintiff's well-pleaded complaint would not demonstrate the presence of an issue of federal law, the case does not fall within the federal question jurisdiction. *Skelly Oil Co. v. Phillips Petroleum Co.*, 339 U.S. 667 (1950).

c. This is because the Declaratory Judgment Act was not designed to expand federal jurisdiction.

d. In *Franchise Tax Board v. Construction Laborers Vacation Trust for Southern California*, 462 U.S. 416 (1983), the Supreme Court held that the principle of *Skelly Oil*, developed originally for suits brought under the Federal Declaratory Judgment Act, applied as well to suits brought under a state declaratory judgment act, and that when applicable, the principle barred removal to federal court, as well as a suit brought originally in federal court.

5

Diversity Jurisdiction

Analysis

I. Introduction: The Scope and Policies of the Diversity Jurisdiction
   A. The Current Statutory Structure
   B. The Purposes and Policies of Diversity Jurisdiction
   C. The "Complete Diversity" Requirement
II. The Meaning of Citizenship
   A. The Concept of Domicile
   B. The Determination of Domicile
III. The Citizenship of Corporations and Associations
   A. Corporations
   B. Associations
   C. Trusts
IV. Judge-Made Exceptions to the Diversity Jurisdiction
   A. Types of Exceptions Fashioned
   B. Rationale of the Exceptions
V. Manufactured Diversity
   A. The Statutory Structure and History
   B. Application of §1359

I. INTRODUCTION: THE SCOPE AND POLICIES OF THE DIVERSITY JURISDICTION

A. THE CURRENT STATUTORY STRUCTURE

1. 28 U.S.C.A. § 1332 extends the diversity jurisdiction of the federal courts, assuming the jurisdictional amount has been met [see Chapter 7], to suits between (1) citizens of different states; (2) citizens of a state and citizens or subjects of a foreign state; (3) citizens of different states and in which citizens or subjects of a foreign state are additional parties; and (4) a foreign state as plaintiff and a citizen of a state or of different states.

2. § 1332 represents an exercise of Congress' power to vest the "judicial power", under Article III, section 2 of the Constitution, in the Article III federal courts. Section 2 extends the judicial power to controversies "between a state and citizens of another state;—between citizens of different states . . . and between a state, or the citizens thereof, and foreign states, citizens or subjects."

B. THE PURPOSES AND POLICIES OF DIVERSITY JURISDICTION

1. *Traditionally, the purpose of the diversity jurisdiction has been thought to be the avoidance of possible prejudice in a state court against out-of-staters.*

2. Today, many commentators argue that, in light of modern communication facilities and transportation systems, the fear of prejudice against out-of-staters is minimal, and that the diversity jurisdiction therefore unduly burdens the federal courts and clogs the federal dockets.

3. Others have responded that in certain instances prejudice may still be a problem, and that in any event federal court interpretation of state law performs an educational function, by providing federal juridical input to the development of state law.

C. THE "COMPLETE DIVERSITY" REQUIREMENT

1. In the well-known decision of *Strawbridge v. Curtiss*, 7 U.S. (3 Cranch) 267 (1806), Chief Justice Marshall held that the federal courts' diversity jurisdiction extended only to cases of "complete" diversity, in other words, those in which all defendants and all plaintiffs are from different states. Thus, the diversity jurisdiction does not extend to cases of "minimal" diversity—those in which at least one plaintiff is from a different state from at least one defendant, but there exists at least some overlap of residence between plaintiffs and defendants.

> *Example 1:* A, from New York, and B, from Illinois, sue C, from Iowa, and D, from Oregon in federal district court. There is "complete" diversity, because both plaintiffs are from states different from those of the two defendants.

Example 2: A, from New York, and B, from Illinois, sue E, from Illinois. "Minimal" diversity is present, because A and E are from different states. But "complete" diversity is absent, because both B and E are from the same state.

   2. It was not clear until 1967 whether the complete diversity requirement represented a construction only of the diversity *statute*, or of the diversity clause of Article III, section 2 of the Constitution. If it were the constitutional provision being interpreted, then Congress would be incapable of extending the diversity jurisdiction to cases of minimal diversity, because Article III, section 2 is generally thought to form the outer potential boundaries of federal court jurisdiction. If it were merely an inference of congressional intent in the fact of congressional silence, then of course Congress could reverse such a construction.

   3. In its decision in *State Farm Fire & Casualty Co. v. Tashire*, 386 U.S. 523 (1967), the Supreme Court finally resolved the issue by holding that the complete diversity requirement was merely a matter of statutory construction. The Court therefore upheld the Federal Interpleader Act, 28 U.S.C.A. § 1335, which extended the diversity jurisdiction to cases of minimal diversity in certain interpleader situations. However, though Congress is now considered empowered to abolish the complete diversity requirement, it has not done so, except in the interpleader context.

   4. There exists some question about the purposes served by the complete diversity requirement. It has been suggested that if parties on opposite sides of the litigation are from the same state, the dangers of prejudice are lessened, since the decision will negatively affect an in-state resident, whichever way the case is resolved. But this will not always be true.

Example: A, from New York and B, from Illinois sue C, from Illinois, in New York state court. If prejudice against out-of-staters is assumed to be a danger, the state court in New York could favor the plaintiffs, and such prejudice would not have a negative impact on a New York resident.

   5. The complete diversity requirement also has what many would consider the beneficial impact of reducing the number of diversity cases.

II. THE MEANING OF CITIZENSHIP

A. THE CONCEPT OF DOMICILE

1. If diversity jurisdiction is to apply, plaintiff and defendant must be citizens of different states. It is not always easy to determine, however, whether a party is a citizen of a particular state.

2. In making the citizenship determination, courts focus on "domicile," rather than "residence."

   a. *"Domicile" refers to an individual's permanent home, to which he plans to return if he has left. "Residence," on the other hand, refers to a location in which an individual spends a substantial period of time, but which he may leave permanently in the foreseeable future.*

   b. An individual may have more than one residence, but only one domicile.

   Example: Al is a law student at Northwestern in Illinois, but his home is in Pennsylvania, where he plans to return after graduation. He has a residence in Illinois, but his domicile is Pennsylvania.

B. THE DETERMINATION OF DOMICILE

1. An individual may change his domicile by moving to another state with the intention of remaining there indefinitely. This does not mean that he must plan on establishing a permanent home in the state, but only that he have no intention at the time to leave.

2. The Supreme Court has held that "jurisdiction, once attached, is not impaired by a party's later change of domicile." *Smith v. Sperling*, 354 U.S. 91, 93 n. 1 (1957).

3. Usually, the court itself, rather than the jury, will make the finding of domicile.

4. An individual's course of conduct, rather than his expressed intentions, will be determinative of the domicile question.

III. THE CITIZENSHIP OF CORPORATIONS AND ASSOCIATIONS

A. CORPORATIONS

1. In *Bank of the United States v. Deveaux*, 9 U.S. (5 Cranch) 61 (1809), Chief Justice Marshall stated that a corporation is an "invisible, intangible, and artificial being" and therefore had the citizenship of all of its stockholders. In light of the complete diversity requirement, this holding

significantly reduced the number of diversity cases involving corporations. This resulted because if a corporation's stockholders reside in numerous states, the likelihood of an absence of complete diversity increases.

2. However, the Court overruled *Deveaux* in *Louisville, Cincinnati & Charleston Railroad Co. v. Letson*, 43 U.S. (2 How.) 497 (1844), holding that a corporation is a citizen for diversity purposes only of the state in which it is incorporated. The Court achieved this end by imposing an irrebuttable presumption that all of the stockholders were citizens of the state of incorporation.

3. In 1958, Congress added 28 U.S.C.A. § 1332(c), which provides that "a corporation shall be deemed a citizen of any state by which it has been incorporated and of the state where it has its principal place of business. . . ."

   a. The effect of this statute is to reduce the number of cases in which diversity jurisdiction will be allowed.

Example: Mammoth Motors Corporation is incorporated in Delaware, but has its principal place of business in Michigan. Prior to the 1958 amendment, Mammoth would be deemed a resident only of the state of Delaware. Hence, if Mammoth were sued by a resident of Michigan prior to 1958, diversity would exist. However, after the 1958 amendment, there would be no diversity in a suit by a Michigan resident against Mammoth, because Mammoth would be deemed a citizen of both Delaware and Michigan.

   b. However, it is not always easy to determine in exactly what state a corporation has its principal place of business. Some courts have employed what has been called the "nerve center" test, which looks for the location in which key decisions are made. This is generally the state in which the "home office" is located. Other courts have relied upon a finding of the "place of operations." The former test focuses on the location of major policy decisions, while the latter test looks to the location at which day-to-day operating decisions are made. It has been suggested that the "nerve center" test is employed when a corporation conducts substantial activities in more than one state, while the "place of operations" test is more likely to be applied when a corporation is incorporated in one state but conducts its affairs in another state.

4. In certain instances, corporations have been allowed to incorporate in more than one state. This creates an obvious problem for the application of the diversity jurisdiction to corporations.

a. Prior to the 1958 amendment, the predominant (though by no means exclusive) approach was the so-called "forum rule," which held that a multiply-incorporated corporation was to be deemed a citizen of the forum state, if that state was one of the places of incorporation.

b. Commentators have suggested that the 1958 amendment had the effect of eliminating the forum rule and instead made a corporation a citizen of every state in which it has been incorporated, though the statute does not explicitly do this.

B. ASSOCIATIONS

1. *Under the rule of* Chapman v. Barney, *129 U.S. 677 (1889), an unincorporated association's citizenship for purposes of the diversity jurisdiction was to be determined by the citizenship of all of its members.*

2. This rule results in a decrease in the availability of the diversity jurisdiction, because it increases the likelihood of an absence of complete diversity.

Example: A private association that has its principal place of business in Illinois has members who live in Illinois, Pennsylvania, Michigan, New York and Idaho. If the association's citizenship for purposes of diversity were determined solely by the location of its principal place of business, a suit brought by the association against a resident of Idaho would come within the diversity jurisdiction. Under the *Chapman* rule, however, the association is deemed to have the citizenship of all of its members, which includes Idaho, and therefore there exists no complete diversity between the association and the Idaho defendant.

3. In the more recent decision in *United Steelworkers of America, AFL-CIO v. R.H. Bouligny, Inc.,* 382 U.S. 145 (1965), the Supreme Court held that the *Chapman* rule continued to be good law, and applied it to labor unions.

a. Though the *Chapman* rule was wholly judge-made, the Court stated that the issue of its repeal was "properly a matter for legislative consideration. . . ."

b. The Court reaffirmed *Chapman*, despite the fact that it recognized the arguable inconsistency between the rule and the standard employed for determining the citizenship of corporations.

C. TRUSTS

1. In *Navarro Savings Association v. Lee,* 446 U.S. 458 (1980), the Supreme Court held that individual trustees of a business may invoke the

diversity jurisdiction on the basis of their own citizenship, regardless of the citizenship of the trust beneficiaries.

2. Though the Court acknowledged that a business trust bears certain similarities to an association, it noted that in some ways it also resembled a corporation.

3. The only question, said the Court, was whether the trustee could be deemed the real party in interest.

IV. JUDGE-MADE EXCEPTIONS TO THE DIVERSITY JURISDICTION

A. TYPES OF EXCEPTIONS FASHIONED
1. *The federal courts have exempted two basic types of cases from the diversity jurisdiction: matters involving* probate, *and cases concerning* domestic relations.

2. The rule as to domestic relations cases derives from a Supreme Court dictum in *Barber v. Barber*, 62 U.S. (21 How.) 582 (1859). While originally the exception was devised for divorce cases, it has since been expanded to apply to most matters involving domestic relations, such as property settlements and child custody cases.

3. However, the domestic relations exception has, in the words of Judge Friendly in *Phillips, Nizer, Benjamin, Krim & Ballon v. Rosenstiel*, 490 F.2d 509 (2d Cir.1973), "been rather narrowly confined."

Examples: The Supreme Court has sustained federal jurisdiction to enforce an alimony award already made by a state court in a divorce proceeding, and to declare a Mexican divorce decree invalid and to order payment of past and future alimony under a previous Ohio decree.

In the *Rosenstiel* case, Judge Friendly, speaking for the Second Circuit, indicated that if a timely motion for a stay had been made, the court would have granted it, even though "the bulk of the complaint is concerned with legal services in no way connected with the matrimonial action. . . . " This was because the plaintiff law firm was an in-state resident and the case required "exploration of a difficult field of New York law with which, because of its proximity to the exception for matrimonial actions, federal judges are more than ordinarily unfamiliar." This dictum represents a substantial expansion of the exception, well beyond its previous narrow confines.

4. The probate exception provides that a federal court will not employ its diversity jurisdiction to probate a will or administer an estate. However, the mere fact that an estate's administrator or executor is a party to a diversity case in a suit involving claims by or against the estate will not preclude the exercise of the court's jurisdiction.

B. RATIONALE OF THE EXCEPTIONS

1. Originally, the probate and domestic relations exceptions were considered to be the result of statutory construction, based on historical English practice.

2. In modern times, however, the exceptions are generally viewed as forms of judge-made abstention.

3. The purported modern rationale for exempting these areas from the diversity jurisdiction is that they may involve complex issues that are of particular concern to the state. It is questionable, however, whether these two areas are significantly more complex or important than numerous other areas of state law traditionally adjudicated by the federal courts in the exercise of their diversity jurisdiction.

V. MANUFACTURED DIVERSITY

A. THE STATUTORY STRUCTURE AND HISTORY

1. 28 U.S.C.A. § 1359 currently provides: "A district court shall not have jurisdiction of a civil action in which any party, by assignment or otherwise, has been improperly or collusively made or joined to invoke the jurisdiction of such court."

2. In its present form, the section was added to the Judicial Code in 1948. Before that, two different statutes dealt with the problem of manufactured diversity:

a. The "assignee clause," that provided, with certain exceptions, that "no district court shall have cognizance of any suit . . . to recover upon any promissory note or other chose in action in favor of any assignee . . . unless such suit might have been prosecuted in such court . . . if no assignment had been made."

Example: A, from Michigan, would like to sue B, from Michigan on a state claim in federal court under the diversity jurisdiction. He assigns his claim to C, from Illinois, who then attempts to sue B in federal court. Under the "assignee clause," diversity could not be found, because absent the assignment, diversity would not have existed.

b. 28 U.S.C.A. § 80, which provided that a district court should dismiss an action whenever "it shall appear to the satisfaction of the . . . court . . . that such suit does not really and substantially involve a dispute or controversy properly within the jurisdiction of [the] court, or that the parties to said suit have been improperly or collusively made or joined . . . for the purpose of creating [federal jurisdiction]."

3. In the 1948 revision of the Judicial Code, § 80 was amended to produce § 1359, and the "assignee clause" was repealed.

B. APPLICATION OF § 1359

1. § 1359 has been applied primarily to assignments and to the appointments of guardians and executors, when those devices have the effect of creating diversity.

2. Unlike the "assignee clause," § 1359 does not automatically deny jurisdiction when the assignment has the effect of creating diversity. It replaces the objective test of the "assignee clause" with a more subjective, motivational test.

a. In *Kramer v. Caribbean Mills, Inc.*, 394 U.S. 823 (1969), the Supreme Court held that § 1359 bars federal jurisdiction when an assignment that has the effect of creating diversity is made to a party totally without a previous connection to the matter who simultaneously reassigns 95% interest in the claim back to the assignor, concluding that the assignment was only for purposes of collection.

b. The Court rejected the argument that the legality, under state law, rendered the assignment non-collusive, because "[t]he existence of federal jurisdiction is a matter of federal, not state, law."

c. In a footnote, the Court noted that it had "no occasion to reexamine the cases in which this Court has held that where the transfer of a claim is absolute, with the transferor retaining no interest in the subject matter, then the transfer is not improperly or collusively made, regardless of the transferor's motive."

3. The Court in *Kramer* also expressly disclaimed consideration of the applicability of § 1359 to the appointment of guardians and administrators. However, the Court did note three possible distinctions between assignments and appointments:

a. In the appointment situation, some representative must be appointed in any event, while an assignor normally can himself bring suit.

b. "[U]nder state law, different kinds of guardians may possess discrete sorts of powers."

c. All appointments are made by state court decree, while assignments are made purely by the actions of private parties.

4. However, the lower federal courts have generally held that appointment of an out-of-state representative for the purpose of creating diversity will not give rise to federal jurisdiction under § 1359. The problems that arise in applying § 1359 to appointments is illustrated by the conflict within the Third Circuit.

a. In *Corabi v. Auto Racing, Inc.*, 264 F.2d 784 (3d Cir.1959), the court found that an appointment used to create jurisdiction fell within the prohibition of § 1359 only if the court found an illegal agreement or understanding between opponents. In the absence of such collusion, said the court, a motive to create federal jurisdiction was irrelevant.

b. However, in McSparran v. Weist, 402 F.2d 867 (3d Cir.1968), *cert. denied*, 395 U.S. 903, the court overruled *Corabi*, holding that appointment of a representative having only nominal duties, motivated by a desire to manufacture jurisdiction, violated § 1359.

5. The Fourth Circuit, in a series of decisions beginning in 1969, has had such difficulty applying § 1359 to unique fact situations that in a footnote the court urged adoption of the American Law Institute's proposal, which suggests imposition of a flat rule deeming the representative to be a citizen of the state in which either the decedent resided or the ward presently resides. The obvious advantage of this proposal is its ease of administration. However, if there still do exist dangers of prejudice to out-of-staters in state courts, and an out-of-state guardian or administrator actually is the best person for the position, the ALI's proposal may undermine achievement of the purposes of the diversity jurisdiction.

6

PENDENT AND ANCILLARY JURISDICTION

Analysis

I. Introduction: The Scope of the Subject
  A. Definitional Matters: The Distinctions and Similarities Between Pendent and Ancillary Jurisdiction
  B. The Hybrid of "Pendent Party" Jurisdiction
  C. The Constitutional Issue
  D. The Purposes and Risks of Pendent and Ancillary Jurisdiction
II. Pendent Jurisdiction
  A. Pendent Power: Development of the "Same Operative Facts" Test
  B. The "Power"—"Discretion" Dichotomy
III. Ancillary Jurisdiction
  A. Historical Development
  B. The Scope and Limits of Ancillary Jurisdiction
IV. Pendent Party Jurisdiction
  A. The Aldinger *Case*
  *B. Post-*Aldinger *Developments and Implications*

I. INTRODUCTION: THE SCOPE OF THE SUBJECT

A. DEFINITIONAL MATTERS: THE DISTINCTIONS AND SIMILARITIES BETWEEN PENDENT AND ANCILLARY JURISDICTION

1. Both pendent and ancillary jurisdiction represent extensions of federal jurisdiction to situations in which statutory jurisdictional requirements have not been met. Federal jurisdiction may be exercised in these situations, under the appropriate circumstances, because they are linked to factual situations which do meet jurisdictional requirements. In other words, the situations in question are "appended" to a case that does meet statutory jurisdictional requirements and therefore is properly in federal court.

2. While significant confusion exists over the distinction between the two concepts, the fundamental difference is that pendent jurisdiction is employed when a single plaintiff has a claim properly in federal court against a single defendant, and he appends onto his claim a claim that could not itself be brought in federal court, while ancillary jurisdiction involves either a third party or the defendant appending or being appended onto the plaintiff's federal court action.

Examples: P sues D, a local policeman, in federal court for violation of P's civil rights, because D allegedly beat P while D was on duty. P appends a state tort law claim against D for battery. Assuming no diversity of citizenship between the parties, P could not bring his state tort claim, standing alone, in federal court. However, under the doctrine of pendent jurisdiction, P may "append" his state claim onto his federal claim against D.

P sues D in diversity, and D attempts to implead T, on the ground that if D is found liable to P, T is liable to D for indemnification. T is from the same state as D and no federal question is present. D's claim against T can be heard in federal court, on the basis of ancillary jurisdiction.

3. It has occasionally been suggested that the difference between ancillary and pendent jurisdiction is that the latter applies when initial federal jurisdiction is premised on diversity while the latter applies when jurisdiction is premised on federal question. This is an inaccurate characterization. It is true that there could not be a *pendent* jurisdiction case in diversity, since in such a case jurisdiction is determined on the basis of the citizenship of the parties, so that if there is federal jurisdiction for one claim there is automatically the same basis of jurisdiction for the other. But, as will be demonstrated below, *ancillary* jurisdiction could easily develop in certain cases where the initial basis of jurisdiction is federal question.

B. THE HYBRID OF "PENDENT PARTY" JURISDICTION

1. The two concepts are, to a certain extent, merged in the so-called "pendent party" concept, which would in certain instances allow a plaintiff to join a defendant over whom he would not have independent jurisdiction.

2. To a large extent, this concept has been rejected by the Supreme Court. *See* Section IV, *infra*.

C. THE CONSTITUTIONAL ISSUE

1. Since the doctrines of both pendent and ancillary jurisdiction may allow a federal court plaintiff to bring suit against a party or over an issue that does not fall within the federal "judicial power" as described in Article III, section 2 of the Constitution (for example, over pure state law issue in the absence of diversity of citizenship between the parties), it might be questioned whether the doctrines are constitutionally valid.

2. The constitutional question was dispelled early in the nation's history, however, by Chief Justice Marshall in *Osborn v. Bank of the United States*, 22 U.S. (9 Wheat.) 738 (1824).

    a. Marshall reasoned that "[t]here is scarcely any case, every part of which depends on the constitution, laws, or treaties of the United States." He concluded "that when a question to which the judicial power of the Union is extended by the constitution forms an ingredient of the original cause, it is in the power of Congress to give the [federal] Circuit Courts jurisdiction of that cause, although other questions of fact or law may be involved in it."

    b. Marshall was saying that the federal judicial power extends to "cases," and that a "case" includes all related facts and issues, not merely those falling within the federal judicial power.

D. THE PURPOSES AND RISKS OF PENDENT AND ANCILLARY JURISDICTION

1. The most often-cited purpose of both pendent and ancillary jurisdiction is the goal of reducing duplication of litigant and judicial time, effort and expense by combining what would otherwise be two separate litigations into one.

2. If this were the sole value of the doctrines, however, it could just as easily be obtained by having the federal and state claims joined in *state* court as in federal court, and thus an important value of the doctrines is that they encourage litigants to seek vindication of their federal claims in federal court, where the judges possess greater sensitivity to and expertise in interpretation of federal rights.

a. Of course, this reasoning would logically not apply to many exercises of *ancillary* jurisdiction, because as previously noted they often involve the exercise of *diversity*, rather than *federal question* jurisdiction.

b. The reasoning is also logically irrelevant when the basis for federal jurisdiction is exclusively within the jurisdiction of the federal courts, since under these circumstances the plaintiff has no choice but to seek federal court vindication of his federal claim.

3. The doctrines have been criticized by some, because they usurp from state courts their responsibility for adjudicating state law, and prevent improvements of state court ability to interpret federal law by keeping federal cases out of the state courts. Of course, the opposite point could just as easily be argued: *limitation* of the doctrines may preclude *federal* courts from exercising their primary responsibility of interpreting and developing federal law, and may limit federal court familiarity with state law issues, matters with which they must deal in the exercise of their diversity jurisdiction.

II. PENDENT JURISDICTION

A. PENDENT POWER: DEVELOPMENT OF THE "SAME OPERATIVE FACTS" TEST

1. The Supreme Court has made clear from the beginning of the pendent jurisdiction doctrine that it may be used only when there exists some conceptual and/or factual linkage between the claim properly in federal court and the claim sought to be appended to it. The exact nature of that linkage, however, has been the subject of both confusion and alteration over the years.

2. In *Hurn v. Oursler,* 289 U.S. 238 (1933), the Supreme Court indicated that pendent jurisdiction could apply only where the federal and state claims are part of the same "cause of action."

a. However, the term, "cause of action" is by no means self-defining; the *Hurn* Court found a state claim arising out of the very same play that had given rise to plaintiffs' federal copyright claim to be part of the same cause of action, because "[t]he bill alleges the violation of a single right, namely, the right to protection of the copyrighted play" and because "the claims of infringement and unfair competition so precisely rest upon identical facts as to be little more than the equivalent of different epithets to characterize the same groups of circumstances."

b. The Court found different "causes of action," however, when the plaintiff sought to append an additional state claim for the copying of a somewhat modified, uncopyrighted version of the plaintiff's play.

c. Though the decision was ambiguous, *Hurn* was generally interpreted to require a total factual identity between state and federal claims before a federal court had power to exercise pendent jurisdiction over the state claim.

3. In *United Mine Workers of America v. Gibbs*, 383 U.S. 715 (1966), the Supreme Court declared the *Hurn* test to be "unnecessarily grudging."

a. In its place, the *Gibbs* Court established the following test of pendent power: "The state and federal claims must derive from a common nucleus of operative fact. But if, considered without regard to their federal or state character, a plaintiff's claims are such that he would ordinarily be expected to try them all in one judicial proceeding, then, assuming substantiality of the federal issues, there is *power* in federal courts to exercise the whole."

4. The meaning of *Gibbs'* "same operative facts" test:

a. Since *Gibbs*, there is no doubt that the key applicable language for determining the existence of federal court power to exercise pendent jurisdiction is the requirement that the state and federal claims concern "the same operative facts." However, the meaning of the phrase is not altogether clear, and the surrounding language in the *Gibbs* opinion only compounds the confusion.

b. The conclusion that is most clear is that whatever "same operative facts" means, it extends beyond the narrow factual identity seemingly required under the *Hurn* test. Quite probably, it requires a common transactional base, and may require some degree (though not a totality) of evidentiary overlap.

c. Also clear is that the exercise of federal court *power* to hear pendent state claims requires a so-called "substantial"—or non-frivolous—question of federal law. Otherwise, the doctrine could be employed as a means of having federal courts adjudicate non-diverse state law claims through the insertion of trumped-up federal issues.

d. The meaning of the Court's "expected-to-try" language provides the primary source of confusion, in part because of the puzzling use of the word, "But" at the sentence's beginning—seemingly implying a contradiction or departure from, rather than an elaboration of, the previously-stated "same-operative-facts" test. Moreover, the Court at no point explains *when* a party would be "expected to try" all his claims together.

B. THE "POWER"—"DISCRETION" DICHOTOMY

1. Everything said to this point about the scope of pendent jurisdiction concerns what the Supreme Court has called the "power" of the federal courts to exercise pendent jurisdiction. As the Court stated in *Gibbs*, however, "[t]hat power need not be exercised in every case in which it is found to exist."

2. The Court thus recognized that a federal court may, under appropriate circumstances, exercise its *discretion* not to hear a pendent state claim, even if the requirements of pendent *power* have been met.

3. The factors the *Gibbs* Court indicated could be relevant to this discretionary determination are:

    a. If the federal claims are dismissed before trial.

    (1) This ground may be criticized as fostering inefficiency, since even if the federal claims are dismissed prior to trial, substantial effort—in the form of pre-trial discovery and motions—may already have gone into the case, effort that will be wasted if the state claim is also dismissed.

    b. If state issues "predominate," even though the federal issue is not "insubstantial."

    c. If there is a likelihood of jury confusion.

    d. In addition to the categories mentioned in *Gibbs*, certain lower federal courts have declined to adjudicate a pendent state claim if the issue of state law is difficult or unresolved by the state courts.

III. ANCILLARY JURISDICTION

A. HISTORICAL DEVELOPMENT

1. The initial Supreme Court case exercising ancillary jurisdiction was *Freeman v. Howe*, 65 U.S. (24 How.) 450 (1860), where the Supreme Court held that a federal court had authority in a diversity case to adjudicate the rights of non-diverse parties whose interests are affected by the disposition of property within the control of the federal court. However, the doctrine has not been limited to such "in rem" cases.

2. In *Moore v. New York Cotton Exchange*, 270 U.S. 593 (1926), the Supreme Court allowed a defendant in a federal antitrust suit to assert a counterclaim under state law, even though there did not exist diversity between the parties, because the defendant's state law counterclaim arose out of the same transaction or occurrence as plaintiff's antitrust claim.

B. THE SCOPE AND LIMITS OF ANCILLARY JURISDICTION

1. *The basic prerequisite to the exercise of ancillary jurisdiction is that the claim sought to be added arise out of the same transaction or occurrence as the claim that is properly in federal court.*

2. Thus, ancillary jurisdiction will be exercised over a compulsory counterclaim under Rule 13(a) of the Federal Rules of Civil Procedure, but not over a permissive counterclaim under Rule 13(b). This is not because one counterclaim is compulsory and the other permissive, but because the tests for exercising ancillary jurisdiction on the one hand and for distinguishing between compulsory and permissive counterclaims on the other are coincidentally identical: whether there exists a common transactional base.

3. Ancillary jurisdiction is applied to cases of impleader under Rule 14 of the Federal Rules of Civil Procedure, but not to cases under Rule 19, concerning indispensable parties.

4. The procedural contexts in which the doctrine will or will not be employed were developed without much rhyme or reason. However, in *Owen Equipment & Erection Co. v. Kroger*, 437 U.S. 365 (1978), the Supreme Court attempted to provide a rationalizing theory.

   a. The case held that while ancillary jurisdiction was appropriate in a traditional impleader context, it could not be employed to allow a non-diverse plaintiff to assert a claim against the third-party defendant brought into the impleader action. To understand the difference, consider the following two hypotheticals:

   Example 1: If A (from New York) sues B (from Illinois) in federal court on the basis of diversity, and B impleads C (also from Illinois), arguing that if B is liable to A, C is liable to B, ancillary jurisdiction will apply. This is the traditional impleader hypothetical.

   Example 2: If A (from New York) sues B (from Illinois) in diversity, and B impleads C (this time from *New York*), clearly the federal court may exercise jurisdiction over the impleader action, because there is diversity between the third-party plaintiff and the third-party defendant. *But:* If, in such a case, A (the original plaintiff, from New York) attempts to assert a state law claim against C (the third-party defendant, also from New York, brought into the impleader action), the federal court, according to *Owen*, is *not* allowed to exercise ancillary jurisdiction.

b. The Court's primary rationale for allowing ancillary jurisdiction in Example 1, while denying it in Example 2, is that in number 1 the benefit of ancillary jurisdiction is sought by the *defendant*, who is attempting to bring in a non-diverse third-party defendant, while in number 2 it is the *plaintiff* who is attempting to invoke the benefits of ancillary jurisdiction.

c. Ultimately, the distinction appears to derive from the Court's fundamental dislike of diversity jurisdiction.

(1) If the Court's goal is to deter the exercise of diversity jurisdiction, it is logical for it to *deny* the benefits of ancillary jurisdiction to the *plaintiffs* who have sought the federal courts—thereby encouraging them to seek the judicial convenience of the state courts—but to *grant* the doctrine's benefits to the *defendants*, who did not choose the federal forum initially.

(2) However, the plaintiff-defendant dichotomy does not provide a perfect fit with the "deterrence-of-diversity" rationale, because in certain instances the federal diversity jurisdiction may in the first instance be invoked by the defendant, who removes the case originally brought in state court to federal court.

(3) The major departure from the plaintiff-defendant dichotomy is the diversity class action context—*i.e.* where the named plaintiff is from a state different from the defendant, absent class members who, are, in fact, from the defendant's state are permitted to have their rights adjudicated in federal court under the ancillary jurisdiction doctrine. *Supreme Tribe of Ben-Hur v. Cauble*, 255 U.S. 356 (1921). However, while the case has not been expressly overruled, subsequent judicial developments in the aggregation of claims for purposes of the jurisdictional amount [*see* Chapter 7, *infra*] have cast serious doubt upon its continued vitality.

IV. PENDENT PARTY JURISDICTION

A. THE *ALDINGER* CASE

1. In *Aldinger v. Howard*, 427 U.S. 1 (1976), *the Supreme Court held that a federal court lacked power to exercise "pendent party" jurisdiction over a state law claim against a non-diverse municipality, even though that claim arises out of the same transaction as a federal civil rights claim under 42 U.S.C.A. § 1983, brought against a state officer, that is properly in federal court.*

a. Ultimately, the Court's holding went only to the question of whether pendent party jurisdiction could be applied to allow a plaintiff in a federal civil rights suit under section 1983 against a "person" acting "under color of" state law to join a state tort law claim under a theory of *respondeat superior* against the municipality that employed the defendant state officer.

(1) The Court cited its earlier conclusion in *Monroe v. Pape*, 365 U.S. 167 (1961), that a municipality was not intended by Congress to be deemed a "person" for purposes of section 1983, and therefore not subject to suit under section 1983.

(2) Thus, the Court concluded that "a fair reading of the [statutory] language . . . requires a holding that the joinder of a municipal corporation . . . for purposes of asserting a state-law claim not within federal diversity jurisdiction, is without the statutory jurisdiction of the district court."

b. However, the Court's opinion, written by Justice Rehnquist, also contained dicta indicating that the entire concept of "pendent party" jurisdiction was invalid, regardless of the basis of the original claim of federal jurisdiction.

(1) For example, the opinion stated: "The situation with respect to the joining of a new party . . . strikes us as being both factually and legally different from the situation facing the Court in *Gibbs* and its predecessors. From a purely factual point of view, it is one thing to authorize two parties, already present in federal court by virtue of a case over which the court has jurisdiction, to litigate in addition to their federal claim a state-law claim over which there is no independent basis of federal jurisdiction. But it is quite another thing to permit a plaintiff, who has asserted a claim against one defendant with respect to which there is federal jurisdiction, to join an entirely different defendant on the basis of a state-law claim over which there is no independent basis of federal jurisdiction, simply because his claim against the first defendant and his claim against the second defendant derive from a common nucleus of operative fact."

(2) The Court concluded that "the addition of a completely new party would run counter to the well-established principle that federal courts . . . are courts of limited jurisdiction marked out by Congress."

B. POST-*ALDINGER* DEVELOPMENTS AND IMPLICATIONS

1. After *Aldinger*, the Supreme Court decided that, under certain circumstances, municipalities were, in fact, to be deemed "persons" for purposes of section 1983. *Monell v. Department of Social Services of the City of New York*, 436 U.S. 658 (1978). However, in the post-*Monell* decision of *Owen Equipment & Erection Co. v. Kroger, supra*, the Court reiterated the continued vitality of the broad contours of *Aldinger*, namely that congressional intent to exclude a party or class of parties from coverage of a federal statutory cause of action will preclude assertion of pendent jurisdiction to state law claims when federal jurisdiction of the primary claim is pursuant to that federal statute.

2. Since *Aldinger*, some lower courts have held, as the *Aldinger* Court itself implied, that pendent party jurisdiction may be employed when the jurisdiction of the federal court on the federal claim is exclusive.

Example: Plaintiff sues the United States in federal court with jurisdiction based on 28 U.S.C.A. § 1346 for suits against the United States. Jurisdiction under this section is exclusive. Plaintiff attempts to join a state law claim, arising out of the same incident, against a non-diverse party. Pendent party jurisdiction is allowed. *Cf. Dick Meyers Towing Service, Inc. v. United States,* 577 F.2d 1023 (5th Cir.1978) (per curiam), *cert. denied,* 440 U.S. 908.

3. Some post-*Aldinger* lower court decisions have allowed pendent party jurisdiction in non-section 1983 suits, while others have construed *Aldinger* to bar any form of pendent party jurisdiction, with the possible exception of the exclusive jurisdiction example.

4. It is conceivable that the logic of *Aldinger*'s approach to section 1983 suits and pendent party jurisdiction—*i.e.* examining congressional intent in establishing the substantive cause of action to determine whether pendent party jurisdiction is appropriate—could be applied even to the pendent *claim* situation.

Examples: Plaintiff sues in federal court under the federal Age Discrimination in Employment Act, with a pendent claim under New York State's age discrimination statute, alleging that her employment was unlawfully terminated because of her age. In her complaint, plaintiff seeks damages for psychological suffering under the state claim. Such damages are recoverable under the state law, but not under the federal law. It might be concluded that under *Aldinger*'s logic, even pendent claim jurisdiction should be denied here, to avoid undermining congressional intent in excluding recovery for such damages under the federal statute.

However, such an extension might be rejected on the grounds that assertion of a federal court's power over a *party* over whom it lacks subject matter jurisdiction is more extreme, and therefore subject to closer scrutiny, then its assertion of power over a *claim* over which it lacks jurisdiction.

7

JURISDICTIONAL AMOUNT

Analysis

I. Introduction: Rationale and Scope of the Jurisdictional Amount Requirement
    A. The Need for a Jurisdictional Amount Requirement
    B. The Applicability of the Jurisdictional Amount Requirement
II. Measurement of the Jurisdictional Amount
    A. The "Legal Certainty" Test
    B. The "Good Faith" Requirement
    C. The "Viewpoint" Issue
III. Aggregation of Claims
    A. Traditional Aggregation Rules
    B. Aggregation Rules and Class Actions
    C. Implications of *Snyder* and *Zahn* *for the Viewpoint Rules*

I. INTRODUCTION: RATIONALE AND SCOPE OF THE JURISDICTIONAL AMOUNT REQUIREMENT

A. THE NEED FOR A JURISDICTIONAL AMOUNT REQUIREMENT

1. The purpose of congressional imposition of a jurisdictional minimum is well accepted: The federal courts possess limited time and resources, and therefore Congress must employ means of limiting what would otherwise be insurmountable judicial burdens. The imposition of a minimum amount requirement reflects congressional judgment that cases not "worth" the specified amount simply do not justify the expenditure of federal judicial time and effort.

2. It is not always clear, however, that it is appropriate to equate "worth" with the measurable amount of money involved in a case. As a result, Congress has in recent years dramatically restricted the reach of the jurisdictional amount requirement.

B. THE APPLICABILITY OF THE JURISDICTIONAL AMOUNT REQUIREMENT

1. *Currently, the primary general jurisdictional heading that contains a jurisdictional minimum is diversity, where the applicable requirement is an amount in excess of $10,000, exclusive of interests and costs.*

2. For many years, cases falling within the general federal question jurisdiction also were required to meet the jurisdictional minimum. However, numerous difficulties arose in cases brought to obtain injunctive relief against federal officers in order to protect federal constitutional rights.

    a. Though suits brought to vindicate constitutional rights against *state* officers were always controlled by a separate jurisdictional grant, 28 U.S.C.A. § 1343, which did not impose a jurisdictional minimum, suits against *federal* officers for constitutional violations have always fallen under the general federal question jurisdictional grant, 28 U.S.C.A. § 1331.

    b. As a result, courts were often faced with the impossible task of deciding whether an individual's right of free speech or privacy could be "valued" at more than $10,000.

Example: Plaintiff, a third-party candidate for President of the United States, sues in federal court to require military officials to allow him to campaign on an army base, arguing that the denial violates his first amendment right of free expression. The government responds that the federal court lacks jurisdiction under 28 U.S.C.A. § 1331, because the requisite $10,000 minimum has not been met. *See Spock v. David*, 502 F.2d 953 (3d Cir. 1974), *rev'd on other grounds*, 424 U.S. 828. In *Spock*, the court was extremely lenient in finding the jurisdictional amount requirement met. Other lower federal courts, however, believed that the problem was one for Congress.

3. In 1976, Congress removed the jurisdictional amount requirement in suits brought against federal officers, and in 1980 Congress amended § 1331 to remove the jurisdictional minimum completely.

II. MEASUREMENT OF THE JURISDICTIONAL AMOUNT

A. THE "LEGAL CERTAINTY" TEST

1. In *St. Paul Mercury Indemnity Co. v. Red Cab Co.*, 303 U.S. 283 (1938), *the Supreme Court held that "the sum claimed by the plaintiff controls if the claim is apparently made in good faith. It must appear to a legal certainty that the claim is really for less than the jurisdictional amount to justify dismissal."*

a. This gave rise to the "legal certainty" test for jurisdictional amount: before a case may be dismissed for failure to meet the jurisdictional amount requirement, it must appear to a legal certainty that plaintiff cannot recover an amount in excess of that amount.

b. It is important to emphasize that this does *not* mean that the plaintiff has the burden to demonstrate that he will "certainly" recover in excess of the jurisdictional minimum; rather, it must be established to a "certainty" that he *cannot* recover in excess of the requisite amount.

Example: Plaintiff sues defendant in a diversity suit for damages suffered allegedly due to defendant's negligence in an auto accident. At the outset of the case, it is impossible to know whether plaintiff's damages actually do exceed the jurisdictional minimum. Plaintiff's claim will not be dismissed for lack of jurisdiction, despite this uncertainty, because it is not certain that plaintiff's damages actually will prove to be less than the jurisdictional minimum.

c. It is not always clear, however, when the court may know to a "legal certainty" that the recovery will be less than the jurisdictional minimum.

2. The clearest cases, of course, are those rare instances in which the sum demanded in the plaintiff's complaint is below the jurisdictional minimum. Also clear are cases where either the applicable substantive state law or a private arrangement between the parties imposes a ceiling on damages that is below the requisite jurisdictional amount.

Example: Plaintiff sues defendant in federal court on the basis of diversity jurisdiction for breach of contract. The terms of the contract contain a liquidated damage clause that provides that neither party may recover more than $5,000 as a result of a breach. Assuming the validity of that term of the agreement, it has been established to "a legal certainty" that the amount in controversy is below the jurisdictional minimum.

3. Even absent a liquidated damage clause or a ceiling imposed by state law, courts have on occasion invoked the *St. Paul* test to deny jurisdiction because the jurisdictional amount had not been met. Usually, these courts reason that if a jury award in excess of the jurisdictional minimum would be vacated as unreasonable on the basis of the available evidence, it is clear to "a legal certainty" that the jurisdictional minimum has not been met.

Example: In a suit for negligence arising out of an auto accident, where plaintiff's total documented medical and property damage were far less than the jurisdictional minimum, and where no loss of employment compensation was claimed, the federal court may dismiss for lack of jurisdiction prior to trial, because a jury award that exceeded the $10,000 jurisdictional minimum would in any event have to be set aside as capricious. *Nelson v. Keefer*, 451 F.2d 289 (3d Cir.1971).

4. 28 U.S.C.A. § 1332(b) provides that if the plaintiff is finally adjudged to be entitled to recover less than the $10,000 minimum, the court may deny an award of costs to plaintiff and in addition may impose costs on plaintiff.

B. THE "GOOD FAITH" REQUIREMENT

1. In *St. Paul Mercury*, the Court also indicated that the amount in excess of the jurisdictional minimum must be claimed in good faith.

2. Such a statement may give rise to confusion over whether "good faith" and "legal certainty" impose distinct, necessary conditions for meeting the jurisdictional minimum, or whether they are simply different characterizations of the same test.

a. While certain courts and commentators have expressed the view that "good faith" merely represents a means of finding "legal certainty," at least as an abstract matter the two might deal with very different questions.

Example: Plaintiff sues defendant for injuries, including pain and suffering, due to defendant's negligence. The amount claimed far exceeds the jurisdictional minimum. The plaintiff and his lawyer say to friends that in reality they do not expect to recover anywhere near $10,000. Under a "good faith" test, plaintiff's complaint might be dismissed. But if plaintiff and his lawyer are undervaluing the worth of their claim, under the "legal certainty" test the claim should not be dismissed.

b. Ultimately, it seems that the motivation for the jurisdictional amount requirement—keeping "worthless" cases out of federal court—dictates that it is the *objective* "legal certainty" test, rather than the *subjective* "good faith" test, that should be deemed primary.

c. Of course, a demonstration that the plaintiff himself does not believe his claim is worth more than the jurisdictional minimum could be valuable evidence in making the objective "legal certainty" finding, and in this sense the two criteria merge.

3. It is important to note that the mere fact that plaintiff ultimately recovers less than the jurisdictional amount will not deprive the federal court of jurisdiction.

C. THE "VIEWPOINT" ISSUE

1. In measuring the jurisdictional amount, there has long existed a controversy over the "viewpoint" from which the jurisdictional amount requirement is to be measured.

2. Under the so-called "plaintiff viewpoint" rule, the jurisdictional amount requirement is met only if the *plaintiff* stands to gain in excess of the minimum; under the "defendant viewpoint" rule, the requirement is met only if the defendant stands to lose in excess of the minimum.

Example: Plaintiff sues in federal court under diversity jurisdiction to enjoin defendant's power plant as a nuisance. Plaintiff's damage is in the largely immeasurable form of air pollution. If defendant's plant is shut down, however, he stands to lose far in excess of the jurisdictional minimum. Under the "plaintiff viewpoint" rule, the jurisdictional amount requirement has not been met; under the "defendant viewpoint" rule, it *has* been met.

3. The argument in favor of the "defendant viewpoint" rule is that it is consistent with the main purpose of the jurisdictional amount requirement—*i.e.*, to keep out of federal court trivial lawsuits: if *either* party stands to gain or lose in excess of the jurisdictional minimum, the case cannot be deemed "trivial."

4. The argument in favor of the "plaintiff viewpoint" rule is that—especially now that the jurisdictional minimum has been removed from federal question cases—use of the "defendant viewpoint" rule would unnecessarily add to the already overcrowded dockets of the federal courts.

5. The lower courts have split on the issue, though it is conceivable that the Supreme Court has, indirectly, adopted the "plaintiff viewpoint" rule. *See infra* at 88.

III. AGGREGATION OF CLAIMS

A. TRADITIONAL AGGREGATION RULES

1. *Under long-accepted principles, a single plaintiff is allowed to aggregate the amounts of all of his separate claims against a single defendant, whether or not those claims arise out of the same transaction or occurrence.*

Example: A sues B in federal court in a diversity suit, joining together a claim for breach of contract, seeking $4,000, and a wholly unrelated tort suit for negligence arising out of an auto accident, seeking $7,000. A is allowed to aggregate the amount of his two claims, for a total of $11,000, thus exceeding the $10,000 jurisdictional minimum.

2. *However, multiple plaintiffs seeking to aggregate their claims against a single defendant, or a single plaintiff seeking to aggregate claims against multiple defendants, have traditionally been allowed to do so only when their claims were deemed "joint," rather than "several," two abstract concepts which the courts never adequately distinguished and which have caused substantial confusion.*

B. AGGREGATION RULES AND CLASS ACTIONS

1. Prior to 1966, the rules concerning class actions in federal court generally paralleled accepted aggregation principles.

   a. Rule 23 prior to 1966 provided for three types of class actions:

   (1) "True": Class actions in which the claims of the parties were "joint."

   (2) "Hybrid:" class actions in which the claims were "several," rather than "joint," but all related to the same property.

   (3) "Spurious:" Class actions in which the claims were "several," or totally separate.

   b. The practical consequences of the distinctions were that the result of a "true" class action was binding on all members of the class; the result of a "hybrid" class bound all members' rights in the property in question; and the result of a "spurious" class action bound only those class members who had formally intervened in the action.

2. The 1966 amendments to the Federal Rules of Civil Procedure rejected the preexisting structure in favor of a new system, under which all class members would be bound by the result, and under which the concepts

of "joint" and "several" were rendered irrelevant, expressly because of the difficulties inherent in distinguishing the concepts.

3. However, in *Snyder v. Harris*, 394 U.S. 332 (1969), the Supreme Court held that the changes in the structure of class actions under Rule 23 did not alter application of the traditional aggregation rules. Hence, plaintiff class members with less than $10,000 claims could not aggregate their claims to exceed the jurisdictional minimum in a diversity class action suit.

   a. The Court rejected the argument that the change in Rule 23 should be deemed to have altered the aggregation rules when applied to class action suits.

   b. Justice Black, speaking for the Court, reasoned that the aggregation rules had been developed entirely separately from the pre-1966 class action rules, and that in effect the use of the "joint"-"several" distinction in both contexts was purely coincidental.

   c. Though dissenting Justice Fortas argued that the aggregation rules should be altered because the concept of a "spurious" class action for "several" rights had been abandoned, meaning that the rights of *all* class members were now implicated in a class action, the majority responded that under Rule 82 a change in the Federal Rules could not alter applicable principles of federal jurisdiction.

   d. The Court might have considered rejecting the traditional aggregation rules, wholly apart from the change in Rule 23, since the relevant statutory phrase in 28 U.S.C.A. § 1332, the diversity jurisdiction statute, was "matter in controversy"; thus, the statute in no way directly commanded use of the aggregation rules, which were totally judge-made. However, the majority concluded that since Congress had never indicated any dissatisfaction with the traditional aggregation rules, even while increasing the jurisdictional amount requirement at various times, the aggregation rules—even though wholly judge-made—could be altered only by congressional action.

4. In *Zahn v. International Paper Co.*, 414 U.S. 291 (1973), the Supreme Court extended the holding in *Snyder*.

   a. The Court held that absent class members whose claims fell below the jurisdictional minimum could not join in a class suit brought by a named plaintiff whose claim did exceed the jurisdictional minimum.

   b. While the majority expressed the view that its holding followed logically from *Snyder*, there existed arguably important differences.

c. In *Snyder,* no plaintiff's claim exceeded the jurisdictional minimum. In contrast, in *Zahn* at least one plaintiff's claim did exceed the requisite minimum; under the theory of ancillary jurisdiction (*see* Chapter 6), the Court might have allowed the absent class members to append their claims to the named plaintiff's claim, which was properly in federal court. The use of ancillary jurisdiction would not have been possible in *Snyder.*

d. The impact of *Zahn* is that no diversity class suit may be brought in federal court, unless *each* class member claims in excess of $10,000, except in the rare case when rights are "joint". Such a rule effectively undermines the class action device, which is designed in part to allow numerous small claims to be joined in one suit when it would be inefficient or impractical for separate suits to be brought. However, it is important to emphasize that under current standards, it is only *diversity* class actions where this will be true, because it is only diversity cases in which the jurisdictional amount requirement is currently imposed.

Example: Plaintiffs file a class action suit in federal court under the federal antitrust laws, alleging price-fixing by defendant supermarkets on the price of bread. Each class member's claim is far below $10,000, but since the applicable jurisdictional statute, 28 U.S.C.A. § 1337, requires no jurisdictional minimum, jurisdiction does not fail as a result of the amount of the class members' claims.

C. IMPLICATIONS OF *SNYDER* AND *ZAHN* FOR THE VIEWPOINT RULES

1. Though the Court never expressly considered the issue in either *Snyder* or *Zahn,* it is conceivable that the holdings in those cases impliedly adopt a "plaintiff viewpoint" rule.

2. The argument for such a position is that if the Court were to accept the "defendant viewpoint" rule, it would have allowed aggregation in both cases, because in both the defendant stood to lose an amount far in excess of the jurisdictional minimum.

3. Since *Snyder* and *Zahn,* the Supreme Court has not dealt with the viewpoint issue. It has been suggested by some lower federal courts that the implication of those cases for the viewpoint issue should be deemed limited to the class action context. However, since the very point of the Court's analysis in *Snyder* was that the traditional aggregation rules were developed wholly apart from class action principles, it is difficult to accept such reasoning.

8

SUPREME COURT JURISDICTION

Analysis

I. Original Jurisdiction of the Supreme Court
   A. Types of Actions Covered
   B. Relation Between the Supreme Court's Original and Appellate Jurisdictions
II. Appellate Jurisdiction of the Supreme Court
   A. The Appeal-Certiorari Distinction
   B. The Final Judgment Rule
   C. The "Independent and Adequate State Ground" Doctrine
   D. Supreme Court Review of State Court Findings of Fact

I. ORIGINAL JURISDICTION OF THE SUPREME COURT

A. TYPES OF ACTIONS COVERED

1. *Article III, section 2 extends the Supreme Court's original jurisdiction only to "cases affecting ambassadors, other public ministers and consuls, and those in which a state shall be a party. . . ."*

2. It is well accepted that the reach of this provision is limited by the general contours of the "judicial power," as set out in Article III, section 2, and thus does not extend the Supreme Court's jurisdiction to cases involving a state or public minister that do not fall within the previous listing.

3. The majority of the Supreme Court's original jurisdiction involves suits between states. Relatively few public minister/ambassador cases are brought originally in the Supreme Court.

B. RELATION BETWEEN THE SUPREME COURT'S ORIGINAL AND APPELLATE JURISDICTIONS

1. *The Supreme Court's appellate jurisdiction extends, at least potentially, to all categories of cases included in the "judicial power" as described in Article III, section 2, and makes up the overwhelming portion of the Court's workload.*

2. In *Marbury v. Madison*, 5 U.S. (1 Cranch) 137 (1803), Chief Justice Marshall indicated his view that the divisions between the Court's original and appellate jurisdictions are rigid.

   a. In other words, he believed that the Court cannot hear cases allocated to its appellate jurisdiction as part of its original jurisdiction, that the Court cannot hear on appeal cases falling within its original jurisdiction, and that only the Supreme Court may hear cases falling within its original jurisdiction.

   b. Marshall's interpretation is largely no longer accepted law. Today, while the Court does adhere to Marshall's view that the Court's original jurisdiction may extend only to the cases specifically described in the original jurisdiction clause of Article III, lower courts are permitted to take jurisdiction over cases falling within the Supreme Court's original jurisdiction and the Supreme Court is allowed to assert appellate jurisdiction over such cases.

   Example: The state of Illinois sues the city of Milwaukee to stop pollution of Lake Michigan. While the case falls within the Supreme Court's original jurisdiction, the Court chose to have the case adjudicated initially in the lower federal courts under their general federal question jurisdiction. *Illinois v. City of Milwaukee*, 406 U.S. 91 (1972).

3. While the Supreme Court's original jurisdiction is assumed to be self-executing, Congress has enacted a jurisdictional structure that sets out the jurisdiction of the lower federal courts over cases falling within the Supreme Court's original jurisdiction.

    a. 28 U.S.C.A. § 1251(a) renders the Supreme Court's original jurisdiction over controversies between two or more states to be exclusive. In *Illinois v. City of Milwaukee*, 406 U.S. 91 (1972), the Supreme Court held that the term "States" in 28 U.S.C.A. § 1251(a) should not be read to include political subdivisions.

    b. 28 U.S.C.A. § 1251(b) indicates that the Supreme Court's original jurisdiction is not exclusive in "(1) All actions or proceedings to which ambassadors, other public ministers, consuls, or vice consuls of foreign states are parties; (2) All controversies between the United States and a State; (3) All actions or proceedings by a State against the citizens of another State or against aliens."

4. In *Ohio v. Wyandotte Chemicals Corp.*, 401 U.S. 493 (1971), the Supreme Court found that while it had jurisdiction of a suit by a state against citizens of other states and a foreign country, it would refuse to exercise that jurisdiction on purely discretionary grounds. This was a result of complex scientific issues involved in the case, which the Court found to be inappropriate for adjudication by means of the Court's original jurisdiction. The Court has indicated that it exercises its "original jurisdiction sparingly and [is] particularly reluctant to take jurisdiction of a suit where the plaintiff has another adequate forum in which to settle his claim." *United States v. Nevada*, 412 U.S. 534 (1972) (per curiam). However, when important state interests are involved, the Court is more likely to exercise its original jurisdiction. *South Carolina v. Regan*, ___ U.S. ___ (1984).

5. One major difference between the Court's original and appellate jurisdictions is the ability of Congress to regulate and limit the Court's appellate jurisdiction (see Chapter 2).

    a. Article III, section 2 of the Constitution expressly provides that the Court's appellate jurisdiction is given "with such exceptions, and under such regulations as the Congress shall make."

    b. No such congressional power exists in regard to the Court's original jurisdiction.

II. APPELLATE JURISDICTION OF THE SUPREME COURT

A. THE APPEAL–CERTIORARI DISTINCTION

1. The statutes describing the Supreme Court's appellate jurisdiction distinguish between two primary methods of obtaining Supreme Court review: appeal and certiorari. Before we can examine the various situations in which each device is to be employed, it is necessary to understand exactly what consequences, if any, flow from the distinction.

2. *Theoretically, the Supreme Court's "appeal" jurisdiction is mandatory, while its "certiorari" jurisdiction is entirely discretionary.* In other words, the Court is required to adjudicate cases falling within its appeal jurisdiction, but retains total discretion to decide whether it will hear cases falling within its certiorari jurisdiction. For certiorari to be granted, at least four of the Justices must vote to grant it.

3. *However, the Court in many ways treats its appeal jurisdiction as if it were discretionary.*

　　a. In *Zucht v. King*, 260 U.S. 174 (1922), the Court held that it lacked jurisdiction to adjudicate an appeal from a state court decision upholding a state statute because the federal question raised was not "substantial."

　　b. It has been suggested by commentators that *Zucht* still imposes a tougher standard for dismissal of an appeal than it does for denial of a writ of certiorari, because for a federal question to be insubstantial it must be plainly wrong, not merely unimportant. As a practical matter, however, the Court appears to treat the two in a very similar manner.

4. One problem in the Court's blurring of the appeal-certiorari distinction derives from the fact that, as a technical matter at least, the dismissal of an appeal or a summary affirmance (used for appeal from the lower federal courts, as opposed to the state courts) constitutes a decision on the merits, while denial of a writ of certiorari implies nothing about the merits of the decision. Thus, the former are theoretically binding precedent, while the latter are not.

　　a. In *Edelman v. Jordan*, 415 U.S. 651 (1974), the Supreme Court deemed itself not to be bound to recent summary affirmances.

　　b. However, in *Hicks v. Miranda*, 422 U.S. 332 (1975), the Court criticized the lower court's statement that it was not bound by the Supreme Court's earlier summary dismissal of an appeal; it noted the obligatory nature of its appellate jurisdiction.

c. When read in combination, decisions such as these appear to establish the principle that while the lower courts are bound by summary dispositions of appeals, they carry far less precedential weight in the Supreme Court.

d. This situation has given rise to substantial confusion, leading to numerous calls for congressional abolition of the distinction, making the Court's appellate jurisdiction completely discretionary.

5. As presently structured, the statutory framework of the Supreme Court's appellate jurisdiction is as follows:

a. Pursuant to 28 U.S.C.A. § 1252, any party may appeal directly to the Supreme Court any interlocutory or final judgment of any court of the United States "holding an Act of Congress unconstitutional in any civil action, suit, or proceeding to which the United States or any of its agencies, or any officer or employee thereof, as such officer or employee, is a party."

b. Pursuant to 28 U.S.C.A. § 1254, the Supreme Court may review a decision of a federal court of appeals by appeal, if sought by a party relying on a state statute held by a court of appeals "to be invalid as repugnant to the Constitution, treaties or laws of the United States," and by writ of certiorari in other cases from a court of appeals, or by a process known as "certification" if a court of appeals certifies a particular question.

c. Pursuant to 28 U.S.C.A. § 1258, by appeal from a final judgment of the state's highest court where a state court has found against the validity of a treaty or statute of the United States or where a federal constitutional challenge to a state statute has been rejected by the state court, and by writ of certiorari where there has been any decision on these same questions, "or where any title, right, privilege or immunity is specially set up or claimed under the Constitution, treaties or statues of, or commission held or authority exercised under, the United States."

d. The Supreme Court has made clear that municipal ordinances and administrative regulations constitute "statutes" for purposes of the extension of the Court's appeal jurisdiction.

e. In *Dahnke-Walker Milling Co. v. Bondurant*, 257 U.S. 282 (1921), the Supreme Court held that challenges to the *application* of a statute constituted challenges to a statute for purposes of the Court's appellate jurisdiction.

B. THE FINAL JUDGMENT RULE

1. *28 U.S.C.A. § 1257 provides for appeal or certiorari from "[f]inal judgments or decrees rendered by the highest court of a State in which a decision could be had. . . ."*

2. The *purposes* of the final judgment rule are:

    a. *Efficiency*, because it avoids piecemeal appeals and may moot numerous potential grounds for appeal because the would-be appellant receives a favorable decision on the merits in the state court.

    b. *Protecting federalism*, by possibly avoiding Supreme Court friction with state courts, that might result from Supreme Court review of state court decisions.

2. However, the phrase "final judgment" turns out to be considerably more ambiguous a term than one might initially suspect. For example, the Court has always been willing to consider the practicalities of the situation, so that if as a practical matter nothing further remains to be done in the state courts, the Court will deem the case "final," even though a technically final judgment has not been entered in the state court.

3. While the Court's *construction* of the final judgment rule has thus taken into account practical realities, the Court has also developed doctrines of appealability under section 1257 that amount to *exceptions* to the statutory requirement of finality.

    a. *Forgay—Radio Station WOW:* In *Forgay v. Conrad*, 47 U.S. (6 How.) 201 (1848) (concerning the separate use of the final judgment rule as it applies to appeals from the trial to appellate federal courts) and *Radio Station WOW, Inc. v. Johnson*, 326 U.S. 120 (1945) (for appeals from state court to Supreme Court), the Court recognized an exception for cases in which property has been ordered transferred and all that remained to be done in the lower court was to conduct an accounting of profits. The Court in *Radio Station WOW* reasoned that the two orders were distinct, and therefore in effect constituted multiple litigation. But in reality, of course, the two orders are still part of the same action.

    b. *The "Collateral Order" Approach:* In *Cohen v. Beneficial Industrial Loan Corp.*, 337 U.S. 541 (1949), the Supreme Court recognized an exception to the finality requirement in appeals from federal district courts to federal courts of appeals "in that small class [of cases] which finally determine claims of right separable from, and collateral to, rights asserted in the action, too important to be denied review and too independent of the cause itself to require that appellate consideration be deferred until the whole case is adjudicated." The Court applied an analogy to this doctrine in allowing appeal from state court under section 1257 in *Construction & General Laborers' Union v. Curry,* 371 U.S. 542 (1963), and *Mercantile National Bank v. Langdeau,* 371 U.S. 555 (1963).

4. The expansion of finality in *Cox.*

a. In *Cox Broadcasting Corp. v. Cohn,* 420 U.S. 469 (1975), the Supreme Court significantly changed the traditional approach to finality and in so doing appeared to expand the concept to the breaking point.

b. The Court described four categories of cases in which appeal might be allowed despite the absence of technical finality:

(1) Cases of "practical finality," where though there exists no technically final judgment, as a practical matter nothing remains to be done in the state court.

(2) Cases, like *Radio Station WOW,* "in which the federal issue, finally decided by the highest court in the State, will survive and require decision regardless of the outcome of future state-court proceedings" [though the *Cox* Court in its description appeared to abandon the earlier prerequisites in such cases that the bulk of the case have been completed in state court and that there exist a danger of irreparable injury if appeal is denied].

(3) Cases where, "if the party seeking interim review ultimately prevails on the merits, the federal issue will be mooted; if he were to lose on the merits, however, the governing state law would not permit him again to present his federal claim for review."

(4) Cases in which the state courts have finally decided the federal issue and in which reversal of the state court on the federal issue would preclude any further litigation and a refusal to provide immediate review "might seriously erode federal policy."

c. The last two categories represent considerably more than a construction of the concept of finality.

(1) In both categories, it is unquestionably true that the case has not been completed in the state court.

(2) Moreover, by so expanding the meaning of "final," the Court may well be undermining many of the purposes behind the final judgment rule of section 1257, primarily avoidance of what may prove to be an unnecessary Supreme Court clash with a state court.

d. The Court applied the fourth category to the specific facts of *Cox* to allow Supreme Court review.

(1) The case was a suit for invasion of privacy brought in Georgia state court by the father of a rape victim, seeking damages from a local television station that had broadcast his daughter's name in connection with the trial of the accused rapists. Defendants contended that the first amendment right of free press precluded the suit.

(2) The state trial court, rejecting the defendants' argument, granted summary judgment against them, leaving damages to be determined at trial.

(3) The state supreme court agreed that the constitutional defense was unacceptable, but reversed the grant of summary judgment and remanded for a trial on the merits to determine if an invasion of privacy had actually occurred.

(4) The Supreme Court allowed appeal under section 1257, even though the state supreme court had remanded for trial. In so holding, the Court noted that the state supreme court's decision "is plainly final on the federal issue and is not subject to further review in the state courts." The Court recognized that the defendants might prevail at trial on state grounds, but asserted that if they were correct on the constitutional issue there should be no trial at all, and in any event, the Court was concerned that if defendants won on non-federal grounds the state court's determination on the first amendment issue would stand unreviewed.

C. THE "INDEPENDENT AND ADEQUATE STATE GROUND" DOCTRINE

1. The concept and rationale.

a. The Supreme Court held in *Murdock v. City of Memphis*, 87 U.S. (20 Wall.) 590 (1875), that the Supreme Court lacks authority to review state court decisions interpreting state law. Though the extent to which this holding is constitutionally required is unclear, it is, at the very least, well established as a matter of Supreme Court doctrine.

b. Related to this principle was the further holding in *Murdock* that *the Supreme Court lacks authority to review federal issues contained in state court decisions when those decisions are premised on independent and adequate state law grounds.*

c. *The doctrine can be divided into two sub-categories:*

(1) *Substantive* state law grounds: where the state court decision rests upon both federal and non-federal grounds, the Supreme Court will not review if the non-federal ground, standing alone, would support the judgment.

(2) *Procedural* state law grounds: where the state court refuses to adjudicate a federal issue because the litigant has failed to comply with a legitimate state procedural rule.

  d. The *substantive* branch of the doctrine is often justified by the "advisory opinion" rationale, which relies on the proposition that the Supreme Court is not permitted to issue advisory opinions which do not resolve actual cases or controversies. *Herb v. Pitcairn*, 324 U.S. 117 (1945). If an adequate state ground would support the state court judgment, no matter how the federal issue is resolved, then a Supreme Court resolution of the federal issue will have no effect on the outcome of the case. However, it may be questioned whether it follows that no real case or controversy exists. This branch of the doctrine could just as easily be rationalized by the prudential principle that the Supreme Court should avoid unnecessary pronouncements of federal law, particularly when friction with state courts or state substantive policies might result.

  e. The *procedural* branch of the doctrine, on the other hand, is never justified on the basis of the "advisory opinion" rationale. Instead, it is generally justified by the Supreme Court's desire to avoid undermining the maintenance of uniform and predictable state procedures. This goal could not be attained if the Supreme Court were to encourage litigants to circumvent state procedures by allowing them to raise their federal issue before the Court even though they had not complied with valid state procedural rules.

  2. Determining the adequacy of the state ground.

  a. *The Supreme Court has made clear that it will not deem itself bound by a state procedural rule or substantive state law holding that it finds to be inadequate.*

  (1) However, the Court has expressed the view that it is less likely to find inadequate a state substantive finding than a state procedural rule.

  (2) This view has been attacked by commentators, who find no basis for the distinction.

  b. Over the years, the Court has established certain categories of procedural rules which it deems inadequate.

  (1) *Arbitrary* state rules: if a state rule "lacks fair or substantial support" or can be characterized as arbitrary, the Supreme Court will deem it nothing more than an attempt to insulate the state court holding from federal review and will disregard it.

Example: The defendant moves to quash a murder indictment on the ground that blacks have been systematically excluded from the grand jury, but the state supreme court refused to consider the motion because it was "prolix", even though the motion took up only two pages in the printed record. The Supreme Court found the state ground to be inadequate, and decided to consider the federal issue. *Rogers v. Alabama*, 192 U.S. 226 (1904).

(2) *"Novel"* state rules: when the state court has applied a state rule that is inconsistent with prior state practice, the Supreme Court has on occasion refused to find the state rule adequate.

(3) *Discretionary* rules: The Supreme Court has closely scrutinized state judicial invocation of procedural rules that are invoked solely at the discretion of the state court, though some have questioned the validity of this exception, suggesting that it unduly interferes with state prerogatives. Its rationale is that such discretionary rules may be employed to insulate the state decision from federal review.

Example: Plaintiff asserts a federal right against racial discrimination, but the state appellate court denies the appeal because opposing counsel had not received reasonable notice and transcript, as required by court rule. Because the state court had not consistently applied its notice requirement to amount to a denial of its power to adjudicate the federal issue, the Court found the state rule "discretionary [rather] than jurisdictional" and adjudicated the federal issue. *Sullivan v. Little Hunting Park, Inc.*, 396 U.S. 229 (1969).

3. The *Henry* decision.

a. The Supreme Court's decision in *Henry v. Mississippi*, 379 U.S. 443 (1965), appeared to expand significantly the scope of the exceptions to the adequate state ground doctrine. In recent years, however, the decision's impact appears to have been reduced significantly.

b. The Mississippi Supreme Court upheld the defendant's conviction, finding that defendant had waived his objection to the introduction of illegally seized evidence by failing to raise a contemporaneous objection to the introduction of the evidence.

c. The Supreme Court remanded for a finding on the issue of defense counsel's conscious waiver. On the general issue of the adequate state ground doctrine, the Court stated: "A litigant's procedural defaults in state proceedings do not prevent vindication of his federal rights unless the State's insistence on compliance with its procedural rule serves a legitimate state interest." This language seemed to indicate an expansion, because while previous exceptions required some affirmative showing as to why the state rule was invalid, the Court's language in *Henry* required that each state rule must be justified before it would be deemed an adequate state ground.

    d. The most controversial aspect of the decision was its implication that the so-called "contemporaneous objection" rule, which requires that before a litigant may challenge the admissibility of evidence on appeal it must object at the time the evidence is introduced at trial.

    (1) While the Court acknowledged that the rule served a legitimate state interest by giving the trial court the opportunity to conduct the trial without the tainted evidence, it noted that that purpose could be equally served by the defendant's motion at the close of the state's evidence on the ground of the improperly admitted evidence.

    (2) This position has been criticized for unduly interfering in the state's choice of procedural rules and for improperly equating the value of the two procedural practices.

    (e) The Court's remand to determine whether the failure to object was because of defense counsel's negligence or conscious choice demonstrated that the Court's potentially broad exception to the adequate state ground doctrine was to be tempered by a waiver doctrine: even if the state rule fails to serve a legitimate state interest, if the defendant consciously chose not to comply with it the rule would still be deemed valid.

    4. Post-*Henry* developments.

    a. The Court decided several adequate state ground cases in the 1960's and early 1970's, but those decisions were largely inconclusive about the continued viability of *Henry*.

    b. Commentators suggest that in recent years the *Henry* rule has lain dormant.

    c. In *Wainwright v. Sykes*, 433 U.S. 72 (1977), the Court, in a habeas corpus case, expressed significant doubt about the assertion, made in *Henry*, that a directed verdict motion could adequately serve as a substitute for the contemporaneous objection rule, pointing out what it considered the unique values of the contemporaneous objection rule. However, the decision did not overrule *Henry*, and did not deal directly with the adequate state ground doctrine as it applies to Supreme Court review of state court decisions.

5. Determining whether the state decision is based on state or federal law.

   a. A state court's decision can serve as an adequate state ground only if the decision is truly a determination of state law.

   b. In certain instances, a state decision will be ambiguous—*i.e.*, unclear whether it is in fact based on state law or federal law. If the decision is based on federal law, then the adequate state ground doctrine becomes irrelevant.

   c. The Supreme Court has, over the years, employed various techniques to determine whether the state decision is premised on state or federal grounds.

   (1) The Court originally *dismissed* unless a federal issue clearly appeared.

   (2) In later years the Court adopted a *vacation* technique—*i.e.*, in the face of an ambiguity, vacate the judgment and return it to state court for clarification.

   d. In *Michigan v. Long*, 463 U.S. 1032 (1983), the Supreme Court held that when the state court's opinion is ambiguous, it will be presumed that the state court intended to decide exclusively or primarily on the basis of federal law, and the Supreme Court may take the case.

D. SUPREME COURT REVIEW OF STATE COURT FINDINGS OF FACT

1. *Traditionally, the Supreme Court denies itself authority to review state court factual findings.*

2. *However, the Court has also stated that it has a duty to make an independent examination of the record when constitutional deprivations are alleged.*

3. If the Court finds that the findings of the state court in such cases lack supporting evidence in the record or if factual findings are so intermingled with the state court's conclusion of law about the federal right, it will make its own independent judgment about the facts.

Example: The state court held that the state Syndicalism Act did not violate the federal Constitution as applied to a specific case in which it found that the defendant was a member of an organization that taught and advocated violent overthrow of the government. The Supreme Court found that there was no evidence to support the state court's conclusion about the organization's aims. *Fiske v. Kansas*, 274 U.S. 380 (1927).

SUPREME COURT JURISDICTION

REVIEW QUESTIONS (PART II)

1. T or F The scope of the current federal question statute is equal to the scope of the "arising under" jurisdiction provision of Article III, section 2.

2. T or F The Supreme Court's decision in *Aldinger v. Howard* precludes the use of any form of pendent party jurisdiction in federal court.

3. T or F In *Gibbs v. United Mine Workers*, the Supreme Court broadened the scope of pendent jurisdiction.

4. T or F The requirement of complete diversity derives from the Constitution.

5. T or F While a corporation may have at most the citizenship of two states, for purposes of diversity jurisdiction, an unincorporated association may have the citizenship of an unlimited number of states.

6. T or F Any case that falls within the Supreme Court's original jurisdiction may not be heard by a lower federal court.

7. T or F The adequate state ground doctrine is designed exclusively to avoid the issuance of advisory opinions by the federal courts.

8. T or F In interpreting the final judgment rule of 28 U.S.C.A. § 1257, the Supreme Court has allowed appeals of orders which could not in any rational sense be classified as "final."

9. T or F To meet the jurisdictional amount requirement of 28 U.S.C.A. § 1332, a plaintiff must establish to a legal certainty that his claim is worth in excess of the statutorily provided minimum.

10. T or F Under applicable principles of ancillary jurisdiction, a plaintiff in a diversity case whose claim is in excess of the jurisdictional minimum may represent a class whose other members do not have claims in excess of the jurisdictional minimum.

11. T or F Even if a case will ultimately turn on issues of federal law, it may not be heard originally in federal court if the federal issues are first introduced in the defendant's answer.

12. T or F The principle described in number 11 derives from the Constitution.

13. T or F The mere fact that a federal court finds that it has power to exercise pendent jurisdiction in a particular case does not mean that the court either will or should actually exercise pendent jurisdiction.

14. T or F While Supreme Court summary affirmances constitute binding precedent on the lower courts, they are of only minimal precedential value in future Supreme Court decisions.

15. T or F In the majority of courts, a case will be held to meet the jurisdictional minimum if *either* party stands to gain or lose in excess of the minimum.

Prepare an answer to the following question:

The legislature of State A, one of the fifty states, enacted the following statute: "Any conduct that would be found to violate the Sherman Antitrust Act if conducted in interstate commerce is hereby deemed to constitute a violation of this law when engaged in solely within the borders of this state."

Paul, a resident of State A, wishes to bring an action under this state statute in federal district court against Monster Corporation and Goliath Corporation, both of which are incorporated and have their principal place of business in State A, for an alleged conspiracy to interfere in Paul's business. None of the parties conducts any business outside of State A. Paul also attempts to append a claim against Monster for an unrelated act of fraud, in violation of state common law.

You are a law clerk to the Federal District Judge hearing the case. He wants to know (1) whether the federal court has subject matter jurisdiction over the antitrust claim, and (2) assuming the court does have jurisdiction over the antitrust claim, whether the federal court may also exercise pendent jurisdiction over the fraud claim.

PART THREE

FEDERAL COURTS, FEDERALISM AND THE STATES

Analysis

9. State Courts and Federal Power
10. State Sovereign Immunity and the Eleventh Amendment
11. Abstention
12. The Anti-injunction Statute
13. "Our Federalism"
14. Removal Jurisdiction
15. Civil Rights Removal Jurisdiction
16. Habeas Corpus
17. The Law to Be Applied in the Federal Courts: The Erie Doctrine
18. Federal Common Law

9

State Courts and Federal Power

Analysis

I. Introduction
   A. Scope of the Inquiry
   B. The Role of State Courts in the Federal System
II. State Court Power to Adjudicate Federal Law
   A. The Concepts of Concurrent and Exclusive Jurisdiction
   B. The Concept of "Implied Exclusivity" and the Claflin Presumption of Concurrent Jurisdiction
   C. State Court Adjudication of Issues Falling Within Exclusive Federal Jurisdiction
III. State Court Power to Control Federal Officers
   A. The Power to Issue Writs of Habeas Corpus: the Doctrine of Tarble's Case
   B. Mandamus and Injunctions
   C. Relevance of Federal Officer Removal
IV. State Court Obligation to Adjudicate Federal Claims
   A. The Traditional Rule
   B. The "Valid Excuse" Doctrine
   C. State Court Obligation to Employ Federal Procedures in Adjudicating Federal Claims

I. INTRODUCTION

A. SCOPE OF THE INQUIRY

1. This chapter examines the relationship between state courts and the conduct and development of federal government policy.

2. It concerns both the power and duty of the state courts to interpret, enforce, and control the execution of federal legislative and executive action.

3. The chapter is divided into three categories:

a. State court power to adjudicate suits arising under federal law.

b. State court power to control the conduct of federal officers.

c. State court obligation to adjudicate federal suits.

B. THE ROLE OF THE STATE COURTS IN THE FEDERAL SYSTEM

1. As described in Chapter 2, since the framing of the Constitution the state courts have been assumed to play an important role in the adjudication and enforcement of federal law.

2. Article VI, clause 2 of the Constitution, the Supremacy Clause, expressly binds state courts to enforce the Constitution, laws and treaties of the United States as "the supreme law of the land . . . anything in the Constitution or laws of any state to the contrary notwithstanding."

3. The Framers of the Constitution chose not to require the creation of lower federal courts, apparently on the assumption that the state judiciaries could always be employed as the trial forums for adjudication of federal law. In fact, though lower federal courts were established immediately by Congress, they were not vested with permanent general federal question jurisdiction until 1875.

4. Thus, it is beyond dispute that the work of the state courts is by no means distinct from the caseload of the federal courts.

5. At the same time, Congress is thought to possess broad power to allocate jurisdiction over federal matters between state and federal courts. It is the delicate interworking of these two principles that is the subject of the following sections.

II. STATE COURT POWER TO ADJUDICATE FEDERAL LAW

A. THE CONCEPTS OF CONCURRENT AND EXCLUSIVE JURISDICTION

1. *When Congress enacts a federal statute creating a cause of action, it has the choice to provide concurrent or exclusive jurisdiction.*

   a. *Concurrent* jurisdiction means that *both* state and federal courts are given authority to enforce claims arising under the federal statute. The plaintiff is given the initial choice of whether to sue in federal or state court, though usually the defendant is given the option of removing a suit filed in state court to federal court. However, Congress may choose to give the plaintiff an irrebuttable option, as it has in the Federal Employers' Liability Act, providing a negligence cause of action to railroad workers, by precluding defendant removal if plaintiff chooses to sue in state court.

   b. *Exclusive* jurisdiction means that only the federal courts are allowed to adjudicate suits arising under the law.

2. Congress' authority to *vest* concurrent jurisdiction in state courts derives from its enumerated powers under Article I of the Constitution, combined with its power under the "Necessary and Proper" clause, read in conjunction with the dictates of the Supremacy Clause.

3. Congress' authority to *exclude* state courts from the adjudication of suits arising under a federal law also derives from its Article I, section 8 powers and the "Necessary and Proper" Clause.

Example: Congress may enact a statute allowing patent holders to sue for patent infringement. It derives this authority from its enumerated power to provide for patents. It derives its authority to exclude state court jurisdiction—as it has in fact done in such cases in 28 U.S.C. § 1338(a)—from its power to do anything "necessary and proper" to the execution of its enumerated power.

B. THE CONCEPT OF "IMPLIED EXCLUSIVITY" AND THE *CLAFLIN* PRESUMPTION OF CONCURRENT JURISDICTION

1. *In* Claflin v. Houseman, *93 U.S. 130 (1876), the Supreme Court held that a "state court has jurisdiction where it is not excluded by express provision, or by incompatability in its exercise arising from the nature of the particular case."*

2. In this statement, the Court effectively adopted the following rule: Where (as is often the case) Congress is silent as to whether federal jurisdiction under a particular federal statute is exclusive, the general prescription will be that jurisdiction is concurrent; however, in certain instances exclusive federal jurisdiction will be inferred from congressional silence.

3. The Court was extremely vague as to exactly how a reviewing court was to determine whether federal jurisdiction was to be found impliedly exclusive. The leading example of such implied exclusivity is jurisdiction to enforce the federal antitrust laws, which are on their face silent on the issue of concurrent jurisdiction. Though the courts have never adequately explained this conclusion, common arguments are the comparative expertise of the federal courts and the danger of widely varying interpretations that would result from state court adjudication.

4. In *Charles Dowd Box Co. v. Courtney,* 368 U.S. 502 (1962), the Supreme Court reaffirmed the *Claflin* presumption of concurrent jurisdiction in the face of congressional silence.

   a. The Court in *Dowd* applied the presumption to find concurrent jurisdiction in suits under section 301(a) of the Labor Management Relations Act.

   b. The Court rejected arguments that the statute's ambiguous scope and the need for uniform interpretation dictated exclusive federal jurisdiction because of the absence in the legislative history of references to concern over the need for exclusivity.

C. STATE COURT ADJUDICATION OF ISSUES FALLING WITHIN EXCLUSIVE FEDERAL JURISDICTION

1. On occasion, state courts are faced with issues of federal law that may form the basis for a suit arising under a law within the exclusive jurisdiction of the federal courts.

   Examples: In the course of a breach of contract suit for a patent licensee's failure to pay royalties, the licensee may raise the defense that plaintiff's patent is invalid. Normally, the issue of a patent's validity would be decided in the course of a suit by the patent holder for infringement—a suit that, under the express terms of 28 U.S.C.A. § 1338(a), must be heard by a federal court.

   A similar situation occurs when a defense grounded in the federal antitrust laws is raised in state court in a breach of contract suit.

2. The dilemma facing the Supreme Court in deciding whether such issues may be considered by the state court is the following:

a. On the one hand, if the state courts are allowed to decide these questions, they will effectively be adjudicating issues of federal law which Congress has deemed to be beyond their competence.

b. On the other hand, if the state courts are prohibited from deciding these matters, important federal policies (*e.g.*, the desire to give monopoly protection only to true innovations; the desire to invalidate agreements in restraint of trade) will be ignored.

3. The Supreme Court has resolved this dilemma by authorizing the state courts to decide such questions. *See, e.g., Lear Inc. v. Adkins*, 395 U.S. 653 (1969).

4. However, the collateral estoppel effect of these decisions in subsequent federal actions is in doubt.

III. STATE COURT POWER TO CONTROL FEDERAL OFFICERS

A. THE POWER TO ISSUE WRITS OF HABEAS CORPUS: THE DOCTRINE OF *TARBLE'S CASE*

1. *In* Tarble's Case, *80 U.S. (13 Wall.) 397 (1871), the Supreme Court denied state courts the power to issue writs of habeas corpus to a federal army officer to determine whether an underage enlistee was improperly restrained.*

a. In the prior decision in *Ableman v. Booth*, 62 U.S. (21 How.) 506 (1858), the Court had held that a state court lacked authority to issue a writ of habeas corpus to obtain release of a prisoner in federal custody and the subject of a criminal action in federal court.

b. The Court in *Tarble* relied heavily upon its earlier analysis in *Booth*, though the earlier case could conceivably have been limited to cases of judicial comity, since it involved friction between the state court and the federal court conducting the criminal prosecution.

2. The Court expressed the fear that if state courts possessed this authority, important operations of the federal government could be disrupted.

3. The decision has been heavily criticized by certain commentators because it appears to disregard the supposedly traditional role of the state courts as enforcers of federal law, equal to the federal courts.

4. However, it can be argued that this view substantially disregards the fundamental changes in the relation between state courts and the federal government and in the general philosophy of federalism growing out of the Civil War and post-Civil War constitutional amendments. *Tarble* might be

viewed as recognizing a type of implied exclusivity under *Claflin*, subject to express congressional reversal.

5. Whatever its merits, the rule of *Tarble's Case* is still good law, and though it has been suggested that the principle be limited to cases of extreme emergency, as in the situation of the military involved in *Tarble* itself, such a nebulous standard is unworkable and has not been adhered to in the courts.

6. Uncertainty over the validity of *Tarble* exists in situations in which Congress has repealed the *federal* judicial avenue for recourse to vindicate federal rights. While the Court in *Tarble* emphasized the availability of federal judicial relief in that case, the opinion was unclear whether that condition was a prerequisite to the Court's ban on state court authority. However, if the ban on state court authority remained and was not removed by Congress, a statutory prohibition of federal habeas corpus jurisdiction would virtually always be unconstitutional, because of the constitutional guarantee of the writ.

B. MANDAMUS AND INJUNCTIONS

1. *Tarble* itself dealt only with the writ of habeas corpus. However, many years earlier, the Supreme Court in McClung v. Silliman, 19 U.S. (6 Wheat.) 598 (1821), had held that state courts lacked authority to issue writs of mandamus to federal officers.

2. The Supreme Court has never definitively decided whether the principle of *Tarble* extends to bar state court *injunctions* against federal officers as well.

   a. The lower federal courts have split on this question, though the majority of these decisions concluded that such writs are also barred.

   b. It has been argued by certain commentators that *Tarble* should not be so extended, but if the reasoning of *Tarble* was that writs of habeas corpus by state courts might significantly disrupt the operation of federal programs, that danger would appear to be at least as substantial in the case of an injunction.

C. RELEVANCE OF FEDERAL OFFICER REMOVAL

1. Federal officers are authorized to remove suits brought against them in state court to federal court pursuant to 28 U.S.C.A. § 1442. *See Tennessee v. Davis*, 100 U.S. 257 (1880).

2. This statute may be employed when a federal officer is sued for damages or criminally prosecuted in state courts—situations to which the *Tarble* rule has been held inapplicable.

IV. STATE COURT OBLIGATION TO ADJUDICATE FEDERAL CLAIMS

A. THE TRADITIONAL RULE

1. State Courts have long been obliged to enforce principles of federal law that become applicable during the course of an adjudication of state claims. Martin v. Hunter's Lessee, 14 U.S. (1 Wheat.) 304 (1816).

2. Though it developed somewhat later, the principle that state courts are generally bound to adjudicate suits arising directly under federal law is also now well established. See, e.g., Testa v. Katt, 330 U.S. 386 (1947); Mondou v. New York, N.H. & H.R.R., 223 U.S. 1 (1912).

    a. The principle derives from the dictates of the Supremacy Clause.

    b. In both *Testa* and *Mondou*, the Supreme Court rejected the argument that the state court could decline to enforce a federal right if that right was found to be inconsistent with state policy; under the logic of the Supremacy Clause, the Court held, federal policy *is* state policy.

B. THE "VALID EXCUSE" DOCTRINE

1. Though state courts are presumptively obligated to provide a forum for federal claims, the Supreme Court has recognized several "valid excuses" which state courts may invoke to decline to assert jurisdiction over federal suits.

    2. The legal rationale of the "valid excuse" doctrine has never been fully explained by the Court.

    a. Since the decision in *National League of Cities v. Usery*, 426 U.S. 833 (1976), recognizing a tenth amendment protection against disruption of important state functions, it is conceivable that the doctrine has a constitutional basis.

    b. However, *National League of Cities* was recently overruled in *Garcia v. San Antonio Metropolitan Transit Authority*, 53 U.S.L.W. 4135 (1985), and the doctrine might instead be considered to be an inference of congressional intent from congressional silence; *i.e.*, though Congress has made no statement as to whether state courts should be obligated to enforce a particular federal cause of action, had Congress foreseen a particular situation it would not have intended to burden the state courts with jurisdiction.

    c. Ultimately, little will turn on which of these two grounds rationalizes the "valid excuse" doctrine, except in the unlikely event that Congress attempts to overturn judicial recognition of a particular valid excuse. If the rationale were solely an inference of congressional intent, then Congress could reverse a particular valid excuse; if the rationale is constitutional, Congress lacks power to overturn the decision.

    3. To date, the Supreme Court has recognized the following situations as "valid excuses":

    a. Where the state court is a court of limited jurisdiction under state law, and that jurisdiction does not extend to the subject matter of the federal suit, wholly apart from its federal nature.

Example: in *Herb v. Pitcairn*, 324 U.S. 117 (1945), a city court in Illinois was allowed to decline jurisdiction over a claim under the Federal Employers' Liability Act because under the Illinois Constitution that court lacked competence to adjudicate such a claim.

    b. Where the doctrine of *forum non conveniens* is found to be applicable (*Missouri ex rel. Southern Ry. v. Mayfield*, 340 U.S. 1 (1950); *Douglas v. New York, N.H. & H.R.R.*, 279 U.S. 377 (1929)).

    c. Where a parallel suit between the parties is pending in federal court.

    d. Some commentators have recognized a "valid excuse" when the state does not have a right "analogous" to the federal right.

    1. The concept of "analogous right" has never been fully defined.

    2. No majority opinion of the Supreme Court has ever recognized such an excuse in its holding.

C. STATE COURT OBLIGATION TO EMPLOY FEDERAL PROCEDURES IN ADJUDICATING FEDERAL CLAIMS

    1. In *Dice v. Akron, Canton & Youngstown R.R. Co.*, 342 U.S. 359 (1952), the Supreme Court held that a state court adjudicating a suit under the Federal Employers' Liability Act was obligated to allocate decisionmaking authority between judge and jury in the same manner as a federal court would.

    2. Though the Court's reasoning was somewhat ambiguous, it appears that the Court relied on the following factors: (a) primary responsibility for the jury was essential to the achievement of Congress' substantive goal in enacting the FELA, and (b) requiring state courts to follow the federal procedure in the FELA suits would not unduly burden the state judicial system.

3. The Court distinguished the case from *Minneapolis & St. Louis R. Co. v. Bombolis,* 241 U.S. 211 (1916), which held that a state court was not bound to employ a unanimous verdict requirement in adjudicating FELA cases, even though such a procedure would be followed in federal court in similar suits, presumably because the unanimity principle was not essential to the vindication of the substantive federal right and might significantly burden and delay the functioning of the state judicial process.

*

10

STATE SOVEREIGN IMMUNITY AND THE ELEVENTH AMENDMENT

Analysis

I. Introduction: The Concept of Sovereign Immunity and the Passage of the Eleventh Amendment
   A. The Concept of Sovereign Immunity
   B. The Chisholm Decision and the Passage of the Eleventh Amendment
II. Construction of the Eleventh Amendment
   A. The Extension of the Eleventh Amendment to Suits by In-State Residents
   B. Alternative Theories of Construction
III. Reconciling the Eleventh Amendment With the Fourteenth Amendment
   A. Statement of the Problem
   B. The Doctrine of Ex parte Young
IV. Constructive Waiver of the Eleventh Amendment Defense
   A. The Traditional Waiver Rule
   B. The Concept of Constructive Waiver
V. The Issue of Congressional Intent
   A. Congressional Intent and the Constructive Waiver Doctrine
   B. Congressional Intent and Section 5 of the Fourteenth Amendment

I. INTRODUCTION: THE CONCEPT OF SOVEREIGN IMMUNITY AND THE PASSAGE OF THE ELEVENTH AMENDMENT

A. THE CONCEPT OF SOVEREIGN IMMUNITY

1. The concept of sovereign immunity is generally thought to derive from the medieval English dictate that "the king can do no wrong," which in turn was said to derive from the precept that no man can be sued in his own court.

2. Some commentators have suggested that the precept that "the king can do no wrong" has been grossly misinterpreted, and that all it meant originally was that the king was not *allowed* to do any wrong. In any event, one may question the logic of applying such a principle, developed in a monarchy, to a democratic society.

3. Nevertheless, there is no doubt that the framers of the Constitution contemplated the existence of some form of sovereign immunity.

4. However, debate continues to this day as to whether that immunity was deemed to have some sort of constitutional status, or instead merely amounted to recognition of a common law doctrine.

B. THE *CHISHOLM* DECISION AND THE PASSAGE OF THE ELEVENTH AMENDMENT

1. In Article III, section 2 of the Constitution, the provision outlining the extent of the federal judicial power, the framers included the category of cases involving suits between a state and citizens of another state.

   a. The provision, as structured, was a special form of diversity jurisdiction.

   b. In response to numerous questions about the provision at the state ratifying conventions, various framers responded that the provision was in no way intended to abrogate state sovereign immunity, and thus was not intended to apply to suits in which the state was the defendant.

2. However, in *Chisholm v. Georgia,* 2 U.S. (2 Dall.), 419 (1793), the Supreme Court, pursuant to this clause of Article III, section 2, asserted original jurisdiction over a suit brought by citizens of the state of South Carolina against the state of Georgia for the purpose of collecting a debt, even though Georgia had not consented to suit.

3. The public uproar over the decision led to rapid passage and ratification of the eleventh amendment, which provides: "The judicial power of the United States shall not be construed to extend to any suit in law or equity, commenced or prosecuted against one of the United States by citizens of another state, or by citizens or subjects of any foreign state."

II. CONSTRUCTION OF THE ELEVENTH AMENDMENT

A. THE EXTENSION OF THE ELEVENTH AMENDMENT TO SUITS BY IN-STATE RESIDENTS

1. An interesting—and often disregarded—aspect of eleventh amendment construction is the extremely narrow language employed.

   a. As structured, the amendment appears to do nothing more than reverse *Chisholm*'s unduly broad construction of the state diversity clause in Article III, section 2. Linguistically, it has no impact on any case brought to federal court pursuant to a different jurisdictional base, such as federal question jurisdiction.

   b. Note that the amendment begins with the words, "The judicial power of the United States shall not be construed to extend to . . . ." This language indicates merely that the Supreme Court improperly *construed* the "judicial power" to "extend" to such suits in *Chisholm*. Also, the amendment's language explicitly concerns only suits against states brought by *out-of-state* residents—the type of suit involved in *Chisholm* and the type of suit dealt with in the state diversity provision of Article III, section 2.

   c. Note also that by its terms, the amendment bars suits only in *federal* court, since it refers only to the reach of the federal "judicial power."

2. A strong argument could therefore be fashioned, strictly on the basis of the amendment's language, that it was in no way intended to constitutionalize a doctrine of state sovereign immunity. Rather, it appears simply to have overruled a Supreme Court construction of a provision of Article III to *revoke* preexisting common law sovereign immunity.

3. However, in *Hans v. Louisiana*, 134 U.S. 1 (1890), the Supreme Court held that suits brought against a state by *in-state* citizens, even when federal jurisdiction is premised on federal question, rather than the provision of Article III interpreted in *Chisholm*, were barred by the eleventh amendment.

   a. The Court employed the dubious reasoning that had the drafters of the amendment included "a proviso that nothing therein contained should prevent a state from being sued by its own citizens in cases arising under the Constitution or laws of the United States," the amendment surely would have been rejected.

B. ALTERNATIVE THEORIES OF CONSTRUCTION

While the eleventh amendment generally receives an interpretation that extends it to *any* suit brought against the state, (though *not*, it should be emphasized, to municipalities or to local governments), Justices Brennan and Marshall, dissenting in their separate opinions in *Employees of Department of Public Health & Welfare v. Department of Public Health & Welfare,* 411 U.S. 279 (1973), have developed their own theories of eleventh amendment interpretation.

    1. Justice Brennan's Theory.

    a. Justice Brennan has argued that the eleventh amendment itself should be given a construction confined to its language, and therefore apply only to suits brought under the state diversity clause of Article III, section 2.

    b. To the extent the concept of sovereign immunity bars suit by *in-state* residents, Justice Brennan reasons, it is solely as a matter of *common law* sovereign immunity, in existence at the time of the Constitution's ratification.

    c. This common law form of sovereign immunity, he argues, was waived by the states at the time of the Constitution's ratification to the extent Article I of the Constitution vests authority in Congress to legislate.

    c. Justice Brennan attempted to explain the *Hans* decision as an illustration of common law sovereign immunity, though most of that opinion tends to undermine Justice Brennan's interpretation.

    d. In any event, the *Hans* case was a suit to recover on a state debt on the grounds that the state had violated the constitutional provision barring state interference with the obligation of contract. It is unclear why whatever common law sovereign immunity existed was not waived by state ratification of the contract clause.

    2. Justice Marshall's Theory.

    a. Like Justice Brennan, Justice Marshall recognizes two forms of state sovereign immunity: Common law and constitutional. However, he defines these two categories in a very different manner from Justice Brennan.

    b. Justice Marshall agrees that common law immunity is waived to the extent of Congress' Article I power.

    c. However, he asserts that the constitutional branch of the doctrine applies not only to suits brought by out-of-state citizens, as the amendment expressly provides, but to suits brought by in-state citizens in federal court. This latter, prohibition, he claims, derives not from the eleventh amendment, but from the limits imposed on federal court jurisdiction by Article III.

d. Justice Marshall would allow Congress to authorize suits by in-state citizens against states in *state* courts, which are not bound by the limits of Article III.

e. The fatal flaw in Justice Marshall's analysis is that at no point does he explain exactly what in Article III precludes suit in federal court against states by in-state citizens.

3. Several commentators have developed the theory that Congress, acting pursuant to its Article I powers, may allow suit in federal court against states, brought by either in-state or out-of-state citizens, despite the eleventh amendment.

a. The argument is in part historical, because it emphasizes that the framers of the amendment were concerned primarily with judicial, rather than congressional interference with state interests.

b. It also is premised on the language of the eleventh amendment, which refers only to the judicial power.

c. The theory is defective, however, because its historical support is questionable and linguistically it disregards the important fact that a constitutional limitation on federal *judicial* power means that Congress cannot vest the federal courts with power to hear the suit, since it is generally accepted that Congress cannot vest the federal courts with jurisdiction over cases falling outside the "judicial power."

III. RECONCILING THE ELEVENTH AMENDMENT WITH THE FOURTEENTH AMENDMENT

A. STATEMENT OF THE PROBLEM

1. The fourteenth amendment imposes substantial limitations on state authority to interfere with the rights of private individuals.

2. To the extent the eleventh amendment precludes suit against the state, at least in federal court, it would cause a significant disruption to congressional efforts to enforce those rights against the states.

3. The simplest answer to this dilemma is to conclude that, because of its later passage and its significant alteration of the concept of federalism, the fourteenth amendment supercedes the eleventh.

4. In fact, the Supreme Court has, at least to a certain extent, reached that conclusion. In *Fitzpatrick v. Bitzer*, 427 U.S. 445 (1976), the Supreme Court found a federal law authorizing damages against a state that

discriminated in employment not to violate the eleventh amendment because the act was passed pursuant to Congress' power under section 5 of the fourteenth amendment.

B. THE DOCTRINE OF *EX PARTE YOUNG*

1. *Long before* Fitzpatrick, *the Supreme Court had developed a fiction in order to reconcile the fourteenth amendment with the eleventh.*

2. *In* Ex parte Young, *209 U.S. 123 (1908), the Court held that when a state officer violates federal constitutional provisions, he or she has in effect been stripped of state authority, because the state could not be presumed to condone or authorize action that violates federal law, and thus he or she may be sued, as an individual, without violating the eleventh amendment.*

3. The doctrine had its origins in decisions prior to *Young*.

   a. *See, e.g., Allen v. Baltimore & Ohio Railroad*, 114 U.S. 311 (1884).

   b. However, prior to *Young* the doctrine required that the state officer's conduct amount to a common law violation.

   c. While *Young* did not expressly reject this limitation, it appeared to disregard it, and it no longer has vitality.

4. There are significant analytical problems with the *Young* doctrine.

   a. It is difficult to see how the actions of a state officer, who is acting either solely to enforce state policy or is enabled to perform his actions because he is vested with state authority, can be thought to be stripped of state authority when he or she violates federal constitutional rights.

   b. Moreover, a prerequisite of a fourteenth amendment violation is the presence of state action. Thus, the *Young* doctrine on the one hand finds the state officer to be a private individual for purposes of the eleventh amendment, yet on the other hand finds the same officer to be part of the state for purposes of the fourteenth amendment. This result-oriented inconsistency is logically indefensible and unprincipled.

5. The main difficulty with the *Young* fiction is that the Supreme Court has, in recent years, selectively attempted to determine whether a suit is *in reality* one against the state, even though the named defendant is a state officer. The problem with this approach is that, ultimately, *all* of these suits are, in practical terms, against the "state." The Court has therefore disregarded the obviously fictitious nature of the *Young* doctrine.

a. For example, in *Edelman v. Jordan*, 415 U.S. 651 (1974), the Supreme Court held that an award of retroactive payments, even if issued in a suit brought nominally against a state officer, constituted an improper suit against the state.

b. The Court reasoned that the money would have to come from state treasuries, and therefore was in violation of the eleventh amendment.

c. The Court distinguished *Young* on the grounds that the relief sought there was prospective (*i.e.* injunctive), though there is no doubt that such prospective relief would have a significant impact on state policies and programs.

6. The Supreme Court distinguished *Edelman* in *Hutto v. Finney*, 437 U.S. 678 (1978), where it affirmed an award of attorney's fees, to be paid by the state, because of the state's bad faith in failing to comply with a prior judicial order. The award, said the Court, was "ancillary" to the prospective relief.

7. *Young* was distinguished in *Pennhurst State School & Hospital v. Halderman*, ___ U.S. ___ (1984), where the Supreme Court held that the eleventh amendment barred a federal court from ordering state officials to conform their conduct to state law, even though a state official was the nominal defendant, because the state was the real party in interest.

a. The Court applied the bar to cases under state law that might be thought to fall within the federal courts' pendent jurisdiction.

b. The majority distinguished *Young* because "*Young* was justified, notwithstanding the obvious impact on the State itself, on the view that sovereign immunity does not apply because an official who acts unconstitutionally is 'stripped of his official or representative character,' . . . . [T]he *Young* doctrine has been accepted as necessary to permit the federal courts to vindicate federal rights and hold state officials responsible to the supreme authority of the United States. . . . Our decisions have repeatedly emphasized that the *Young* doctrine rests on the need to promote the vindication of federal rights."

c. The decision is to be commended for stripping away the fictional aspect of the *Young* doctrine, though this only tends to raise more serious question about the logic of *Edelman*'s prospective-retroactive dichotomy: That dichotomy was purportedly based on the assumption that retroactive relief was in actuality a suit against the state. Yet *Pennhurst* openly acknowledges that the *Young* doctrine allows suits that are in reality against the state, but are justified because the fiction created by *Young* enables such actions to be brought to vindicate federal rights. But if that is true, the same logic seems to dictate that retroactive relief necessary to vindicate federal rights is also proper, even though cases in which it is awarded might ultimately be deemed suits against the state.

d. The dissent of Justice Stevens relied on extensive precedent to demonstrate that the *Young* exception to the eleventh amendment had never been confined to cases alleging violation of federal rights, but the majority responded that "[u]nder the dissent's view of the *ultra vires* doctrine, the Eleventh Amendment would have force only in the rare case in which a plaintiff foolishly attempts to sue the State in its own name, or where he cannot produce some state statute that has been violated to his asserted injury," and that as phrased the exception "would swallow the general rule that a suit is against the State if the relief will run against it."

IV. CONSTRUCTIVE WAIVER OF THE ELEVENTH AMENDMENT DEFENSE

A. THE TRADITIONAL WAIVER RULE

1. *It has long been understood that a sovereign may waive its defense of sovereign immunity, and allow itself to be sued.*

2. It was in fact this principle that led Justice Brennan to criticize Justice Marshall's theory that sovereign immunity was dictated by the limits of Article III, since traditionally the limits of Article III are deemed unwaivable.

B. THE CONCEPT OF CONSTRUCTIVE WAIVER

1. *On occasion, the Supreme Court has found a state's waiver of its eleventh amendment defense on the basis of state conduct that does not expressly waive its immunity.*

a. For example, in *Parden v. Terminal Railway*, 377 U.S. 184 (1964), the Court held that the operation of an interstate railroad by the state of Alabama after passage of the Federal Employers Liability Act, which rendered railroad employers subject to negligence suits in federal court by their employees, constituted a waiver of the state's immunity to suit in federal court.

b. The reasoning was that when the state undertook operation of the interstate railroad, it was presumed to be aware of the condition set by Congress for the operation of such a railroad—i.e., potential suit in federal court.

c. The decision was somewhat confused, however, by Justice Brennan's intertwining of his theory of "waiver" of common law sovereign immunity by ratification of the Constitution.

2. The constructive waiver principle has been criticized for conflicting with the "unconstitutional conditions" doctrine, which posits that the government may not condition the loss of a constitutional right on the receipt of a benefit. However, some have questioned whether the logic of the "unconstitutional conditions" doctrine—developed to protect individuals against the state—has any place in the relationship between federal and state governments.

V. THE ISSUE OF CONGRESSIONAL INTENT

A. CONGRESSIONAL INTENT AND THE CONSTRUCTIVE WAIVER DOCTRINE

1. The logic of the constructive waiver doctrine requires that Congress have intended to condition the receipt of a benefit or the participation in an activity by a state as a waiver.

2. Determining whether Congress actually has so intended has not always proven to be a simple task.

a. In *Parden*, the Federal Employers' Liability Act provided that "[e]very common carrier by railroad while engaging in commerce between any of the several States . . . shall be liable in damages to any person suffering injuries while he is employed by such carrier in such commerce." Though the statutory language did not on its face provide that operating such railroads would be subject to suit, the Supreme Court reasoned that a state operating an interstate railroad fell within the statutory terms.

b. However, in *Employees of Department of Public Health & Welfare v. Department of Public Health & Welfare*, 411 U.S. 279 (1973), the majority refused to find the requisite congressional intent to subject states to suit in the Fair Labor Standards Act, even though the 1966 amendment to the statute had altered the original exception to the Act's reach for any state or political subdivision to exclude suits brought by state employees who worked in hospitals or schools. The majority's conclusion represented a blatant misreading of congressional intent.

3. The approach used by the Court in *Employees* is referred to as the "clear statement" rule, which posits that even where Congress possesses power to revoke state immunity, it must say so explicitly. While the requirement makes sense as a means of avoiding interfederal friction, its application in *Employees* carried the requirement too far.

B. CONGRESSIONAL INTENT AND SECTION 5 OF THE FOURTEENTH AMENDMENT

1. *As previously noted, since Fitzpatrick v. Bitzer Congress is recognized to have authority under section 5 of the fourteenth amendment to subject states to suit for fourteenth amendment violations.*

2. The issue of determining congressional intent to subject the states to suit is as much an issue here as it is under the constructive waiver doctrine.

3. In *Edelman v. Jordan, supra,* Justice Marshall, dissenting, argued that in section 1983 of the Civil Rights Laws Congress had expressed its intent generally to subject states to suit for fourteenth amendment violations.

4. The position was rejected by Justice Rehnquist, speaking for the majority, because section 1983 subjected to suit only any "person" acting under color of state law, and not the state itself.

5. Justice Brennan has suggested that since the Court has now held—contrary to its previous understanding—that municipalities may under certain conditions be deemed "persons" for purposes of section 1983, perhaps states should as well. However, in dictum, the Court, per Justice Rehnquist, rejected this suggestion. *Quern v. Jordan,* 440 U.S. 332 (1979).

11

ABSTENTION

Analysis

I. Introduction
   A. The Concept of Judge-Made Abstention
   B. The Forms of Judge-Made Abstention
II. Pullman Abstention
   A. The Pullman Case
   B. Purposes of Pullman Abstention
   C. Harms of Pullman Abstention
   D. The Confines of Pullman Abstention
III. Thibodaux Abstention
   A. The Thibodaux Case
   B. The Rationale of Thibodaux Abstention
   C. The Confusion Caused by Mashuda
IV. Burford Abstention
   A. The Burford Decision
   B. The Rationale of Burford Abstention
V. Colorado River Abstention
   A. The Colorado River Case
   B. The Colorado River Criteria
   C. The Will Case

    VI. Procedural Aspects of Abstention
       A. The England *Doctrine*
       B. Certification

I. INTRODUCTION

A. THE CONCEPT OF JUDGE-MADE ABSTENTION

1. *The abstention doctrine is a label used to describe several distinct but related doctrines under which the federal courts will decline to exercise or postpone an otherwise valid application of their jurisdiction in order to defer to various interests of the state courts or to state policies.*

2. While abstention may be legislatively ordered—as it is in the Anti-Injunction Act and the Tax Injunction Act—the abstention doctrines discussed in this chapter are entirely judge-made.

B. THE FORMS OF JUDGE-MADE ABSTENTION

1. Since the dividing lines among the different forms of the doctrine are not always clear, they have generally come to be known by the cases in which they were first developed.

2. The forms of judge-made abstention are: *Pullman, Thibodaux, Burford* and *Colorado River.*

II. *PULLMAN* ABSTENTION

A. THE *PULLMAN* CASE

1. In *Railroad Commission of Texas v. Pullman,* 312 U.S. 496 (1941), the Commission had ordered that "no sleeping car shall be operated on any line of railroad in the State of Texas . . . unless such cars are continuously in the charge of an employee . . . having the rank and position of Pullman Conductor," apparently in order to eliminate the practice of employing porters—who were black—to be in charge of a sleeping car in those trains not carrying a conductor. The Pullman Company challenged the order in federal court on grounds of equal protection and due process, and the porters challenged it on grounds of racial discrimination. However, another issue in the case concerned whether the Commission lacked statutory authority under Texas law to issue such an order.

2. The Supreme Court, noting that the meaning of the Texas statute was "far from clear", ordered the federal court to abstain, while the parties could obtain a definitive interpretation of the state law from the state courts. When and only when such a determination was made could the

parties return to the federal court to have their constitutional claims adjudicated if they were still relevant.

B. PURPOSES OF *PULLMAN* ABSTENTION

1. *Avoidance of constitutional questions.*

   a. *One obvious purpose of the doctrine is to avoid what may prove to be a needless conflict between state law and the Constitution, by having ambiguous state laws construed in a manner that renders them constitutional.*

   b. Presumably the federal court itself could impose this interpretation, but since any federal court interpretation of state law would not be definitive, it was apparently deemed wiser to defer to state court interpretation of its own law.

2. *Avoidance of interference with important state functions.*

   a. *The Court has also noted that the doctrine is designed to avoid "interference with important state functions. . . ." Harman v. Forssenius,* 380 U.S. 528, 534 (1965).

   b. However, it is not clear exactly how the doctrine achieves this end; if the state law was in fact intended to reach a particular result, there is no way that *Pullman* abstention can avoid a conflict between the state policy embodied in the statute and federal constitutional provisions. If such a conflict is to be reconciled, it must be in the course of a decision on the constitutional merits, the very result which *Pullman* abstention is intended to avoid.

3. Reduction in federal court caseloads.

   a. If the state court interprets the statute in a manner that renders it constitutional, naturally the federal action need not proceed and the federal court caseload will thereby be reduced.

   b. While this reason has on occasion been asserted as a justification, it is questionable whether the desire to reduce caseloads should be used to justify abstention when important federal issues are raised.

C. HARMS OF *PULLMAN* ABSTENTION

1. Whatever one thinks of the asserted benefits of *Pullman* abstention, there can be little doubt that the doctrine imposes serious costs.

   a. Often there will be significant delays in the resolution of a litigant's federal constitutional claims.

b. There may also be the need for two distinct trials, with all of the waste normally involved in the conduct of duplicative proceedings.

2. In order to avoid the harms caused by the delay inherent in the abstention process, the Supreme Court has held that in cases in which the need for resolution of the constitutional claims is great, resort to abstention is less likely. This is especially true in cases challenging state statutes which may chill the exercise of the first amendment right of free expression.

D. THE CONFINES OF *PULLMAN* ABSTENTION

1. *Before* Pullman *abstention will apply, a state law must be ambiguous, to the extent that one interpretation will render the law constitutional while another will render it unconstitutional.*

a. The mere fact that a state law is challenged as unconstitutionally vague does not automatically implicate *Pullman* abstention.

b. Such a limitation flows from the underlying purposes of the doctrine.

c. The fact that a state statute has not yet been interpreted by the state courts does not itself implicate *Pullman* abstention.

2. *Pullman* abstention also will not apply when there is unavailable an adequate opportunity in the state courts to have the state issue adjudicated.

3. *Pullman* abstention may apply, even if the challenged state statute is itself not ambiguous, but there exists a unique state constitutional provision that may be held to invalidate the law.

a. However, the Supreme Court has made it clear that the mere fact that a state constitution contains a provision paralleling the due process or equal protection clauses of the fourteenth amendment does not mean that abstention is appropriate.

b. The doctrine will apply only when the constitution contains a unique provision dealing with the subject of the case, and the subject is a matter of special concern to the state. See, e.g., *Reetz v. Bozanich*, 397 U.S. 82 (1970).

III. *THIBODAUX* ABSTENTION

A. THE *THIBODAUX* CASE

1. In *Louisiana Power & Light Co. v. City of Thibodaux*, 360 U.S. 25 (1959), the Supreme Court affirmed the lower federal court's decision to abstain in a case involving a city's petition for expropriation of private

property, removed to federal court by the Company, a Florida corporation, on the basis of diversity of citizenship.

2. The Supreme Court emphasized that the state statute on which the city's expropriation was premised had never been construed by the state supreme court.

B. THE RATIONALE OF *THIBODAUX* ABSTENTION

1. Unlike *Pullman* abstention, *Thibodaux* abstention was not designed to avoid determination of a federal constitutional question, since the basis of federal jurisdiction in *Thibodaux* was diversity of citizenship, rather than federal question.

2. Though the actual rationale of this form of abstention has never been made entirely clear, the factor emphasized by the Court was "[t]he special nature of eminent domain" which is "intimately involved with sovereign prerogative."

C. THE CONFUSION CAUSED BY *MASHUDA*

1. Significantly confusing the basis for *Thibodaux* abstention was a decision handed down the same day in *County of Allegheny v. Frank Mashuda Co.*, 360 U.S. 185 (1959), where the Supreme Court reversed the lower federal court's decision to dismiss in a local condemnation case, noting that "the fact that a case concerns a State's powers of eminent domain no more justifies abstention than the fact that it involves any other issue related to sovereignty."

2. A possible basis of distinction is that in *Mashuda* the meaning of the applicable state law was clear, and only factual issues remained to be litigated, while in *Thibodaux* the state law was, in fact, ambiguous.

3. More recently, *Thibodaux* abstention has been tied by the courts to concern over interfering with some not-fully-defined notion of state "sovereignty".

IV. *BURFORD* ABSTENTION

A. THE *BURFORD* DECISION

1. In *Burford v. Sun Oil Co.*, 319 U.S. 315 (1943), the Supreme Court held federal abstention appropriate in a case involving a challenge to a Texas Railroad Commission order granting Burford a permit to drill oil wells.

2. Though federal jurisdiction was based in part on diversity, a federal constitutional challenge to the Commission's order was also made.

B. THE RATIONALE OF *BURFORD* ABSTENTION

1. *Burford* has been called "administrative" abstention, because in ordering abstention the Supreme Court emphasized the importance to the state of the subject of the regulation and the complex nature of the relation between the Commission and the reviewing state courts.

2. In recent years, the Supreme Court has characterized *Burford* as a case in which "exercise of federal review of the question in a case and in similar cases would be disruptive of state efforts to establish a coherent policy with respect to a matter of substantial public concern."

V. *COLORADO RIVER* ABSTENTION

A. THE *COLORADO RIVER* CASE

1. In *Colorado River Water Conservation District v. United States*, 424 U.S. 800 (1976), the Supreme Court explored the circumstances under which a federal court should choose to stay itself because of the existence of a parallel state court proceeding.

2. The case was a suit by the United States against local water users to obtain a declaration of its rights and those of Indian reservations to certain Colorado waters and to seek appointment of a special master.

B. THE *COLORADO RIVER* CRITERIA

1. Despite the Court's ultimate decision to defer to a parallel state action, the decision emphasized that such deference was to be the exception, not the rule.

2. The Court noted the applicable federal statutory policy of avoiding piecemeal adjudication of water rights, as well as the federal government's current participation in state water litigation.

C. THE *WILL* CASE

1. In *Will v. Calvert Fire Insurance Co.*, 437 U.S. 655 (1978), the Supreme Court reversed the court of appeals' order to a district judge to proceed in a parallel federal action.

2. The Court emphasized that mandamus was involved, and a district judge's discretion had to be recognized.

3. Though the decision was sharply split and is unclear in its scope, it appears that the Court was departing substantially from *Colorado River*'s notation of "the virtually unflagging, obligation of the federal courts to exercise the jurisdiction given them."

4. In *Moses H. Cone Memorial Hospital v. Mercury Construction Corp.*, 103 S.Ct. 927 (1983), the Court refused to allow a federal court to defer to a parallel state proceeding in a contract dispute. *Calvert* was distinguished on the ground that mandamus had been involved there, while in *Moses H. Cone* review was by means of direct appeal.

VI. PROCEDURAL ASPECTS OF ABSTENTION

A. THE *ENGLAND* DOCTRINE

1. In *England v. Louisiana State Board of Medical Examiners*, 375 U.S. 411 (1964), *the Supreme Court made clear that once the state law issue is resolved in state court, the plaintiff has the option to return the case to federal court for the adjudication of the federal constitutional issues.*

2. *The Court held that when the state issue is presented to the state court, the federal issue must be presented, even though the plaintiff has retained the option to return to federal court.*

    a. The reason for this requirement is that the state court should be given the opportunity to narrow the construction of the ambiguous state statute in order to avoid constitutional problems.

    b. The difficulty with this requirement is that if the plaintiff raises the federal constitutional issue in the state court, as required, it will often be unclear whether the plaintiff has waived his right to return to federal court.

    c. To avoid this problem, the Supreme Court has required that waiver of the option to return to federal court be made explicitly.

3. The *England* doctrine has been attacked because of the long delays it causes. Nevertheless, the Court has reaffirmed its commitment to the doctrine.

B. CERTIFICATION

1. One possible method of avoiding the waste and delays of abstention is by resort to a process known as certification, which may be employed by a federal court only if the state has chosen to adopt the procedure.

2. Under this procedure (sometimes adopted by state statute and sometimes by state court rule), the federal court may refer unsettled state law questions directly to the state's highest court, thereby avoiding the necessity of proceeding through the entire state judicial system.

3. The Supreme Court has indicated that if a state certification procedure is available, it is highly advisable for a federal court to resort to it in the presence of an unclear issue of state law. See *Lehman Brothers v. Schein,* 416 U.S. 386 (1974).

12

THE ANTI-INJUNCTION STATUTE

Analysis

I. Introduction
   A. The Statutory Provision
   B. History and Policy
II. The Scope of the Exceptions
   A. The "Relitigation" Exception
   B. The "Expressly Authorized" Exception
   C. The "In Aid of Jurisdiction" Exception
III. Other Statutory Restrictions on Federal Injunctions Against State Activities
   A. The Tax Injunction Act of 1937
   B. The Johnson Act of 1934
IV. Injunction of Federal Judicial Proceedings
   A. Injunction by a Federal Court
   B. Injunction by a State Court

I. INTRODUCTION

A. THE STATUTORY PROVISION

1. *The Anti-Injunction Statute, 28 U.S.C.A. § 2283, provides that "[a] court of the United States may not grant an injunction to stay proceedings in a State court except as expressly authorized by Act of Congress, or where necessary in aid of its jurisdiction, or to protect or effectuate its judgments."*

2. The three exceptions are generally referred to as:

   a. The "expressly authorized" exception

   b. The "in aid of jurisdiction" exception, and

   c. The "relitigation" exception.

3. The Supreme Court has stated that the three statutory exceptions exhaust the list of exceptions to the Act's prohibition, and that no other exceptions may be created. *Atlantic Coast Line R.R. v. Brotherhood of Locomotive Engineers*, 398 U.S. 281 (1970).

4. However, in *Leiter Minerals, Inc. v. United States*, 352 U.S. 220 (1957), the Court held that the Act's prohibitions were inapplicable to a suit brought by the United States, even though the Act itself makes no provision for such an exception. In *NLRB v. Nash-Finch Co.*, 404 U.S. 138 (1971), the Court expanded this exception to include suits by federal agencies. Note that the prohibitions of the Anti-Injunction Statute must be considered in conjunction with non-statutory comity restrictions that the Supreme Court has imposed on federal court injunctive power, discussed in Chapter 13.

B. HISTORY AND POLICY

1. History of the Anti-Injunction Statute.

   a. The original version of the Act appeared in section 5 of the Judiciary Act of 1793.

   b. For most of its history, the Act was largely absolute in its prohibition on federal court authority to enjoin state proceedings. However, over the years various common law exceptions were recognized.

   (1) The primary common law exception was the "res" exception, which allowed a federal court to enjoin a subsequent state court proceeding that might interfere with the federal court's jurisdiction over a piece of property.

   c. The current version of the Statute was enacted in 1948, primarily to overrule the Supreme Court's decision in *Toucey v. New York Life*

Insurance Co., 314 U.S. 118 (1941), which had held that no common law exception existed for cases in which a party sought to relitigate in state court a case or factual question that had previously been litigated in a completed federal court proceeding.

    2. Policies behind the Anti-Injunction Statute.

        a. It is likely that part of the reason for the Statute's original enactment was concern about the extension of equity jurisdiction.

        b. More important, at least today, are the federalism considerations that lie behind the Statute.

        (1) The Statute reflects the Framers' original understanding that the state courts were fully competent to interpret and enforce federal law.

        (2) Any federal "policing" of state court interpretations of federal law may come on direct review in the United States Supreme Court, rather than through the disruptive device of a collateral federal court injunction.

        (3) However, the assumed fungibility of state and federal courts is a matter for Congress' judgment. Thus, Congress has provided for the specified exceptions to the otherwise absolute bar on federal court power to enjoin state court actions.

II. THE SCOPE OF THE EXCEPTIONS

A. THE "RELITIGATION" EXCEPTION

    1. The policy behind this exception was described by Justice Reed, dissenting in *Toucey*, when he argued that absent such an exception "a federal judgment entered perhaps after years of expense in money and energy and after the production of thousands of pages of evidence comes to nothing that is final."

    2. It is not always easy, however, to determine whether a particular question was actually decided in the federal proceeding. See *Atlantic Coast Line R.R. v. Brotherhood of Locomotive Engineers*, 398 U.S. 281 (1970).

B. THE "EXPRESSLY AUTHORIZED" EXCEPTION

    1. This exception codifies Congress' authority to withdraw the bar of the Anti-Injunction Statute whenever Congress deems it appropriate.

    2. The term "expressly" has never been held to require that the Act of Congress specifically refer to the Anti-Injunction Statute.

3. Nor must the Act specifically provide that a federal court is authorized to enjoin a state court proceeding.

4. In *Mitchum v. Foster*, 407 U.S. 225 (1972), the Supreme Court held that the Civil Rights Act of 1871, today commonly referred to as section 1983, constitutes an "expressly authorized" exception, even though that Act makes no express reference to a federal injunction of state court proceedings.

   a. The Court there developed the following test to determine whether a federal statute is an "expressly authorized" exception: "whether an Act of Congress, clearly creating a federal right or remedy enforceable in a federal court of equity, could be given its intended scope only by the stay of a state court proceeding."

   b. The Court found the test to be met by section 1983, because

   (1) the Act specifically provides for equitable relief, and

   (2) legislative history established that the Act was passed largely because of congressional mistrust of state court ability or willingness to protect federal constitutional rights.

   c. In effect, the *Mitchum* Court developed an "implied" version of the "expressly authorized" exception.

   d. The *Mitchum* test was applied by the Court to the federal antitrust laws in *Vendo Co. v. Lektro-Vend Corp.*, 433 U.S. 623 (1977). The opinion announcing the judgment of the Court concluded that the *Mitchum* test was not met by the antitrust laws, because while those laws did provide for equitable relief, there existed no basis in the legislative history to indicate that Congress believed the laws could be given their intended scope only by means of a stay of state court proceedings. However, the dissent, speaking for four Justices, concluded that the antitrust laws were in fact exceptions to the Anti-Injunction Statute, and the two concurring Justices concluded that the antitrust laws were an exception, but that the activity in question did not constitute a violation of those laws.

C. THE "IN AID OF JURISDICTION" EXCEPTION

1. Though the language of this exception is arguably not so confined, the exception has generally been limited to the "res" cases, described previously.

2. Thus, a federal court may not enjoin a parallel state proceeding when the rights are in personam and jurisdiction is not premised on the attachment of specific property.

3. This was the rule established in *Kline v. Burke Construction Co.*, 260 U.S. 226 (1922), prior to the 1948 revision and generally continues to be accepted as an interpretation of the current "in aid of jurisdiction" exception.

4. According to the Reviser's Note to the 1948 revision, this exception was also intended to authorize federal injunction of state proceedings following removal of a case to federal court, but traditionally such power has been thought to fall within the "expressly authorized" exception.

III. OTHER STATUTORY RESTRICTIONS ON FEDERAL INJUNCTIONS AGAINST STATE ACTIVITIES

A. THE TAX INJUNCTION ACT OF 1937

1. *This Act provides that "[t]he district courts shall not enjoin, suspend or restrain the assessment, levy or collection of any tax under State law where a plain, speedy and efficient remedy may be had in the courts of such State."*

   a. The Supreme Court has interpreted the phrase, "plain, speedy and efficient" to require the meeting of only *procedural* criteria, and not to concern a state's unwillingness to pay interest. *Rosewell v. La Salle National Bank*, 450 U.S. 503 (1981).

   b. The "plain, speedy and efficient" requirement is not violated by a procedure that makes a defense to a suit to collect the tax the taxpayer's only remedy.

   c. However, the requirement is not met if state procedure requires a multiplicity of suits.

2. In addition to the statutory bar, the Court has recognized non-statutory limits of comity on the power of federal courts to interfere with state taxing systems. *Fair Assessment in Real Estate Association, Inc. v. McNary*, 454 U.S. 100 (1981).

3. The Act has been construed to prohibit issuance of a declaratory judgment, as well as an injunction.

B. THE JOHNSON ACT OF 1934

1. *This statute, now 28 U.S.C.A. § 1342, prohibits a district court in diversity cases from enjoining, suspending or restraining the operation of or compliance with a public utility rate set by a state or local administrative agency when the order does not interfere with interstate commerce, reasonable notice and hearing have been given, and a "plain, speedy and efficient remedy" is available in the state courts.*

2. The "plain, speedy and efficient" requirement is interpreted in the same manner as it is in the Tax Injunction Act.

IV. INJUNCTION OF FEDERAL JUDICIAL PROCEEDINGS

A. INJUNCTION BY A FEDERAL COURT

1. *The Supreme Court has held that the lower federal courts have considerable discretion in deciding whether to stay proceedings when parallel federal proceedings are taking place in a different district.*

2. However, the Court has not definitively decided the power of a federal court to enjoin a proceeding in another federal court. *Kerotest Manufacturing Co. v. C-O-Two Fire Equipment Co.*, 342 U.S. 180 (1952).

B. INJUNCTION BY A STATE COURT

1. *State courts are generally prohibited from enjoining federal judicial proceedings.* *Donovan v. City of Dallas*, 377 U.S. 408 (1964).

2. However, a state court may enjoin a federal court action when the state court initially obtained jurisdiction over property and the federal court is attempting to interfere with the exercise of that jurisdiction.

13

"OUR FEDERALISM"

Analysis

I. Introduction
  A. The Concept of "Our Federalism"
  B. Relationship to the Anti-injunction Statute
  C. The Contours of "Our Federalism"
II. Historical Development
  *A. Pre-*Younger v. Harris
  B. The Dombrowski *Decision*
III. Younger v. Harris *and the Modern Development of "Our Federalism"*
  A. The Younger *Decision*
  B. The Rationale of "Our Federalism"
  C. Exceptions to "Our Federalism"
IV. Timing of Federal Intervention
  A. The Distinction Between Future and Ongoing Prosecutions
  B. Limitations on the Steffel *Doctrine*
  C. Post-Trial Intervention
V. Applicability to Civil Proceedings
  A. Background
  *B. Post-*Younger *Developments*

    VI. Applicability to Non-judicial State Action
        A. State Executive Actions
        B. State Administrative Actions

I. INTRODUCTION

A. THE CONCEPT OF "OUR FEDERALISM"

1. *"Our Federalism" is a non-statutory doctrine, developed by the Supreme Court, imposing significant restrictions on the authority of federal courts to interfere with certain state functions, primarily state criminal prosecutions.*

2. Traditionally, the doctrine has limited only federal judicial interference with state judicial proceedings. However, more recently the doctrine has occasionally been deemed relevant in cases in which no state judicial proceeding is either pending or contemplated.

B. RELATIONSHIP TO THE ANTI-INJUNCTION STATUTE

1. Usually, federal court authority to interfere with state judicial proceedings is prohibited by the Anti-Injunction Statute, 28 U.S.C.A. § 2283 [see Chapter 12].

2. However, the Supreme Court held in *Mitchum v. Foster*, 407 U.S. 225 (1972), that federal civil rights suits under section 1983 constituted an "expressly authorized" exception to the Anti-Injunction Statute. Thus, if federal courts are to be limited in their power to interfere with state court actions in order to protect federal civil rights, it must be because of non-statutory considerations.

3. A year prior to *Mitchum*, the Supreme Court held in *Younger v. Harris*, 401 U.S. 37 (1971), the seminal case in the development of "Our Federalism," that even if the Anti-Injunction Statute were held inapplicable to section 1983 suits to enjoin state judicial proceedings, the federal courts would generally not be allowed to take such action.

C. THE CONTOURS OF "OUR FEDERALISM"

1. *In its classic form, the doctrine prohibits a federal court from enjoining an ongoing state criminal judicial proceeding.*

2. *However, the Court has also applied the bar to issuance of most declaratory judgments against ongoing state criminal judicial proceedings.* *Samuels v. Mackell*, 401 U.S. 66 (1971).

    a. The Court reasoned that the level of interference caused by a declaratory judgment was generally as high as that caused by an injunction, because the federal court's conclusion would have to receive collateral estoppel effect in the state proceedings, and, pursuant to the terms of the Declaratory Judgment Act, the declaratory judgment could form the basis for a subsequent injunction.

    b. The Court did leave open the possibility that exceptions might be recognized, but gave no indication as to what they were.

    3. In varying degrees, described in detail in subsequent sections, the Court has extended the doctrine to limit federal court authority to interfere with (a) state civil judicial proceedings, (b) future state judicial proceedings, and (c) state administrative and executive action.

II. HISTORICAL DEVELOPMENT

A. PRE-*YOUNGER v. HARRIS*

    1. In a series of decisions between the 1920's and 1940's, the Supreme Court developed the principle that a federal court could not enjoin the bringing of a state prosecution except in the most extraordinary circumstances. *E.g. Fenner v. Boykin*, 271 U.S. 240 (1926); *Douglas v. City of Jeannette*, 319 U.S. 157 (1943).

    2. Several modern commentators contend that these cases represent departures from long-established Supreme Court doctrine. However, their analysis is limited primarily to injunction of future, rather than ongoing, state prosecutions.

B. THE *DOMBROWSKI* DECISION

    1. In *Dombrowski v. Pfister*, 380 U.S. 479 (1965), the Supreme Court authorized a federal injunction of a threatened state prosecution of civil rights workers in Louisiana that was alleged to have been brought to harass the federal plaintiffs in the exercise of their first amendment right of freedom of expression.

    2. While the Court acknowledged that usually raising a defense to a state prosecution would provide an adequate means of protecting federal constitutional rights, that would not be the case here, largely because of the chilling effect on free speech rights that would be caused by the delay prior to adjudication. The Court also noted that the prosecution was alleged to have been brought in bad faith.

    3. After the *Dombrowski* decision, the federal courts began to exercise a significant role in protecting constitutional rights in the course of state criminal proceedings.

III. *YOUNGER v. HARRIS* AND THE MODERN DEVELOPMENT OF "OUR FEDERALISM"

A. THE *YOUNGER* DECISION

1. Harris, a member of the Progressive Labor Party, had been indicted for distributing leaflets allegedly in violation of the California Criminal Syndicalism Act. He sought an injunction of the prosecution on the grounds that the law under which he was prosecuted violated his constitutional rights.

2. The Supreme Court refused to allow the injunction, and in so doing developed the modern version of "Our Federalism."

   a. The Court relied heavily on the earlier Supreme Court decisions of the 1920's through 1940's.

   b. It distinguished *Dombrowski* on the grounds that no bad faith was alleged in the present prosecution.

B. THE RATIONALE OF "OUR FEDERALISM"

1. *In* Younger, *the Court described its deference in terms of "equity," "comity," and "federalism."*

2. "Equity" refers to the traditional equitable principles that an equity court will not enjoin a criminal prosecution and that equity will not act when there exists an adequate remedy at law.

   a. Since a defendant in a state criminal prosecution may always raise his constitutional argument as a defense in the course of that prosecution, the Court concluded that he had available an adequate remedy at law.

   b. In so holding, however, the Court disregarded the long established principle that adequacy of remedy for purposes of equitable federal jurisdiction was to be determined exclusively on the basis of available remedies within the *federal* court system.

   c. The Court also rejected the argument that the possible chilling effect caused by the delay in adjudication of first amendment rights renders the availability of a criminal defense an inadequate remedy.

3. The "federalism" and "comity" justifications concern what the Court called "a proper respect for state functions."

4. More particularly, as the *Younger* doctrine has developed, the deference is to both state courts and state substantive policies.

    a. It is thought that allowing a federal court to enjoin a state prosecution would reflect negatively on the abilities of state judges to interpret and enforce federal constitutional rights.

    b. It is also thought that allowing state, rather than federal, courts to adjudicate the constitutionality of state laws will provide a more appropriate, presumably more substantial deference to state policies, whether manifested in state legislation or in the discretionary activities of state executive officers.

    c. Finally, it is feared that exercise of widespread federal court injunctive authority could seriously disrupt the smooth operation of the state judicial process.

C. EXCEPTIONS TO "OUR FEDERALISM"

1. In *Younger*, the Court recognized the existence of several conceivable exceptions to the otherwise absolute bar to federal court injunctive power:

    a. Where the prosecution was brought in bad faith, or where it was part of a series of harassing prosecutions.

    b. Where there exist "extraordinary circumstances," as where the state law is "flagrantly and patently violative of express constitutional prohibitions in every clause, sentence and paragraph, and in whatever manner and against whomever an effort might be made to apply it." However, the Court has construed this exception in an extremely narrow manner. *See, e.g., Trainor v. Hernandez*, 431 U.S. 434 (1977).

    c. Where "[t]he injunction was not directed at the state prosecutions as such, but only at the legality of pretrial detention without a judicial hearing, an issue that could not be raised in defense of the criminal prosecution." This exception was established in *Gerstein v. Pugh*, 420 U.S. 103 (1975).

IV. THE TIMING OF FEDERAL INTERVENTION

A. THE DISTINCTION BETWEEN FUTURE AND ONGOING PROSECUTIONS

1. *Younger* itself dealt with an injunction of an ongoing criminal prosecution.

2. Though the earlier cases relied upon in *Younger* had prohibited federal injunctive relief against *future* prosecutions, the Court in *Younger* left unresolved whether its limits on federal equity power extended this far.

3. In *Steffel v. Thompson*, 415 U.S. 452 (1974), the Supreme Court held that the *Younger* doctrine did not apply at least to the issuance of declaratory relief against future state prosecutions.

    a. The decision did not explicitly deal with the question of whether injunctive relief could also be obtained against future prosecutions.

    b. Though the decision emphasized the less invasive nature of declaratory relief, such an assumption appears to depart from the analysis in *Samuels v. Mackell*, 401 U.S. 66 (1971), which generally equated the invasiveness of declaratory and injunctive relief.

    c. Other portions of the opinion emphasized that the interests of the *Younger* doctrine were largely inapplicable to future prosecutions, arguably leading to the conclusion that any form of federal relief could be appropriate against a future state prosecution.

4. In *Doran v. Salem Inn, Inc.*, 422 U.S. 922 (1975), the Supreme Court held that at least *preliminary* injunctive relief—where appropriate—could be obtained against a future state prosecution. However, some of the Court's language tended to indicate that it might draw a distinction between *preliminary* and *permanent* injunctive relief.

5. In *Wooley v. Maynard*, 430 U.S. 705 (1977), the Supreme Court authorized permanent injunctive relief against a future state prosecution. However, the decision was somewhat ambiguous as to whether it represented a full extension of *Steffel* and *Doran* to permanent injunctive relief, or whether it merely fell within one of the exceptions recognized in *Younger*. Most commentators view the decision as a full extension of *Steffel*. See also *Zablocki v. Redhail*, 434 U.S. 374 (1978).

B. LIMITATIONS ON THE *STEFFEL* DOCTRINE

1. In *Hicks v. Miranda*, 422 U.S. 332 (1975), the Supreme Court held that *Steffel* does not authorize a federal court injunction of a state proceeding, even if the injunction was initially sought prior to the filing of the state prosecution, if, at the time the injunction is to be issued, a state proceeding is pending, unless "proceedings of substance on the merits" had already taken place in the federal action prior to the filing of the state action.

2. The Court gave no real indication as to the meaning of that phrase, and its interpretation remains ambiguous.

3. Dissenting Justice Stewart noted that after *Hicks*, when notified of a pending federal court action for an injunction, a state prosecutor could simply file a state prosecution instead of responding in the federal

proceeding, thereby significantly reducing any benefit to the private litigant deriving from the *Steffel* doctrine.

C. POST-TRIAL INTERVENTION

1. *Younger* held that a federal court could not enjoin an ongoing state criminal proceeding.

2. The Court has also held, however, that "a necessary concomitant of *Younger* is that a party . . . must exhaust his state appellate remedies before seeking relief in the District Court." *Huffman v. Pursue, Ltd.*, 420 U.S. 592, 608 (1975).

3. The Court reasoned that "[v]irtually all of the evils at which *Younger* is directed would inhere in federal intervention prior to completion of state appellate proceedings, just as surely as they would if such intervention occurred at or before trial."

4. However, in *Wooley v. Maynard, supra*, the Court allowed a party who had been repeatedly convicted in state court for a continued violation of state law to seek equitable relief against future prosecutions in federal court following completion of those convictions, because he was not seeking to review the validity of the earlier convictions.

V. APPLICABILITY TO CIVIL PROCEEDINGS

A. BACKGROUND

1. *Younger* itself applied only to a *criminal* proceeding, leaving unresolved the doctrine's applicability to purely civil proceedings.

2. On the one hand, it might be argued that the logic of "Our Federalism" dictates its application to state civil proceedings, because whatever insult to state judges that derived from enjoining state criminal proceedings would also seem to flow from injunction of state civil proceedings.

3. On the other hand, the traditional equitable concern about enjoining a criminal prosecution is not present in the case of a civil proceeding, and it is arguable that the substantive state legislative policies are not as compelling in civil proceedings.

B. POST-*YOUNGER* DEVELOPMENTS

1. In *Huffman v. Pursue, Ltd., supra*, the Supreme Court was presented with an attempt to obtain a federal court injunction against state judicial enforcement of a state public nuisance statute. The state law had been used against the exhibiting of certain films alleged to be obscene.

2. Though the state proceeding was not technically criminal, the Court held that "we deal with a state proceeding which in important respects is more akin to a criminal prosecution than are most civil cases," and that the federal injunction "has disrupted [the] State's efforts to protect the very interest which underlie its criminal laws. . . ."

3. Though *Huffman* extended *Younger* to quasi-criminal civil proceedings, it left unresolved the doctrine's applicability to purely civil proceedings.

4. In *Trainor v. Hernandez*, 431 U.S. 434 (1977), the Court extended *Younger* to a state civil proceeding brought by the Illinois Department of Public Aid to recoup welfare payments allegedly obtained through fraud. The defendant in the state action sought federal equitable relief against the state's use of the Illinois Attachment Act to attach his funds, arguing that the Attachment Act was unconstitutional.

5. The Supreme Court held that *Younger* applied because "the State was a party to the suit in its role of administering its public-assistance programs," and "[b]oth the suit and the accompanying writ of attachment were brought to vindicate important state policies such as safeguarding the fiscal integrity of those programs." Thus, the Court's extension of *Younger* was limited to suits "brought by the State in its sovereign capacity," though Justice Brennan argued that the case was simply another step on the road toward full extension of *Younger* to all state civil proceedings.

6. In *Juidice v. Vail*, 430 U.S. 327 (1977), the Supreme Court applied *Younger* to a federal suit against state statutory contempt procedures, and in *Moore v. Sims*, 442 U.S. 415 (1979), the Court applied *Younger* to a federal suit to enjoin the operation of Texas' judicial protection of minors.

VI. APPLICABILITY TO NON–JUDICIAL STATE ACTION

A. STATE EXECUTIVE ACTIONS

1. In *Rizzo v. Goode*, 423 U.S. 362 (1976), the Supreme Court relied, in part, on *Younger* in overturning federal injunctive relief restructuring the Philadelphia Police disciplinary system, though no state judicial proceeding existed or was even contemplated.

2. Many lower courts since *Rizzo* have construed the decision merely to dictate significant concern on the part of the federal court for state executive officer discretion, but not to require the rigid and total federal judicial abdication of *Younger*.

B. STATE ADMINISTRATIVE ACTIONS

1. Though the Supreme Court has held that a litigant need not exhaust state administrative remedies prior to seeking relief in federal court under section 1983, the Court has indicated that *Younger* may play at least some role in certain types of state administrative proceedings.

2. In *Middlesex County Ethics Committee v. Garden State Bar Association*, 457 U.S. 423 (1982), the Court held that *Younger* bars federal injunctive relief against a state attorney disciplinary proceeding, which had been challenged on first amendment grounds.

    a. The Court noted that the proceedings "bear a close relationship to proceedings criminal in nature, as in *Huffman* . . . ", and emphasized "the unique relationship" between the state supreme court and the local ethics committee.

    b. The Court also noted that prior to the filing of the petition for certiorari in the Supreme Court the state Supreme Court had, on its own, entertained the constitutional issues. Thus, the decision might be limited to cases in which the administrative action is closely intertwined with the state judicial process.

*

14

REMOVAL JURISDICTION

Analysis

I. Introduction: The Concept and Structure of Removal
    A. The Concept of Removal
    B. Types of Removal Jurisdiction
    C. The "Derivative Jurisdiction" Limitation
II. Removal and Original Jurisdiction Contrasted
    A. Federal Question Jurisdiction
    B. Diversity
    C. Counterclaims
III. Procedure on Removal
    A. The Statutory Framework
    B. Injunction of State Proceedings
    C. Remand

I. INTRODUCTION: THE CONCEPT AND STRUCTURE OF REMOVAL

A. THE CONCEPT OF REMOVAL

1. Traditionally, assuming appropriate jurisdiction, a plaintiff is given the option of choosing the forum. This prerogative, denied to the defendant, is usually deemed to be part of the plaintiff's role as the aggressor in the litigation process.

2. In certain situations, however, Congress has authorized the defendant to modify plaintiff's forum choice if he so chooses, by means of the removal process.

3. When applicable, removal jurisdiction effectively provides both plaintiff and defendant with the absolute power to select a federal forum.

   a. If the plaintiff selects the federal forum and the requirements of subject matter jurisdiction are met, the defendant has no power to veto plaintiff's choice and have the case sent to the state court.

   b. However, if the plaintiff has chosen to sue in state court and the requirements of removal jurisdiction are met, the defendant may remove the case to federal court, and the plaintiff has no authority to have the case returned to state court.

4. As will be seen in section II, however, the requirements for original jurisdiction are on occasion different from those relevant to resort to removal jurisdiction.

B. TYPES OF REMOVAL JURISDICTION

1. *Most removal is authorized by 28 U.S.C.A. § 1441, which provides for removal in both federal question and diversity cases.*

2. 28 U.S.C.A. § 1442 provides for removal of either civil actions or criminal prosecutions commenced in a state court against any officer of the United States or agency thereof for any act under color of his office.

   a. Until 1948, the federal officer removal provision was limited to actions against revenue officers. In that year, Congress expanded the provision to include all federal officers.

   b. The constitutionality of federal officer removal jurisdiction was upheld in *Tennessee v. Davis*, 100 U.S. 257 (1879). Even though the state proceeding is brought pursuant to state law, the possible availability of a federal defense and the "protective jurisdiction" interest of the federal government in insulating its programs from state attack are deemed sufficient bases to fall within the "federal question" jurisdiction of Article III, section 2 of the Constitution.

    c. The availability of federal officer removal jurisdiction and the extent to which state courts may control the activities of federal officers present important issues relevant to the areas of congressional power to control federal court jurisdiction (Chapter 2) and state courts and federal power (Chapter 9). Consult those chapters for more detailed discussions of the implications of federal officer removal.

    3. 28 U.S.C.A. § 1443 provides for so-called civil rights removal. Because of an extremely narrow construction, this provision has atrophied to the point of virtual uselessness. Civil rights removal is examined in detail in Chapter 15.

C. THE "DERIVATIVE JURISDICTION" LIMITATION

    1. *One judge-made limitation on the use of removal jurisdiction is the principle of "derivative jurisdiction," i.e., that a court on removal can have no jurisdiction beyond that of the court from which the case has been removed.*

    2. If the state court in which the case has been originally brought lacks jurisdiction because the case falls within the exclusive jurisdiction of the federal courts, the federal court on removal also lacks jurisdiction, even though the case could, and should, have been filed originally in federal court.

Example: Plaintiff sues in state court for patent infringement, an area within the federal courts' exclusive jurisdiction. Defendant removes to federal court. The federal court must dismiss, because the state court lacked original jurisdiction. This is so, even though the case should have been filed in federal court in the first place.

II. REMOVAL AND ORIGINAL JURISDICTION CONTRASTED

A. FEDERAL QUESTION JURISDICTION

    1. *28 U.S.C.A. § 1441(a) provides that "[e]xcept as otherwise expressly provided by Act of Congress, any civil action brought in a state court of which the district courts of the United States have original jurisdiction, may be removed by the defendant or the defendants, to the district court of the United States for the district and division embracing the place where such action is pending."*

    2. One important point to note about this provision is its initial qualification: "Except as otherwise expressly provided by Act of Congress. . . ."

a. An example of such an Act of Congress is the Federal Employers' Liability Act, authorizing railroad employee negligence suits against employers. See 28 U.S.C.A. § 1445(a). In these cases, Congress has chosen to leave the plaintiff with an unchallengeable option to proceed in either state or federal court.

3. Another point to note about the language of section 1441(a) is its limitation to cases which fall within the federal court's original jurisdiction.

a. The effect of this limitation is to preclude removal in cases brought pursuant to state law but in which the defendant raises a federal defense, even if the federal issue raised in that defense will ultimately prove to be dispositive of the entire case.

b. Cases of this type have been excluded from the federal courts' original "federal question" jurisdiction by the "well-pleaded complaint" rule of *Louisville and Nashville Railroad Co. v. Mottley*, 211 U.S. 149 (1908) (discussed in Chapter 4, *supra*).

c. While a practical argument may be fashioned to justify the exclusion of such cases from the federal courts' original jurisdiction on the ground that federal judicial time could be wasted if no federal defense is actually raised (a fact that cannot be known when the complaint is filed), it is considerably more difficult to justify applying the same limitation to a defendant's removal. After all, the defendant can guarantee the presence of a federal issue, simply by raising it in the removal petition.

d. The American Law Institute has proposed a statute allowing removal in many of these cases.

4. Traditionally, it has been thought that if a state court plaintiff includes only a state cause of action in his complaint, his failure to raise a federal cause of action, even though one would clearly be applicable, precludes removal of the case to federal court under "federal question" jurisdiction.

5. However, in *Federated Department Stores, Inc. v. Moitie*, 452 U.S. 394 (1981), the Supreme Court held that a state plaintiff cannot employ artful pleading to avoid removal by the defendant.

a. The state complaints in that case purported to raise only state law claims, though they tracked closely the federal government's action under the federal antitrust laws.

b. The Supreme Court, in a footnote, indicated that the court of appeals had correctly affirmed the district court's conclusion that removal was proper because the claims presented were "federal in nature."

c. The main question about this reasoning concerns the nature of the issues to be litigated once the case has been removed to federal court. Presumably, the plaintiff cannot be forced to argue issues of federal law if he chooses not to, and one may wonder whether the requirements of the "federal question" statute have been met in a litigation in which the plaintiff never raises an issue of federal law.

B. DIVERSITY

1. *One major difference between original and removal jurisdiction in diversity cases is that while a plaintiff invoking the original diversity jurisdiction may be a resident of the state in which the action is brought, a defendant may not remove a case, even though complete diversity is present, if either he or any co-defendants who have been served is a resident of the state in which suit has been filed.*

Example: A, a resident of Illinois, sues B, a resident of New York, and C, a resident of Pennsylvania, on a state cause of action in state court in Pennsylvania. Neither B nor C is allowed to remove the case to federal court.

2. The rule on removal appears more consistent with the accepted purpose of the diversity jurisdiction to avoid state court prejudice against out-of-state residents, because an in-state plaintiff presumably suffers no prejudice in state court.

3. A problem arises, however, if one defendant is an out-of-state resident, but another is an in-state resident. Under 28 U.S.C.A. § 1441(b), a diversity action may be removed "only if none of the parties in interest properly joined and served as defendants is a citizen of the State in which such action is brought."

4. Under § 1441(c), "[w]henever a separate and independent claim or cause of action which would be removable if sued upon alone, is joined with one or more otherwise non-removable claims or causes of action, the entire case may be removed and the district court may determine all issues therein, or, in its discretion, may remand all matters not otherwise within its original jurisdiction."

a. The apparent reason for the statute is to allow removal where the claim against the party who could remove if sued alone is so distinct from the claims against the parties who could not remove (*e.g.*, non-diverse or in-state defendants) that the state court could invoke its jurisdiction distinct from the claims against the parties who could not remove (*e.g.*, non-diverse or in-state defendants) that the state court could invoke its prejudice against the out-of-state defendant without prejudicing the in-state defendants.

    b. However, in *American Fire & Casualty Co. v. Finn*, 341 U.S. 6 (1951), the Supreme Court indicated that a purpose of this 1948 statute was to reduce the number of cases removable to federal court.

    1. In *Finn*, the Court denied removal under § 1441(c) in a suit by a Texas citizen against two out-of-state insurance companies and their local agent, who was also a citizen of Texas. The complaint had alleged that the two companies were alternatively liable for fire loss or that the agent was liable for failing to keep the property insured.

    2. The Supreme Court held that the claims against the diverse and non-diverse parties were not "separate," because there had only been a single wrong to plaintiff—failure to pay compensation for the loss of the property.

    3. However, as commentators have noted, in such a case a state court could easily exercise prejudice against out-of-staters without harming the in-state resident.

    4. Because of *Finn*'s extremely narrow construction, relatively few cases are removable under § 1441(c).

C. COUNTERCLAIMS

    1. The greatest problem concerning removal of counterclaims involves the jurisdictional amount requirement, largely limited to diversity cases.

    a. If a diverse plaintiff sues for less than $10,000, a defendant cannot remove.

    b. If the defendant counterclaims for an amount in excess of $10,000, the plaintiff is not allowed to remove.

    c. The defendant in such a case may not remove if his counterclaim is permissive, although some courts allow him to remove if his counterclaim is compulsory under state law.

    2. These rules are basically judge-made, since the removal statutes do not refer to the jurisdictional amount issue, and the jurisdictional amount requirement in the diversity statute makes no specific reference to counterclaims.

REMOVAL JURISDICTION

III. PROCEDURE ON REMOVAL

A. THE STATUTORY FRAMEWORK

1. The current statutory procedure on removal is the result of a substantial congressional revision in 1948.

2. *Pursuant to 28 U.S.C.A. § 1446, a state defendant who wishes to remove the action to federal court must file "a verified petition containing a short and plain statement of the facts which entitle him . . . to removal" in the federal district court for the district and division within which the state action is pending. He must also include "a copy of all process, pleadings and orders served upon him . . . in such action."*

3. The removal petition for a civil action must be filed within thirty days after the defendant's receipt of the initial pleading. If the case in its initial form is not removable, it may be removed within thirty days of receipt of an amended complaint rendering the case removable. A removal petition in a criminal case must be filed within thirty days after arraignment in state court, or at any time prior to trial, whichever is earlier. However, for good cause shown the district court may grant permission to file the petition at a later time.

4. 28 U.S.C.A. § 1446(e) provides that in a civil action once the defendant provides written notice of the filing of the removal petition to all adverse parties and files a copy of the petition with the clerk of the state court, "the State court shall proceed no further unless and until the case is remanded." In a criminal prosecution, 28 U.S.C.A. § 1446(c)(3) provides that the filing of the removal petition "shall not prevent the State court in which such prosecution is pending from proceeding further, except that a judgment of conviction shall not be entered unless the petition is first denied."

5. If the federal court does not summarily deny the petition, it must order a prompt evidentiary hearing.

6. Each removal petition in a civil action, except in behalf of the United States, must be accompanied by a bond, assuring that the defendant will pay all costs if it is determined that the case was not removable or was improperly removed.

B. INJUNCTION OF STATE PROCEEDINGS

1. 28 U.S.C.A. § 1446(e) as already noted, provides that upon the filing of the removal petition, proceedings in the state court shall cease. This provision has been interpreted as a congressional exception to the Anti-Injunction Statute, 28 U.S.C.A. § 2283 [*see* Chapter 12], allowing a federal court to enjoin the plaintiff from proceeding further in the state action if the state court does not itself decline to continue with its proceedings.

2. In addition, the Reviser's Note to § 2283 indicates that the explicit exception in aid of the federal court's jurisdiction was added to cover such removal cases.

C. REMAND

1. *According to 28 U.S.C.A. § 1447(c), the federal court must remand the case to state court "[i]f at any time before final judgment it appears that the case was removed improvidently and without jurisdiction. . . ."*

2. Remand for lack of federal jurisdiction may be undertaken by the court on its own motion.

3. A decision to remand is not reviewable, except in the case of civil rights removal.

15

CIVIL RIGHTS REMOVAL JURISDICTION

Analysis

I. Introduction: The Structure and History of Civil Rights Removal—An Overview
   A. Current Status and Structure
   B. Historical Development
II. The Distinction Between State Statutes and State Practice: The Strauder-Rives *Doctrine*
   A. The Strauder *Decision*
   B. The Rives *Decision*
III. Modern Case Law
   A. Background
   B. The Rachel *Decision*
   C. The Peacock *Decision*
IV. The Meaning of "Equal Civil Rights"
   A. The History of the "Equal Civil Rights" Language
   B. Interpretation

I. INTRODUCTION: THE STRUCTURE AND HISTORY OF CIVIL RIGHTS REMOVAL—AN OVERVIEW

A. CURRENT STATUS AND STRUCTURE

1. *28 U.S.C. § 1443, the civil rights removal provision, provides:*

Any of the following civil actions or criminal prosecutions, commenced in a state court may be removed by the defendant to the district court of the United States for the district and division embracing the place wherein it is pending:

(1) Against any person who is denied or cannot enforce in the courts of such state a right under any law providing for the equal civil rights of citizens of the United States, or of all persons within the jurisdiction thereof;

(2) For any act under color of authority derived from any law providing for equal rights, or for refusing to do any act on the ground that it would be inconsistent with such law.

2. Fundamentally, the statute contains three clauses, each of which describes a situation in which removal will be allowed:

   a. *The "denial" clause.*

   b. *The "authority" clause.*

   c. *The "refusal" clause.*

3. By far the greatest judicial attention has been given to the "denial" clause. However, under modern Supreme Court interpretation, none of the three clauses plays any significant role.

B. HISTORICAL DEVELOPMENT

1. The origin of the modern-day civil rights removal statute is the Civil Rights Act of 1866.

2. The Revised Statutes of 1875 significantly altered previous practice.

   a. Under the original version of the removal procedure, removal was authorized either before or after trial in the state court.

   b. The 1875 statutes made post-trial removal unavailable, even though it was apparently Congress' original understanding that post-trial removal would function as the primary means of enforcing the Act.

3. As a result of the revision, removal decisions would have to be based on a *prediction* as to whether the state court would deny the

defendant a civil right of equality, since removal could be obtained only prior to trial.

4. Such a procedure necessarily contains within it a substantial amount of potential friction between state and federal courts, and it is largely for this reason that the Supreme Court has declined to provide the Civil Rights Removal Statute a broad scope.

5. The following sections describe exactly how the Court has construed the Statute to give it such a limited scope.

II. THE DISTINCTION BETWEEN STATE STATUTES AND STATE PRACTICE: THE *STRAUDER-RIVES* DOCTRINE

A. THE *STRAUDER* DECISION

1. In *Strauder v. West Virginia*, 100 U.S. 303 (1879), a black indicted for murder attempted to remove the prosecution from state court to federal court, arguing that his equal rights would be denied in state court, since only white males were allowed by state statute to serve on a grand or petit jury.

2. The Supreme Court held that pretrial removal should have been granted, since the defendant had demonstrated that he would be unable to enforce his equal civil rights in state court because of the state's juror selection statute, which the Court found to violate the fourteenth amendment.

B. THE *RIVES* DECISION

1. Decided the same day as *Strauder* was *Virginia v. Rives*, 100 U.S. 313 (1879). The state court defendants had argued that while there did not exist a state statute excluding blacks from jury service in Virginia, blacks had never been permitted to serve on county petit juries in cases concerning a black, and that their requests that blacks be included had been rejected in the state courts.

2. The Supreme court denied removal in *Rives*, distinguishing *Strauder* because there a state statute had expressly prohibited black jury participation, and therefore it could be presumed that the state courts would consider themselves bound by it. The same was not true of non-statutory state practice.

3. The distinction is highly questionable.

a. State Courts are bound by the Supremacy Clause of the Constitution to enforce federal law, including all constitutional provisions. Thus, there is no inherent reason to believe that the state courts would fail to enforce the fourteenth amendment by holding contrary state statutes unconstitutional.

    b. Moreover, if state courts are not to be trusted to invalidate state statutes that clearly violate the fourteenth amendment, one may wonder whether they can be trusted to invalidate unconstitutional non-statutory state practice.

    c. Finally, if the Supreme Court desires to reduce friction between federal and state courts, it is questionable whether a holding that exposes inherent mistrust of state court ability or willingness to invalidate a plainly unconstitutional state statute achieves that goal.

    4. Nevertheless, the Supreme Court adhered to the dichotomy in a series of subsequent decisions.

III. MODERN CASE LAW

A. BACKGROUND

1. For a number of years, the Supreme Court refrained from considering the civil rights removal law, because of statutory limitations on appellate review of removal denials.

2. However, in 1964, Congress amended the law, so that the Supreme Court could reconsider its earlier position on the question.

3. In 1966, the Supreme Court decided two cases the same day, in which it reexamined—and in certain ways altered—preexisting principles.

B. THE *RACHEL* DECISION

1. In *Georgia v. Rachel*, 384 U.S. 780 (1966), blacks who had sought service at certain hotels and restaurants were indicted under a local trespass statute for refusing to leave when so requested.

2. The Supreme Court allowed removal under the Civil Rights Removal Statute, finding a "denial" of defendants' rights in state court because of the unique nature of the federal right the defendants were asserting.

    a. That right was the right to equal service at public accommodations, guaranteed by the 1964 Civil Rights Act.

    b. That right the Court had previously construed to preclude not only *conviction*, but also the very act of *prosecution* in state court.

3. Therefore the Court found a "denial" of equal, rights in state court, even absent the existence of an express statutory denial of equality.

4. However, the Court failed to explain why removal to federal court necessarily constituted a violation, because after removal, the prosecution would still take place; the only difference would be that it would be conducted in federal, rather than in state court.

   a. The federal court might dismiss the prosecution immediately upon removal, but presumably the state court could have done the same.

   b. Moreover, factual issues may well exist—for example, whether the defendants were told to leave because they were rowdy, rather than because of their race—so in either federal or state court, it is conceivable that the prosecution could not properly be dismissed at the outset.

C. THE *PEACOCK* DECISION

1. In *City of Greenwood v. Peacock*, 384 U.S. 808 (1966), civil rights workers in Mississippi were charged with such offenses as obstructing the public streets, assault, disturbing the peace, creating a public disturbance, and inciting to riot.

2. Defendants sought removal, arguing that they had been prosecuted because of their efforts to register black voters.

3. The Supreme Court refused to allow removal.

   a. *Rachel* was distinguished on the ground that the statutory right invoked there involved a protection against even an *attempt* to prosecute, while the relevant civil rights statute in *Peacock*, unlike the public accommodations provision, contained no such protection.

   b. The Court also noted that, unlike the situation in *Rachel*, "no federal law confers an absolute right on private citizens . . . to obstruct a public street" or commit any other of the violations with which the defendants were charged.

4. Thus, after the decisions in *Rachel* and *Peacock*, civil rights removal continued to receive an extremely narrow construction.

   a. The *Strauder-Rives* dichotomy remained in force, meaning that only in the comparatively rare instance in which state *statutes*, rather than state *practice*, deny equal rights in state judicial procedures will civil rights removal be authorized.

b. A limited exception to this rule was recognized for the rare case in which the state prosecution is for conduct protected by a federal right against the very initiation of a prosecution.

5. The limited construction of civil rights removal jurisdiction was reaffirmed by the Supreme Court in *Johnson v. Mississippi,* 421 U.S. 213 (1975).

IV. THE MEANING OF "EQUAL CIVIL RIGHTS"

A. THE HISTORY OF THE "EQUAL CIVIL RIGHTS" LANGUAGE

1. Though the present Civil Rights Removal Statute is limited to cases in which the federal right asserted is "under any law providing for the equal civil rights of citizens of the United States," the original statutory framework did not include this wording.

2. The language was added in the 1875 revisions.

B. INTERPRETATION

1. *The Supreme Court has made clear that the phrase, "equal civil rights" applies only to rights of racial equality.*

2. Such a limitation appears nowhere on the face of the statute, though it is true that concern with racial equality was of primary importance to the statute's original drafters.

16

HABEAS CORPUS

Analysis

I. Introduction: The Origins of the Writ
   A. The Concept of Habeas Corpus
   B. History of the Writ
II. Current Statutory Structure
   A. The Basic Statute
   B. Habeas Corpus for State Prisoners
   C. Exhaustion of State Remedies
   D. Review of State Court Findings
   E. Habeas Corpus and the Exclusionary Rule
   F. Habeas Corpus for Federal Prisoners
III. Habeas Corpus, Waiver and the Adequate State Ground
   A. Applicability of the Adequate State Ground Doctrine to Habeas Corpus
   B. The Doctrine of Fay v. Noia *and Subsequent Developments*

I. INTRODUCTION: THE ORIGINS OF THE WRIT

A. THE CONCEPT OF HABEAS CORPUS

1. *Habeas corpus, often referred to as the "Great Writ", is a means to test judicially the legality of a person's detention by government authority.*

2. The writ thus provides an important means of preventing lawless government and of protecting the individual from secret and unjustified restraint.

B. HISTORY OF THE WRIT

1. The writ developed in England, and was firmly codified by the Habeas Corpus Act of 1679.

2. *The framers inserted the protection of the writ in Article I, section 9 of the Constitution, which provides: "The privilege of the writ of habeas corpus shall not be suspended, unless when in cases of rebellion or invasion the public safety may require it."*

3. Congress first vested jurisdiction in the federal courts to issue the writ in section 14 of the Judiciary Act of 1789.

II. CURRENT STATUTORY STRUCTURE

A. THE BASIC STATUTE

1. *28 U.S.C.A. § 2241(a) currently provides that "[w]rits of habeas corpus may be granted by the Supreme Court, any justice thereof, the district courts and any circuit judge within their respective jurisdictions."*

2. Section 2241(b) imposes certain limits on the use of the writ. It may not be issued unless:

    a. the prisoner "is in custody under or by color of the authority of the United States or is committed for trial before some court thereof," or

    b. he "is in custody for an act done or omitted in pursuance of an Act of Congress, or an order, process, judgment or decree of a court or judge of the United States," or

    c. "he is in custody in violation of the Constitution or laws or treaties of the United States;" or

    d. "It is necessary to bring him into court to testify or for trial."

e. Additional provision is made for issuance of habeas corpus for citizens of foreign states in custody for acts done under color of their government's authority and which are to be judged by international law.

B. HABEAS CORPUS FOR STATE PRISONERS

1. *28 U.S.C.A. § 2254 covers the issuance of writs of habeas corpus for prisoners held in state custody. Section 2254(a) provides that the writ may be issued for a prisoner in custody pursuant to a state court judgment "only on the ground that he is in custody in violation of the Constitution or laws or treaties of the United States."*

C. EXHAUSTION OF STATE REMEDIES

1. *Section 2254(b) provides that before the writ may issue, it must appear "that the applicant has exhausted the remedies available in the courts of the State, or that there is either an absence of available State corrective process or the existence of circumstances rendering such process ineffective to protect the rights of the prisoner."*

a. The exhaustion requirement was originally developed judicially, primarily in order to avoid unnecessary friction between state and federal courts and to avoid undue burdens on federal court dockets. *Ex parte Royall,* 117 U.S. 241 (1886).

b. Congress codified the exhaustion requirement in 1948.

c. Though exhaustion of state remedies is required in habeas corpus, it is not required in suits for deprivation of federal civil rights by state officers pursuant to 42 U.S.C.A. § 1983. It is often difficult to determine whether a particular case should be classified as one or the other, when prisoners sue to challenge the imposition of penalties by prison officials.

Examples: State prisoners, deprived of good-conduct-time credits by prison authorities as a result of disciplinary proceedings, sued in federal court, claiming that the authorities had acted unconstitutionally. If the credits were restored, the prisoners' immediate release from confinement would result, because of the length of time left on their sentences. The Supreme Court held that even if restoration would not result in release, the suits were governed by the habeas corpus statute, and therefore required exhaustion, because habeas corpus concerns the length of confinement. *Preiser v. Rodriguez,* 411 U.S. 475 (1973).

Plaintiff prisoner files a federal court suit pursuant to section 1983, alleging that the procedures followed by prison authorities in revoking good-time credits failed to meet due process requirements. As relief, the suit seeks both restoration of credits and damages. The Supreme Court held that while the restoration of credits was governed by the exhaustion requirement, the suit for damages was a proper § 1983 suit, and therefore could proceed without exhaustion of state remedies. In such a suit, a litigant could obtain as "ancillary relief an otherwise proper injunction enjoining the prospective enforcement of invalid prison regulations." *Wolff v. McDonnell*, 418 U.S. 539 (1974).

    d. When a prisoner combines in one habeas corpus suit both exhausted and non-exhausted claims, the federal court must dismiss the petition. *Rose v. Lundy*, 455 U.S. 509 (1982).

D. REVIEW OF STATE COURT FINDINGS

    1. *While traditionally a state court judgment and its factual findings will be res judicata or collateral estoppel in a subsequent federal court proceeding, this is not so in the case of federal habeas corpus for state prisoners.* See *Brown v. Allen*, 344 U.S. 443 (1953).

    2. Given the exhaustion requirement, the value of the writ would be effectively destroyed if the state decision were to bar the federal court from acting.

    3. However, a federal court in a habeas case is not totally free to ignore state court factual findings.

    a. Originally, the federal courts were authorized to disregard basic factual findings of the state court only if there had been a "vital flaw" in the state court proceedings. *Brown v. Allen*, 344 U.S. 443 (1953).

    b. However, in *Townsend v. Sain*, 372 U.S. 293 (1963), the Supreme Court held that a federal court on a habeas petition must re-examine state factual findings if the state court had not afforded the petitioner a "full and fair hearing" at trial.

    c. In 1966, Congress codified standards for determining under what circumstances state factual findings were to be reviewed in a habeas case. 28 U.S.C.A. § 2254(d) currently provides that state findings are presumed to be correct, unless it is established that (1) the merits of the factual dispute were not resolved in the state proceeding; (2) the state's factfinding procedure was inadequate to afford a full and fair hearing; (3) "that the material facts were not adequately developed at the State court hearing"; (4) that the state lacked subject matter jurisdiction; (5) that the applicant, an indigent, was not appointed counsel; (6) that the applicant did not receive a full and fair hearing; (7) "that the applicant was otherwise denied due process of law in the State court proceeding"; or (8) if the federal court concludes that the state court's factual determination "is not fairly supported by the record. . . . "

E. HABEAS CORPUS AND THE EXCLUSIONARY RULE

1. *In* Stone v. Powell, *428 U.S. 465 (1976), the Supreme Court held that a state prisoner who had been afforded the opportunity in state court for full and fair consideration of a claim that evidence was illegally seized and therefore should have been excluded from trial, could not have that issue reviewed by the federal court in a habeas corpus petition.*

    a. The decision represented an expansion over *Townsend* and section 2254(d), since the issue involved in *Stone* was a question of law, rather than of basic fact.

    b. The Court reasoned that the value of the exclusionary rule is questionable, because though illegally seized the evidence may nevertheless be probative, and that while the rule should still apply at trial, its costs did not justify its further use in a habeas corpus proceeding.

2. Some commentators have suggested that the key to *Stone* is that the excluded evidence did not undermine a proper finding of guilt or innocence, since the illegal nature of the seizure did not affect the evidence's accuracy. Therefore habeas review should be deemed improper unless the challenged evidentiary ruling might undermine a correct finding of guilt or innocence (e.g., a coerced confession). However, the Court never explicitly adopted this standard, and in any event it is not clear how such a standard would work in practice.

Example: Petitioner seeks federal habeas corpus, alleging that the state court improperly denied his claim of racial discrimination in the selection of the grand jury that issued the indictment. Held: *Stone v. Powell* does not apply to preclude federal review of the state court ruling. *Rose v. Mitchell,* 443 U.S. 545 (1979). If the standard to be employed were whether the constitutional challenge might go to the issue of guilt or innocence, it is difficult to determine whether racial discrimination in the grand jury would meet it.

F. HABEAS CORPUS FOR FEDERAL PRISONERS

1. 28 U.S.C.A. § 2255 governs the issuance of habeas corpus for federal prisoners.

2. The section provides that an application for relief "shall not be entertained if it appears that the applicant has failed to apply for relief, by motion, to the court which sentenced him, or that such court has denied him

relief, unless it also appears that the remedy by motion is inadequate or ineffective to test the legality of his detention."

III. HABEAS CORPUS, WAIVER AND THE ADEQUATE STATE GROUND

A. APPLICABILITY OF THE ADEQUATE STATE GROUND DOCTRINE TO HABEAS CORPUS

1. The adequate state ground doctrine, traditionally applied to Supreme Court review of state court decisions [see Chapter 8, *supra*], provides in relevant part that a federal court will not review a federal issue arising in a state case if the state court declined to decide the federal issue because the litigant who sought to raise it failed to comply with a legitimate state procedural requirement.

2. In *Daniels v. Allen*, 344 U.S. 443 (1953), the Supreme Court held that the doctrine applies to habeas corpus, and that therefore the federal court could not consider constitutional challenges when the petitioner had failed to appeal his conviction in the state system until one day after the prescribed limit.

3. *Daniels* was abandoned ten years later in the controversial decision in *Fay v. Noia*, 372 U.S. 391 (1963).

B. THE DOCTRINE OF *FAY v. NOIA* AND SUBSEQUENT DEVELOPMENTS

1. In *Fay*, the Court abandoned *Daniels*, holding that a state defendant's failure to comply with state procedural requirements would not preclude federal review of his constitutional claims on habeas corpus unless the defendant had consciously by-passed his state judicial remedies. Thus, inadvertent failure to comply with state procedure, regardless of the merits of that state procedure, would not bar federal consideration of a constitutional challenge.

2. In a vigorous dissent, Justice Harlan argued that the adequate state ground doctrine should apply to habeas cases.

3. In *Wainwright v. Sykes*, 433 U.S. 72 (1977), the Supreme Court effectively abandoned *Noia*, by holding that a state defendant's failure to raise a contemporaneous objection to the admission of certain evidence (even though not a deliberate by-pass) precluded Supreme Court review of his claim in a habeas proceeding.

   a. The Court indicated that before the reviewing Court would consider the issue, the habeas petitioner must first establish both cause for his failure to object and prejudice from admission of the challenged evidence.

b. The *Sykes* Court relied heavily on *Francis v. Henderson*, 425 U.S. 536 (1976), where the Court had effectively applied the adequate state ground doctrine in habeas corpus, without dealing with *Noia*.

c. While the Court in *Sykes* did not explicitly overrule *Noia*, it severely criticized the rule of that case, and both its comments and holding indicate that the *Noia* rule is not likely to be considered valid.

*

17

THE LAW TO BE APPLIED IN THE FEDERAL COURTS: THE *ERIE* DOCTRINE

Analysis

I. The History and Meaning of the Rules of Decision Act
   A. Historical Development
   B. The *Erie* Decision and the Rules of Decision Act
II. Post-*Erie* Developments
   A. The *York* Decision and the "Outcome Determination" Test
   B. The *Byrd* Decision and the Balancing of State and Federal Interests
III. The *Hanna* Decision: Recognition of the Statutory and Constitutional Origins of the *Erie* Doctrine
   A. The Facts of *Hanna*
   B. *Hanna's* Three-Part Structural Analysis
   C. The Constitutional Test
   D. The Rules of Decision Act: Development of the Modified Outcome Determination Test
   E. The Rules Enabling Act
   F. Post-*Hanna* Developments
IV. Specific Applications of the *Erie* Doctrine
   A. Choice of Law
   B. Interpleader

    V. Determining the Applicable State Law
        A. Statement of the Problem
        B. The General Approach to the Issue of Uncertain State Law

I. THE HISTORY AND MEANING OF THE RULES OF DECISION ACT

A. HISTORICAL DEVELOPMENT

1. *The Rules of Decision Act, presently codified at 28 U.S.C.A. § 1652, provides: "The laws of the several states, except where the Constitution or treaties of the United States or Acts of Congress otherwise require or provide, shall be regarded as rules of decision in civil actions in the courts of the United States, in cases where they apply."* The statute is basically the same as in its original form as section 34 of the Judiciary Act of 1789. While the Act usually requires the use of state "rules of decision" only in diversity cases because most federal question cases arise under an act of Congress, by its terms the Act is not limited to diversity cases, and conceivably could have an impact in non-diversity situations.

2. In the well-known decision of *Swift v. Tyson*, 41 U.S. (16 Pet.) 1 (1842), Justice Story held that while state statutes were "rules of decision" which the Rules of Decision Act required the federal courts to follow, state judicial decisions were generally not "laws" of the several states and therefore need not be observed. In such cases, *Swift* allowed the federal courts to develop a "general federal common law," that superceded state common law in federal suits. However, Story recognized two exceptions, where state decisions did have to be followed:

    a. state decisions interpreting state statutes, and

    b. state decisions concerning common law matters of peculiarly local concern.

3. Story's goal was to create uniformity of law among the federal courts. However, experience under the *Swift* rule demonstrated that such uniformity was difficult to attain. In any event, the effect of *Swift* was to establish different legal standards between state and federal courts in the same state, giving rise to significant uncertainty for potential litigants, who could not know whether they would be sued in state or federal court. Use of different legal standards in state and federal court therefore might result in substantial difficulties in planning day-to-day behavior.

B. THE *ERIE* DECISION AND THE RULES OF DECISION ACT

1. *Swift* was overruled in *Erie Railroad v. Tompkins*, 304 U.S. 64 (1938).

2. In his famous opinion for the Court, Justice Brandeis rejected *Swift* because of:

    a. *Historical* inaccuracies in Justice Story's construction of the word, "laws" in the Rules of Decision Act to exclude judicial decisions.

    b. *Social* difficulties resulting from *Swift,* including (1) the danger that out-of-state plaintiffs would "forum shop" between state and federal court, depending on which substantive law the plaintiff found more beneficial; (2) the inequality among sets of defendants—those sued by out-of-state residents were subjected to the harms of forum shopping, while those sued by in-state plaintiffs did not suffer this disadvantage, and (3) the resulting uncertainty in the planning of day-to-day "primary" conduct.

    c. *Constitutional* problems raised by the federal courts' displacement of state common law with federal common law, because "Congress has no power to declare substantive rules of common law applicable in a state whether they be local in their nature or 'general,' be they commercial law or a part of the law of torts. And no clause in the Constitution purports to confer such a power upon the federal courts."

    d. *Philosophical* fallacies in Justice Story's implicit assumption that judicial decisions were not "law," but merely "evidence" of a higher law, which the federal courts could discern as easily as the state courts.

II. POST-*ERIE* DEVELOPMENTS

A. THE *YORK* DECISION AND THE "OUTCOME DETERMINATION" TEST

1. In *Guaranty Trust Co. of New York v. York,* 326 U.S. 99 (1945), the Supreme Court held that a federal court sitting in a diversity case must apply the relevant state law on the issue of the timeliness of the suit.

2. In so holding, the Court assumed that *Erie* had barred the development of only *substantive* federal common law, and that federal courts could still develop their own *procedural* principles, even in diversity cases, where the source of the substantive cause of action was purely state-created.

3. However, the Court noted that the dichotomy between "substantive" and "procedural" was not a fixed one for all contexts. In applying *Erie,* the Court found the dichotomy to turn on the effect of the relevant legal principle on the outcome of the case. If the use of a federal rule rather than a state rule would affect the case's outcome, the rule was deemed "substantive" and the state law had to be followed.

    a. The reason for such a dichotomy, stated the Court, was that "[t]he nub of the policy that underlies Erie . . . is that for the same transaction the accident of a suit by a non-resident litigant in a federal court instead of in a State court a block away, should not lead to a substantially different result."

    b. In effect, the Court was focusing on the forum-shopping concern cited in *Erie*: if the laws applied in state and federal court on an issue that will affect the outcome of the case differ, forum shopping may result.

    3. An important point to note about *York* is that instead of focusing on the meaning of the Rules of Decision Act, the opinion spoke of the "policy of federal jurisdiction which Erie . . . embodies." Thus, the Court began a shift away from the *Erie* doctrine as a matter of statutory and constitutional construction, and toward the view of *Erie* as merely a matter of social and federalism "policy."

    4. The difficulty with the "outcome determination" test of *York* is that conceivably *any* legal rule might ultimately have an impact upon the outcome of the case, if not followed by the litigants. For example, if court rules require that briefs be submitted with red covers, a litigant who stubbornly insists on submitting a blue-covered brief might not have that brief accepted by the court, clearly affecting the case's outcome.

    5. In the years following *York*, the Supreme Court made clear that to come within the "outcome determination" test, a rule need not inescapably affect the outcome. The mere possibility that the outcome would be different because of the use of a separate federal standard would be sufficient to require that state law be followed. *Bernhardt v. Polygraphic Co. of America, Inc.*, 350 U.S. 198 (1956).

B. THE *BYRD* DECISION AND THE BALANCING OF STATE AND FEDERAL INTERESTS

    1. In Byrd v. Blue Ridge Rural Electric Cooperative, Inc., 356 U.S. 525 (1958), the Court, as it had in York, seemingly abandoned a search for the meaning of the Rules of Decision Act in favor of an exposition of the wisest "policy" on the issue of what law to apply in the federal courts. Unlike York, however, in answering that question Byrd focused largely on the competing interests of the state and federal systems, rather than on the concerns of forum shopping and litigant inequality.

    2. In *Byrd*, the Court held that in a federal diversity suit the factual issue of whether a plaintiff in a negligence case was an employee for purposes of workmen's compensation was to be determined by the jury, pursuant to the federal standard, rather than by the judge, which was the state practice.

3. In reaching this conclusion, the Court examined three distinct factors:

a. Whether the state rule of having the judge decide the issue was "bound up" with "the rights and obligations of the parties"—*i.e.*, whether the use of the judge as the decisionmaker was in some way designed to further the state's substantive objectives in its workmen's compensation statute;

b. Whether use of the federal rule would likely result in a difference in outcome (*i.e.*, the "outcome determination" element, used as the exclusive standard in *York*); and

c. "countervailing considerations" favoring the federal rule in the role of the federal courts as an "independent system for administering justice to litigants who properly invoke its jurisdiction" (*i.e.*, the interests of the federal system in applying its own procedural rules).

4. The Court answered the first inquiry in the negative, finding no state purpose to further the substantive objectives of the statute through use of its procedural rule. It answered the second question by noting the possibility of an impact on outcome, but found to be overriding the federal interest in distributing the judge-jury function "under the influence—if not the command—of the Seventh Amendment" guarantee of a right to a jury trial in civil cases in federal court.

5. The *Byrd* opinion was not entirely clear how these three factors were to be examined.

a. Under a literal reading of the Court's opinion, an initial, separate inquiry must be made into whether the state rule furthers a substantive purpose; if it does, the rule must be followed, regardless of any possible competing federal interest. Under this reading, only if no state interest in the procedural rule was found (as in *Byrd* itself) would the Court proceed to balance the interest in avoiding a difference in outcome against the federal interest in employing its own rule.

b. Some lower courts, however, interpreted *Byrd* to impose merely a one-step analysis, in which the state's substantive interest and the possible effect on outcome were balanced against the competing federal interest.

c. Still other courts excluded the "outcome effect" element from the *Byrd* analysis, and instead engaged in a direct balancing of state and federal interests.

6. The primary difficulty with the *Byrd* balancing approach was the great uncertainty to which it gave rise, largely because of the unguided, subjective nature of the balancing process.

III. THE *HANNA* DECISION: RECOGNITION OF THE STATUTORY AND CONSTITUTIONAL ORIGINS OF THE *ERIE* DOCTRINE

A. THE FACTS OF *HANNA*

1. In *Hanna v. Plumer*, 380 U.S. 460 (1965), the issue was whether a federal court sitting in diversity was required to follow a state rule requiring in-hand service of process on state executors, despite the existence of Rule 4(d)(1) of the Federal Rules of Civil Procedure, which permits service at "the dwelling house of the defendant."

2. The Court of Appeals, applying *Byrd*'s balancing test, inquired into the "importance" of the state rule, and concluded that a substantive state purpose was being served. It therefore affirmed the district court's decision to apply the state rule.

3. The Supreme Court reversed, holding that the Federal Rule was to apply. In so doing, the Court substantially restructured the approach to the *Erie* doctrine.

B. *HANNA*'S THREE-PART STRUCTURAL ANALYSIS

1. *Instead of the broad policy focus of both York and Byrd, the Court in Hanna recognized three distinct issues of statutory or constitutional construction relevant to the Erie doctrine:*

   a. *Whether a federal court may, under the Constitution, displace the state rule with its own;*

   b. *assuming the constitutionality of the use of a distinct federal rule, whether Congress has in fact authorized the creation of such a rule in a specific federal statute, such as the Rules Enabling Act, the statute authorizing the Supreme Court to promulgate the Federal Rules of Civil Procedure; and*

   c. *assuming no specifically applicable federal statute, whether the federal courts are authorized by the Rules of Decision Act to displace state law through the creation of federal common law. The Rules of Decision Act will apply only to those rules of procedures not covered by another statute, and will therefore include only those rules developed by the federal courts themselves.*

C. THE CONSTITUTIONAL TEST

1. The Court in *Hanna* recognized that the Constitution imposed certain limits on the power of both Congress and the federal courts to supplant state law. These limits derived from the limited nature of federal power under Article I of the Constitution.

a. Congress may only act when authorized to do so by the enumerated powers delegated in Article I, § 8 of the Constitution.

b. The only enumerated power conceivably relevant to federal court power to develop its own rules is the provision enabling Congress to establish inferior federal courts.

c. While the Court found that the "necessary and proper" clause (enabling Congress to do anything that is "necessary and proper" to the achievement of one of its enumerated powers) authorized Congress to allow the federal courts to develop *procedural* rules to govern the procedures employed in federal court, it declined to find a similar power to develop *substantive* rules in diversity cases.

2. The Court recognized that it would not always be easy to determine whether a particular rule was "substantive" or "procedural;" in fact, it is conceivable that a rule could be both "procedural" (in that it concerns matters of the fairness or efficiency of the litigation process) and "substantive" (concerning some interest other than the fairness or efficiency of the litigation process).

3. Therefore, the Court indicated that if a particular rule was rationally capable of being classified as "procedural," it could constitutionally be developed by the federal courts, even in diversity cases.

4. Thus, under *Hanna*, it is only purely substantive matters on which the federal courts are constitutionally incapable of developing common law rules in diversity areas.

5. While this constitutional construction leaves broad authority to Congress to allow the federal courts to displace state rules, it is important to recall that the mere fact Congress has power to allow the federal courts to displace state law does not necessarily mean that Congress has actually exercised its broad power. In fact, it is arguable that Congress, in relevant statutes, has imposed limitations not required by the Constitution.

D. THE RULES OF DECISION ACT: DEVELOPMENT OF THE MODIFIED OUTCOME DETERMINATION TEST

1. The *Hanna* Court's discussion of the appropriate Rules of Decision Act test was dictum, because the Court ultimately decided that whether a Federal Rule of Civil Procedure is employed rather than state law is controlled by the test of the Rules Enabling Act, rather, than the Rules of Decision Act.

2. However, the Court discussed how the issue would be resolved if the Rules of Decision Act did apply.

3. Unlike the *Byrd* balancing of competing state and federal interests, *Hanna* returned to the "forum shopping" concerns expressed in *Erie* and *York*.

4. Like *York*, *Hanna* focused on the effect on outcome that use of the federal, rather than state standard, would have. Unlike *York*, however, the Court did not impose a rigid outcome determination test.

   a. The *Hanna* Court indicated that outcome determination "cannot be read without reference to the twin aims of the *Erie* rule: discouragement of forum-shopping and avoidance of inequitable administration of the laws."

   b. In effect, the Rules of Decision Act test adopted by the Court was a "modified outcome determination" test: if use of a distinct federal standard would provide a plaintiff with such an advantage or disadvantage that it would cause a reasonable plaintiff to choose one forum rather than another, the state standard must be used. If not, the separate federal standard is to be used.

   c. Since differences in method of service of process would not likely cause a litigant to choose one forum over another, even though failure to follow the applicable procedural rule would result in a technical difference in outcome, said the Court, under a Rules of Decision Act analysis the federal standard would be used.

E. THE RULES ENABLING ACT

1. It is important to recall that the Court's Rules of Decision Act analysis did not determine the Court's actual holding, because the federal procedural standard, dealing with method of service of process, was covered by Federal Rule of Civil Procedure 4(d)(1), and the Federal Rules of Civil Procedure were in turn controlled by a distinct federal statute, the Rules Enabling Act.

2. The Rules Enabling Act, 28 U.S.C.A. § 2072, provides in relevant part: "The Supreme Court shall have the power to prescribe by general rules, the forms of process, writs, pleadings and motions, and the practice and procedure of the district courts and courts of appeals of the United States in civil actions. . . .

   "Such rules shall not abridge, enlarge or modify any substantive right. . . ."

3. The *Hanna* Court found Rule 4(d)(1) to be a valid exercise of the Supreme Court's rulemaking power delegated in the Rules Enabling Act.

4. There exists some confusion, however, as to how the Court intended the Rules Enabling Act to be construed.

a. One possible construction is the one employed by the Court a number of years prior to *Hanna* in *Sibbach v. Wilson & Co., Inc.*, 312 U.S. 1 (1941). There the Court held that Rule 35 of the Federal Rules, dealing with the ordering of mental and physical examinations for discovery purposes, was a valid exercise of the power delegated by the Rules Enabling Act. It rejected the argument that the Rule violated the Enabling Act directive that the rules "shall not abridge, enlarge or modify any substantive right" because the Rule regulated procedure, and therefore by definition could not violate a substantive right. The test, in other words, views "procedural" and "substantive" as mutually exclusive: if a Rule regulates procedure, it cannot simultaneously be considered substantive. This test is Equivalent (in impact, if not analysis) to the test employed by the *Hanna* Court to determine a rule's constitutionality: if in some sense it regulates procedure, it is deemed "procedural," even if it also affects substance.

b. An alternative construction argues that Rules can simultaneously regulate procedure yet have an impact upon a substantive right.

Example: A statute of limitations is "procedural," in that it is in part concerned with assuring the fairness of the truthfinding process by deterring the use of stale and therefore possibly unreliable evidence. Yet it is also designed to protect an interest concerned with something other than the fairness of the truth-finding process, because it is aimed in part at allowing a potential defendant to "breath easy" after a specified period, and no longer worry about a suit.

c. Under this alternative construction, the mere fact that a Federal Rule in some sense regulates procedure is not sufficient, although it is a necessary condition; additionally, the rule would be required not to have an impact upon a non-procedural, or substantive, interest protected by the state.

d. The Court in *Hanna* did not make clear which of these two constructions it intended, and one cannot infer which it preferred from its conclusion that Rule 4(d)(1), regulating method of service, was valid. The Rule would have been valid under either construction, since method of service deals exclusively with procedural issues.

F. POST-*HANNA* DEVELOPMENTS
1. The *Walker* Decision

a. In *Walker v. Armco Steel Corp.*, 446 U.S. 740 (1980), the Supreme Court held that Rule 3 of the Federal Rules of Civil Procedure, which provides that "[a] civil action is commenced by filing a complaint with the Court," is not directed to the issue of when a statute of limitations period ceases to run, and therefore presents no conflict with a state rule that measures the tolling of the statute of limitations from the date of service of the complaint on the defendant, rather than from the date the case is filed.

    b. Since there is no applicable Federal Rule of Civil Procedure, or other applicable federal statute, whether a federal court sitting in diversity may ignore the state standard and develop its own rule as a matter of federal common law is controlled by the Rules of Decision Act.

    c. In holding that the state rule must be used, the Court in some ways appeared to return to a strict outcome determination test, since it concluded that the state rule must be followed even though it acknowledged that "in this case failure to apply the state service law might not create any problem of forum shopping. . . ."

    d. The Court also seemed to reintroduce some of the systemic concerns manifested in *Byrd* by noting that the state rule "is a statement of a substantive decision by that State that actual service on, and accordingly actual notice by, the defendant is an integral part of the several policies served by one statute of limitations."

    2. It should be noted that at least prior to *Walker*, many lower courts continued to apply the *Byrd* balancing test to issues not controlled by the Federal Rules of Civil Procedure, despite the *Hanna* dictum to the contrary.

IV. SPECIFIC APPLICATIONS OF THE *ERIE* DOCTRINE

A. CHOICE OF LAW

    1. *In* Klaxon Co. v. Stentor Electric Manufacturing Co., Inc., *313 U.S. 487 (1941), the Supreme Court held that a federal court sitting in diversity must employ the choice-of-law rule of the state in which it sits, rather than employ its own choice-of-law rule.*

    2. *Klaxon* has on occasion been criticized, because it reduced the certainty that a uniform federal choice-of-law rule would provide. However, such criticism represents much of the same rejected logic that underlies *Swift v. Tyson*, in that it seeks uniformity of decision among federal courts, at the expense of consistency between state and federal courts within the same state. Whatever uncertainty that derives from *Klaxon's* use of state choice-of-law rules is no different from the uncertainty facing any potential litigant involved in multi-state activities.

    3. Moreover, though *Klaxon* preceeded both *Byrd* and *Hanna*, the decision appears consistent with both the systemic concerns of *Byrd* and the forum-shopping concerns of *Hanna*.

B. INTERPLEADER

1. In Griffin v. McCoach, *313 U.S. 498 (1941)*, *the Supreme Court held that state rules must be applied in a diversity case brought pursuant to the Federal Interpleader Statute.*

2. That Statute authorizes nationwide service of process, a practice not allowed in state court. Thus, certain parties in the suit could not have been brought into a corresponding state court suit.

3. One might therefore criticize *Griffin*, because there was no danger of forum shopping resulting from use of a distinct federal standard. However, state policies might nevertheless be undermined by use of a distinct federal rule, even though suit could not have been brought in state court.

V. DETERMINING THE APPLICABLE STATE LAW

A. STATEMENT OF THE PROBLEM

1. Once it has been determined that a federal court is to employ state law, and that the law of a particular state, under relevant choice-of-law principles, is to be used, the federal court faces the problem of determining exactly what that state law is.

2. In many instances, this will not prove to be a difficult task, because there exists recent and unambiguous statements of the state supreme court on the issue.

3. However, on occasion there may exist no relevant statements of the state supreme court, and instead exist only statements of intermediate appellate courts. On the other hand, there may exist a technically applicable state supreme court decision, but one that is old and inconsistent with the modern trend in other jurisdictions, rendering uncertain whether the state supreme court would today adhere to it.

B. THE GENERAL APPROACH TO THE ISSUE OF UNCERTAIN STATE LAW

1. *While a number of lower federal courts have expressed the view that they are bound by intermediate state appellate court decisions, the majority have asked, what would the state supreme court likely hold if the case were to reach them today?*

Example: In 1957, a federal court sitting in diversity is required to determine the law of Mississippi on the issue of whether privity is required in negligence suits. In 1928, the state supreme court had held that privity was required, even though many state courts had by that time rejected the requirement. By 1957, virtually no other state required privity in negligence suits. In 1954, the state supreme court had indicated, in dicta, doubts about its earlier rule, though it did not overrule it. The federal court held that at that time Mississippi law should be construed to reject the privity requirement. *Mason v. American Wheel Works*, 241 F.2d 906 (1st Cir.1957).

2. The reason why a federal court should apply what it thinks the state supreme court would hold the law to be today is that the opposite approach might well give rise to a type of "reverse" forum shopping: *i.e.*, a plaintiff who prefers the law as it was formally held many years ago, but who realizes that today the state supreme court would likely change it, would be likely to choose the federal forum, knowing that the federal courts would consider themselves bound by the old rule. If he sued in state court, however, the case would eventually reach the state supreme court, which would likely change the law.

3. In *Commissioner v. Estate of Bosch*, 387 U.S. 456 (1967), the Supreme Court stated in dicta that "under some conditions, federal authority may not be bound even by an intermediate state appellate court ruling. . . . [T]he underlying substantive rule involved is based on state law and the State's highest court is the best authority on its own law. If there be no decision by that court then federal authorities must apply what they find to be the state law after giving 'proper regard' to relevant rulings of other courts of the State. In this respect, it may be said to be, in effect, sitting as a state court."

4. If the state has authorized the practice (either by court rule or statute), a federal court uncertain of the meaning of state law may employ a *certification* procedure, in which it refers the state law question directly to the state supreme court for clarification. The Supreme Court has indicated that if the state has made such a procedure available and a federal court is faced with ambiguous state law, the federal court would be well advised to make use of the procedure. *Lehman Brothers v. Schein*, 416 U.S. 386 (1974).

18

FEDERAL COMMON LAW

Analysis

I. Introduction: The Sources of and Justification for Federal Common Law
    A. Federal Common Law and the Erie Doctrine
    B. Federal Common Law and the Rules of Decision Act
    C. The Reach of Federal Common Law

II. Areas of Federal Common Law
    A. Description of Categories
    B. Federal "Proprietary" Interests
    C. International Relations
    D. Admiralty
    E. Interstate Disputes
    F. Interstate Pollution
    G. Enforcement of Constitutional Rights

I. INTRODUCTION: THE SOURCES OF AND JUSTIFICATION FOR FEDERAL COMMON LAW

A. FEDERAL COMMON LAW AND THE *ERIE* DOCTRINE

1. In *Erie Railroad Co. v. Tompkins*, 304 U.S. 64 (1938), the Supreme Court overruled the controversial holding in *Swift v. Tyson*, 41 U.S. (16 Pet.) 1 (1842), that there existed a general federal common law which the federal courts could develop and apply, even in cases falling only within their diversity jurisdiction. For a variety of reasons [*see* Chapter 17, *supra*], the *Erie* Court concluded that "[t]here is no federal general common law."

2. However, the same day that *Erie* was decided, the Court also handed down the decision in *Hinderlider v. La Plata River & Cherry Creek Ditch Co.*, 304 U.S. 92 (1938), in which it concluded that federal common law controlled the issue of whether an interstate stream must be apportioned between two states. Thus, while after *Erie* there may exist no *general* federal common law, the *Erie* decision was in no way designed to do away with all forms of federal common law. However, under exactly what circumstances the creation of federal common law is appropriate is not totally clear.

B. FEDERAL COMMON LAW AND THE RULES OF DECISION ACT

1. The Rules of Decision Act, 28 U.S.C.A. § 1652, which was the subject of interpretation in both *Swift* and *Erie*, provides: "The laws of the several states, except where the Constitution or treaties of the United States or Acts of Congress otherwise require or provide, shall be regarded as rules of decision in civil actions in the courts of the United States, in cases where they apply."

2. Both the language and history of the Act contain ambiguities, but it is at least arguable that the creation of federal common law not specifically authorized by the Constitution or an Act of Congress constitutes a violation of the Act.

3. The Supreme Court has never directly considered this question. However, the Court has on occasion reasoned that the creation of federal common law is designed to fill "gaps" left in federal statutory schemes, implying that the common law development is authorized by an act of Congress. But in a number of instances, the relation of the federal common law to a specific federal statutory scheme is at best remote.

C. THE REACH OF FEDERAL COMMON LAW

1. *Where federal common law is used, it is applicable even when the case is filed in state, rather than federal court.*

2. This is so, because the federal interest that led to the creation of federal common law in the first place may be as undermined by use of a different state law standard in a state court suit as in a federal action.

II. THE AREAS OF FEDERAL COMMON LAW

A. DESCRIPTION OF CATEGORIES

1. *The Supreme Court has recognized certain forms of federal common law in the following areas:*
   a. *Federal "proprietary" interests*
   b. *International relations*
   c. *Admiralty*
   d. *Interstate disputes*
   e. *Interstate pollution*
   f. *Enforcement of constitutional rights*

B. FEDERAL "PROPRIETARY" INTERESTS

1. The *Clearfield Trust* Decision

   a. In *Clearfield Trust Co. v. United States*, 318 U.S. 363 (1943), the Supreme Court held that federal common law controlled the issue of liability for a cashed stolen check issued by the United States. The Court reasoned that "[w]hen the United States disburses its funds or pays its debts, it is exercising a constitutional function or power. . . . The authority to issue the check had its origin in the Constitution and the statutes of the United States. . . ."

   b. As stated in *Clearfield*, the doctrine of federal common law is broad indeed, since every instance in which the United States acts presumably "had its origin in the Constitution and the statutes of the United States." Moreover, the Court's vague assertions about the Constitution and federal statutes hardly brings the case within the exceptions to the Rules of Decision Act. Finally, the Court's expressed concern for uniformity in the interstate commercial dealings of the United States may lead one to question why the government should be any better off than a private interstate commercial enterprise, that must deal with various state choice-of-law problems.

2. Adoption of state law as the federal standard.

   a. *Though Clearfield has received substantial criticism, it has never been overruled. It is presently the law that federal, rather than state law controls whenever the United States acts. However, the Court has made clear that it may choose to adopt state law and incorporate it as the federal standard, rather than develop a distinct federal standard (as it had done in* Clearfield*).*

Example: The Small Business Administration, a federal agency, makes a loan to a Texas family. The family defaults on the note and the SBA forecloses on the mortgage, suing the family for the deficiency. The wife argues that under Texas law's doctrine of "coverture" she lacked the capacity to bind herself contractually. The government argues that federal common law, rather than Texas law should apply. Held: State law is applied as the federal standard. *Clearfield* is distinguished because the contract was not part of a nationwide scheme, and the state has a strong interest in applying its own law of domestic relations. *United States v. Yazell*, 382 U.S. 341 (1966).

b. In *United States v. Kimbell Foods, Inc.*, 440 U.S. 715 (1979), the Court reaffirmed *Clearfield*'s holding "that federal law governs questions involving the rights of the United States arising under nationwide federal programs." However, the Court developed a balancing test to determine whether state law was to be adopted as the federal standard in such cases. The Court balanced the need for uniformity and the danger that state law would "frustrate specific objectives of the federal program" against "the extent to which application of a federal rule would disrupt commercial relationships predicated on state law." The underlying tone of the Court's opinion indicated that cases in which state law is *not* adopted as the federal standard will be relatively rare. If this perception is accurate it represents a substantial shift in the Court's attitude from the days of *Clearfield*.

3. Use of federal common law when the federal government is not a party to the litigation.

a. It is conceivable that the Supreme Court will apply federal common law, in lieu of state law, even when neither the United States nor one of its agents is a party to the case, if important federal interests are implicated. However, the Court is reluctant to reach such a result.

Examples: A bank brings a diversity suit in federal court for conversion of bonds issued by a federal agency. Payment on the bonds is guaranteed by the United States. One of the main issues is whether plaintiff or defendant has the burden of proof on the issue of defendant's good faith in receiving the bonds. *Held:* state law controls the issue. However, federal law controls the issue of whether the bonds could be deemed "overdue." *Bank of America National Trust & Savings Association v. Parnell*, 352 U.S. 29 (1956).

Survivors of deceased air passengers bring diversity action against a municipality on the theory that they are third-party beneficiaries of a contract between the municipality and the

Federal Aviation Administration in which the municipality agreed to maintain activities around the airport compatible with normal aircraft operations—a contract that was allegedly breached by the maintenance of a garbage dump near the airport, attracting birds which were ingested into the aircraft's engines. *Held:* The right of one plaintiff to sue third-party beneficiaries and the interpretation of the contract are governed by state, rather than federal law.

Plaintiff files a libel suit against a former Navy officer because of alleged statements about plaintiff's job performance. *Held:* Whether defendant's defamatory statements are privileged is controlled by federal, rather than state common law, because important federal interests are implicated. *Howard v. Lyons*, 360 U.S. 593 (1959).

C. INTERNATIONAL RELATIONS

1. The Supreme Court held in Banco Nacional de Cuba v. Sabbatino, *376 U.S. 398 (1964), that common law issues that implicate the foreign relations of the United States are to be controlled by federal, rather than state common law.*

a. Specifically, the decision held that federal common law determines whether Cuban nationalization of a shipment of sugar was protected by the "act of state doctrine" in a federal diversity case.

b. The Court reached this conclusion, even though the cause of action was state-created.

c. The Court reasoned "that the problems involved are uniquely federal in nature."

2. Use of federal common law in this area has been criticized by certain commentators because, unlike cases falling under the *Clearfield* heading, no basis could be found in a federal statute to authorize the creation of federal common law.

3. Though the Court recognized the relevance of federal common law in this area, it acknowledged that ultimately the decisions concerning foreign relations are for Congress and the Executive, and therefore that federal common law developed in the field of foreign relations may be superceded by the political branches.

D. ADMIRALTY

1. It is well established that federal courts have authority to develop a federal common law of admiralty. The power is thought to derive from the provision of Article III, § 2, extending the federal "judicial power" to "all cases of admiralty and maritime jurisdiction."

2. One may question, however, why the extension of the federal judicial power to such cases logically leads to the conclusion that federal courts possess authority to develop substantive federal common law. For example, the federal "judicial power" also extends to diversity cases, but in *Erie* the Court made clear that federal courts lacked authority to develop substantive common law in cases falling under this jurisdictional heading.

3. Originally, federal court authority to create federal common law did not apply to inland waterways. However, by 1851 the Supreme Court had extended the authority to include these waters.

4. Federal courts do not develop a distinct federal common law standard in every conceivable admiralty case. Rather, the Supreme Court has employed a form of a balancing test to decide whether federal common law should supercede otherwise applicable state law. Use of this test has led to substantial confusion and uncertainty.

a. In *Southern Pacific Co. v. Jensen*, 244 U.S. 205 (1917), the Supreme Court overturned a state workmen's compensation award to relatives of a deceased stevedore because use of state law would undermine the uniformity of federal maritime law. But this extreme supremisist view has since been significantly modified, allowing state law a significant—if uncertain—role in the maritime area.

Examples: The Supreme Court has held that state law requiring unemployment compensation contributions from employers of individuals working on navigable waters may apply, even though the cases could conceivably have been controlled by federal common law. *Standard Dredging Corp. v. Murphy*, 319 U.S. 306 (1943).

On the other hand, the Court held that federal common law, rather than state law, applied to a suit brought by a crew member's guest injured on board a ship berthed in a New York pier. *Kermarec v. Compagnie Generale Transatlantique*, 358 U.S. 625 (1959).

The Supreme Court has held that Texas law applies to the issue of insurance coverage for a houseboat fire occurring on an inland lake between Texas and Oklahoma, even though the case fell within the federal admiralty jurisdiction. *Wilburn Boat Co. v. Fireman's Fund Insurance Co.*, 348 U.S. 310 (1955).

The Court has also held, however, that federal law applied to a diversity suit between a seaman and a shipowner for breach of an oral agreement to assume responsibility for improper medical treatment. *Kossick v. United Fruit Co.*, 365 U.S. 731 (1961).

b. The line to be drawn among these cases is by no means clear.

E. INTERSTATE DISPUTES

1. As the *Hinderlider* case demonstrates, the Court has held that federal common law controls disputes among states.

2. Federal law is used in order to avoid the friction that would result from choosing one state's law over the other's in a dispute between them.

F. INTERSTATE POLLUTION

1. In *Illinois v. City of Milwaukee*, 406 U.S. 91 (1972) (*"Milwaukee I"*) the Court held that although no federal statute created a remedy for a suit by the State of Illinois against the municipality to stop them from polluting Lake Michigan, federal common law could provide a remedy.

2. The Court emphasized that Congress had enacted numerous laws generally concerning pollution of interstate waters.

3. In *City of Milwaukee v. Illinois and Michigan*, 451 U.S. 304 (1981) (*"Milwaukee II"*), the Court held that the Federal Water Pollution Act Amendments of 1972 displaced federal common law, and that federal common law could not be created to impose standards more stringent than those imposed by the federal statute.

G. ENFORCEMENT OF CONSTITUTIONAL RIGHTS

1. In *Bivens v. Six Unknown Named Agents of Federal Bureau of Narcotics*, 403 U.S. 388 (1971), the Supreme Court recognized a private damage remedy for a violation of the Fourth Amendment prohibition against unreasonable searches and seizures, even though the constitutional provision, by its terms, makes no reference to a damage remedy (or any other means of enforcement), and Congress had not provided a statutory remedy.

2. The Court reasoned that "the absence of affirmative action by Congress" did not bar judicial creation of the damage remedy when the Court deemed the remedy an appropriate means of enforcing the constitutional right.

3. The Court applied the *Bivens* damage remedy in *Davis v. Passman*, 442 U.S. 228 (1979), in a suit brought against a Congressman under the "equal protection" component of the Fifth Amendment.

4. Since the *Bivens* remedy is not expressly authorized by the Constitution, there exists a question whether Congress may repeal or modify it, as it may do with any area of federal common law, but which it may not do to a constitutionally-created right.

   a. In *Carlson v. Green*, 446 U.S. 14 (1980), the Supreme Court stated that a *Bivens* cause of action may be defeated only (1) "When defendants demonstrate 'special factors counseling hesitation in the absence of affirmative action by Congress'" and (2) "when defendants show that Congress has provided an alternative remedy which it explicitly declared to be a *substitute* for recovery directly under the Constitution and viewed as equally effective. . . ."

   b. The Court appeared to cut back on *Bivens* by implicitly expanding the situations in which the *Bivens* remedy may be replaced in *Bush v. Lucas*, 462 U.S. 367 (1983). There the Court found that "[w]hen Congress provides an alternative remedy, it may, of course, indicate its intent, by statutory language, by a clear legislative history, or perhaps even by the statutory remedy itself, that the Court's [common law] power should not be exercised." In *Carlson*, it should be recalled, the Court had indicated that Congress' alternative remedy must *"explicitly"* declare itself to be a substitute—a requirement that seems to have been abandoned in *Bush*.

   c. In *Bush*, the Court held that a *Bivens* remedy was not available in a suit under the First Amendment for damages by a federal employee who had been demoted for making critical statements, alleged by his superior to be false, to the news media about the facility at which he worked. The Court reached this conclusion because the plaintiff's claim arose out of a government relationship controlled by comprehensive procedural and substantive provision providing remedies against the United States.

REVIEW QUESTIONS (PART III)

1. T or F   When Congress is silent on the issue of state court jurisdiction to enforce claims under a federal statute, it is presumed that state and federal court jurisdictions are concurrent.

2. T or F   The three exceptions to the Anti-Injunction Act described in that statute are exhaustive.

3. T or F   The doctrine of *Younger v. Harris* applies only to ongoing state criminal proceedings.

FEDERAL COMMON LAW

4. T or F   When the federal government exercises one of its constitutional powers, any issue arising in a suit concerning the exercise of those powers that is not controlled by statute is to be decided as a matter of federal common law.

5. T or F   When a Federal Rule of Civil Procedure applicable in a diversity case differs from the applicable state procedural standard, the Federal Rule will not be employed if its use would likely influence an out-of-state plaintiff in choosing between state and federal court.

6. T or F   Under all judge-made forms of abstention, the plaintiff may ultimately return to federal court for a final adjudication.

7. T or F   A state prosecution may be removed to federal court pursuant to the civil rights removal statute if the state prosecution will preclude the defendant from enforcing a federal right, regardless of which federal right is involved.

8. T or F   Though section 1983 is an expressly authorized exception to the bar of the Anti-Injunction Act, the federal courts will nevertheless generally not interfere with an ongoing state prosecution, even to vindicate federal rights protected by section 1983.

9. T or F   Though sovereign immunity will generally not bar a suit against a state officer for the purpose of vindicating constitutional rights, such a suit that is deemed to be in reality against the state is barred in federal court.

10. T or F   A case removed to federal court from state court that falls within the exclusive jurisdiction of the federal court must be dismissed by the federal court.

11. T or F   The Supreme Court has held that state courts may not issue writs of mandamus, habeas corpus or injunction against federal officers.

12. T or F   Though generally state courts are obligated to adjudicate suits under federal law, the Supreme Court has recognized several "valid excuses" which allow the state courts to decline jurisdiction of such suits.

13. T or F   The "in aid of jurisdiction" exception to the Anti-Injunction Statute applies only when a state court suit attempts to interfere with a federal court's disposition of property within its control.

14. **T or F** Because state courts are barred from adjudicating suits arising under the patent laws, they may not adjudicate the validity of a patent when the issue is raised as a defense to a suit for breach of a patent royalty agreement.

15. **T or F** Under current standards, a state criminal defendant's failure to raise a contemporaneous objection to the admission of evidence will not preclude Supreme Court review of his objection in a habeas corpus proceeding.

Prepare a response to the following question:

A tenured public school teacher was relieved of his duties because he taught the use of birth control devices in a high school sexual education class. The action was taken pursuant to a state statute providing that a tenured teacher may be removed for "teaching matter not in the best interests of the students." The statute provides that the initial removal decision is to be made by the school principal, and that an appeal may be taken to an administrative review board, consisting of several state-appointed educators. The review board's decision, according to the statute, may receive very limited judicial review in the state courts.

Instead of pursuing the state statutory procedure, the teacher filed suit in federal district court, challenging the state statute as a violation of his first amendment right of free expression because it was unconstitutionally vague, and seeking an injunction, ordering the principal to reinstate him. The principal urges the federal court to abstain, on grounds of *Pullman*, *Burford* and *Younger* abstention. Discuss how the court should rule on each of these contentions.

APPENDIX A

ANSWERS TO REVIEW QUESTIONS

PART I

1. ***False*** The plaintiff has not suffered injury in fact, a prerequisite of the standing rules.

2. ***False*** Because the plaintiff has actually been threatened with prosecution, there exists a live controversy. The plaintiff need not wait until the prosecution has actually been filed to challenge its constitutionality in federal court.

3. ***True*** The political question doctrine does not apply to questions concerning the constitutionality of *state* governmental action, only to those involving the *federal* government.

4. ***False*** However broad Congress' Article III power is found to be, it may be limited by other provisions of the Constitution, particularly those contained in the amendments. The law in question would clearly violate the Fifth Amendment's Due Process Clause, held to incorporate an equal protection component.

5. *False*   While it is true that the Supreme Court's existence is mandated by Article III, its appellate jurisdiction is conveyed, subject to Congress' power to impose regulations and make exceptions.

6. *True*   The principle of separation of powers has been construed to mean that even though Congress may exclude the jurisdiction of the Article III federal courts completely, it may not undermine their integrity by ordering them to act in an unconstitutional manner.

7. *False*   The Supreme Court has viewed administrative agencies simply as adjuncts to the Article III federal courts.

8. *True*   Though the Supreme Court has not formally resolved this specific question, it has held that the political question doctrine will be invoked to prevent a federal court from possibly embarrassing the executive branch in the conduct of foreign policy.

9. *False*   An organization's special interest in an area is an insufficient basis on which to establish standing. To have standing, a plaintiff must have suffered some injury in fact.

10. *True*   Though the mootness doctrine is said to derive from the constitutional requirement of case or controversy, the Supreme Court has on occasion developed exceptions, largely because of the public interest in having the legal issue resolved.

11. *True*   Under the holding of *Crowell v. Benson*, the principle of separation of powers dictates that some Article III court have final power to rule upon constitutional questions. While the case has been much undermined, that is largely because the case concerned property rights, which are not accorded as much weight today by many as they were at the time of the decision.

12. *False*   While there is language in *McCardle* which seems to justify broad congressional power over the Supreme Court's appellate jurisdiction, the Court there also emphasized that Congress had not totally removed all procedural avenues to obtain Supreme Court review.

13. *False*   Though the Due Process Clause has been usually construed to require an independant forum prior to the deprivation of property or liberty, it has not been construed to require any level of appellate review.

14. *False*   Although three justices in *Tidewater* accepted this view, a majority of the Court rejected it.

ANSWERS TO REVIEW QUESTIONS

15. *True*   Such a practice would violate the case or controversy requirement of Article III.

Essay

Proposal 1: Of all the proposals, this is probably the most clearly unconstitutional. While Article III may grant Congress power to limit federal court jurisdiction, it says nothing about congressional authority to employ its jurisdiction-curbing authority to overrule Supreme Court constitutional determinations. Under *Crowell v. Benson*, the courts, independent of majoritarian pressures, must make the final determination of the meaning of constitutional provisions.

Proposal 2: Under traditional thinking, this proposal would be held constitutional. Under the Madisonian Compromise, it is widely thought that, because Congress need not have created lower federal courts, it may abolish them. Therefore it may take the lesser step of limiting their jurisdiction. Similarly, Congress is thought to have broad power under the Exceptions Clause of Article III to regulate the Supreme Court's appellate jurisdiction. The due process right to an independent forum is not violated, because the state courts remain available. However, certain modern theories, such as the "essential functions" thesis, would, if accepted, render the proposal unconstitutional.

Proposal 3: Such a statute would be unconstitutional, because it deprives all judicial forums of their function as enforcer and interpreter of the Constitution and constitutional rights.

Proposal 4: This statute poses difficult questions concerning the interrelation of due process and Article III's principle of separation of powers. Traditionally, the courts have assumed that while due process requires an independent adjudicator, such independence need not include the Article III protections of judicial tenure and salary. Thus, it is conceivable that a non-Article III legislative court could meet the due process requirement of independence. While of course such a court does not meet the requirement of Article III independence, it is questionable whether that Article can be construed to require the use of an Article III court. *Crowell v. Benson* does seem to require such a result (or at least the use of state courts), but the basis in Article III for such a position has never been fully explained.

ANSWERS TO REVIEW QUESTIONS (PART II)

1. *False*   While the language of both the statutory and constitutional provisions are very similar, the courts have assumed that Congress

would not intend to clutter federal courts with any case only remotely implicating federal law.

2. **False**   The actual holding of *Aldinger* was only that there could be no pendent party jurisdiction over municipalities in section 1983 civil rights actions against state officers. Though there was language in Justice Rehnquist's opinion for the Court expressing doubt about the validity of pendent party jurisdiction in general, the Court has never held this. Moreover, the opinion indicated that pendent party jurisdiction may be valid in cases of exclusive federal jurisdiction.

3. **True**   The Court in *Gibbs* deemed the previous "same-cause-of-action" test of *Hurn v. Oursler* as "unnecessarily grudging." In its place, the Court required only that the original and pendent claims arise from a "common nucleus of operative fact."

4. **False**   Though in establishing the requirement in *Strawbridge v. Curtiss* Chief Justice Marshall failed to make clear whether he was construing the constitutional or the statutory diversity provision, the Supreme Court in recent years made clear that the requirement is a matter of statutory construction, and therefore can be overturned by Congress.

5. **True**   In recent years, the Supreme Court refused to reconsider the longstanding rule that unincorporated associations have the citizenship of all its members for purposes of diversity jurisdiction.

6. **False**   The Supreme Court has held that certain matters falling within the Court's original jurisdiction may also be adjudicated by the lower federal courts.

7. **False**   The advisory opinion rationale cannot explain the procedural branch of the adequate state ground doctrine. In large part, the doctrine is premised on grounds of comity and federalism.

8. **True**   In applying an analogy to the "collateral order" doctrine of *Cohen v. Beneficial Industrial Loan Corp.*, the Court has authorized appeals that could not be deemed technically "final", because the case in the state court has in no way been completed. Also, in *Cox Broadcasting Corp. v. Cohn*, the Court described certain categories of cases in which appeal could be taken in which the appealed order could not be considered "final".

9. **False**   The "legal certainty" test requires only that it not appear to a legal certainty that the plaintiff's claim is less than the jurisdictional minimum.

ANSWERS TO REVIEW QUESTIONS

10. *False*   Under the Supreme Court's decision in *Zahn v. International Paper Co.*, each member of a plaintiff class in a diversity case must meet the jurisdictional minimum.

11. *True*   This describes the "well-pleaded complaint" rule.

12. *False*   The "well-pleaded complaint" rule is a matter of statutory construction.

13. *True*   In *Gibbs*, the Supreme Court established a dichotomy between power and discretion to exercise pendent jurisdiction. The mere fact that the federal court finds that it has power to exercise pendent jurisdiction does not mean that it should actually exercise it.

14. *True*   While the Supreme Court has criticized lower courts for not adhering to their summary affirmances, it has indicated that it does not deem itself bound by them.

15. *False*   The majority of lower courts employ the "plaintiff viewpoint" rule, which dictates that the jurisdictional minimum is met only if the plaintiff stands to gain or lose in excess of the amount.

Essay

1. *Subject Matter Jurisdiction:* There is little doubt that the federal court lacks subject matter jurisdiction over the suit. There is clearly no diversity of citizenship between the parties. Nor does it appear that federal question jurisdiction can be found. While it is no longer required that a suit present a federal cause of action before federal question jurisdiction will be found, there must exist in the plaintiff's well-pleaded complaint some issue of federal law, the resolution of which will determine whether the plaintiff wins or loses.

In the present case, ultimately all that is at stake are matters of state law. No federal statute is directly in point, since the statute in question has an impact only upon *intrastate* commerce—an area which Congress is not constitutionally empowered to regulate. Since interpretation of the state law can have no effect on any federal interests, there is no justification for the invocation of federal court power. This is so, even though the state has chosen to incorporate the federal standard by reference.

2. *Pendent Jurisdiction:* The second part of the question asks the student to assume that the federal court has subject matter jurisdiction over the antitrust claim. Even making this assumption, however, it is clear that the federal court lacks power to exercise pendent jurisdiction over the unrelated fraud claim. Under the standard of *United Mine Workers v. Gibbs*, a federal

court does not even have *power* to exercise pendent jurisdiction unless the two claims arise out of a "common nucleus of operative fact." Since that is clearly not the case here, we need not examine the various discretionary factors a federal court is to consider once the power issue is resolved. Here, the claim cannot overcome the initial "power" hurdle.

ANSWERS TO REVIEW QUESTIONS (PART III)

1. *True* — This is the rule of *Claflin v. Houseman*. It should be noted, however, that under *Claflin*, this presumption may be rebutted in an individual case, as has happened in the case of suits to enforce the federal antitrust laws.

2. *False* — While the Supreme Court has so indicated on certain occasions, the Court has recognized an additional exception for suits by the United States or one of its agents.

3. *False* — While the *Younger* doctrine has its greatest force in the area of ongoing state criminal proceedings, it has also been employed to prevent federal judicial interference with certain state civil proceedings in which important elements of state sovereignty were implicated.

4. *True* — This is the rule of *Clearfield Trust*, which, though criticized, has never been overruled. It is important to note, however, that while technically federal common law is always applied in those cases, today the Supreme Court will often choose to adopt state law as the federal common law standard.

5. *False* — The forum-shopping test is the standard adopted by the Supreme Court in *Hanna v. Plumer* in dictum for the Rules of Decision Act, applicable only when no other federal statute is in point. When a Federal Rule of Civil Procedure is in point, the applicable test is that of the Rules Enabling Act, pursuant to which the Federal Rules are promulgated.

6. *False* — While this is true of *Pullman* abstention and possibly *Colorado River* abstention, it is not so for other forms of judge-made abstention.

7. *False* — Both by its terms and construction, the civil rights removal statute is limited to federal rights of equality.

8. *True* — This is basically the *Younger* abstention doctrine.

9.	**True**	This was the position taken in *Edelman v. Jordan.*
10.	**True**	This describes the so-called "derivative jurisdiction" rule.
11.	**False**	While the Supreme Court has so held for writs of mandamus and habeas corpus, it has never dealt directly with the injunction issue. However, a majority of lower federal courts to have considered the issue have held that state courts lack power to issue injunctions to federal officers.
12.	**True**	The primary illustrations of the "valid excuse" doctrine are for state courts of limited jurisdiction and for forum non conveniens. However, a state court is not allowed to discriminate against federal law in declining to adjudicate federal cases.
13.	**True**	This is the rule of *Kline v. Burke Construction Co.*
14.	**False**	The Supreme Court has held that, in order to assure enforcement of federal patent policy, state courts may adjudicate issues of patent validity that arise in state suits, even though they could not directly adjudicate a suit under the patent laws for patent infringement.
15.	**False**	While this was true under *Fay v. Noia,* it is no longer good law in light of *Wainwright v. Sykes.*

Essay

1. *Pullman Abstention:* The argument in support of *Pullman* abstention here is that the state statute is inherently ambiguous and therefore the state courts should be given the opportunity to construe the statute narrowly. For two reasons, however, it is unlikely that the federal court would invoke the doctrine.

First, the fact that the state statute may be unconstitutionally vague does not mean that it is "ambiguous" for purposes of *Pullman* abstention. The vagueness does not mean that the statute lends itself to two constructions, one of which would render it unconstitutional. Moreover, the case involves the exercise of first amendment free speech rights, where the delay in ultimate vindication of the federal right may increase the chilling effect.

However, certain members of the Supreme Court, such as Justice Rehnquist and Chief Justice Burger, would probably wish to provide the state court the opportunity to narrow the statute.

2. *Burford Abstention:* At least a plausible argument could be made to support the applicability of *Burford* abstention to this case. The issue of public education is a matter of great importance to the state, and, as in *Burford*, the state has established a complex network of administrative and judicial review. However, a federal court could decide that *Burford* should be limited to truly complex matters of state law, and not apply to cases in which the central issue will be a matter of federal constitutional law.

3. *Younger Abstention:* *Younger* abstention has been applied primarily to cases of state criminal prosecutions. However, it has also been applied to certain state civil proceedings brought by the state to vindicate important sovereign interests (see, e.g., *Trainor v. Hernandez*.).

In the present case, the federal interference would not be with an ongoing *judicial* proceeding of any kind, but rather one that is—at least at the present time—administrative. Though state judicial review is provided, it is only after the administrative process is completed, a point which may unduly delay vindication of first amendment rights. While the basic assumption of the *Younger* doctrine is that state *courts* are constitutionally and historically capable of enforcing federal rights, the same cannot be said of state administrative agencies.

In *Middlesex County Ethics Committee v. Garden State Bar Association*, the Supreme Court held that *Younger* barred federal injunctive relief against a state attorney disciplinary proceeding which had been challenged on first amendment grounds. The Court did note the important state interest involved, which arguably renders the case relevant to this one. However, the case might be distinguished because the Court emphasized the "unique relationship" between the administrative ethics committee and the state supreme court, which appointed and supervised it. This may indicate that the case is limited to such instances of close judicial and administrative interaction.

APPENDIX B

MODEL EXAMINATION

I.

In response to rising concern over undue judicial interference in the operation of federal prisons, Congress has enacted and the President signed into law the Judicial Prison Review Act of 1985. The Act provides:

Section 1. No federal district court may review the constitutionality of decisions by federal prison officials regarding the confinement or discipline of prisoners.

Section 2. Any prisoner may seek review of a decision by federal prison officials in the Federal Prison Review Board, which is to be comprised of three individuals, appointed by the President and confirmed by the Senate, who sit at the discretion of the President.

Section 3. Decisions of the Federal Prison Review Board are not subject to review in any federal court.

Write a memorandum discussing the constitutionality of the Act.

II.

A, a resident of Illinois, filed suit in federal district court in New York against B Corporation, for breach of contract. B Corporation is incorporated in the state of New York, where its board of directors meets, but conducts all of its manufacturing in the state of Illinois. B Corporation moved to dismiss for lack of subject matter jurisdiction, but the motion was denied.

B Corporation then impleaded C, a resident of the state of Illinois. C sought to file a state law claim against A, and A sought to amend to file a state law claim against C. The district court allowed C to file a claim against A, but held that it lacked subject matter jurisdiction over A's claim against C.

Write a memorandum discussing the correctness of each of the district court's rulings.

III.

A filed suit against B in state court under state unfair competition law. Both A and B are residents of the same state. B answered, arguing that its alleged unfair competition was justified by its interest in protecting its federally issued patent. B then sought to remove the case to federal district court, but that court remanded to the state court.

The state court denied defendant's motion for summary judgment, holding that because the federal courts have exclusive jurisdiction over patent cases, it lacked authority to rule upon the relevance of defendant's patent as a justification for its actions. Under state law, interlocutory appeals can be taken directly to the state supreme court. B took such an appeal to the state supreme court, which affirmed the lower court's decision. B then sought review in the United States Supreme Court, which agreed to hear the case and reversed the state courts' conclusion that they could not take into account the relevance of B's patent.

Write a memorandum considering the correctness of each judicial ruling.

ANSWER TO MODEL EXAMINATION

I.

All conceivable constitutional objections to the Act flow either from Article III or from the fifth amendment's due process clause.

Article III

The Act's clear impact is to exclude the Article III federal courts (including the Supreme Court) from review of significant constitutional issues. Under traditional thinking, Congress need not vest the federal judicial power in any Article III court. It need not vest the judicial power in the lower federal courts, because Article III expressly allowed Congress not to have created lower courts, and in light of this power it has been assumed that Congress could abolish such courts. If Congress has power to abolish them, the argument proceeds, it has power to take the lesser step of curbing their jurisdiction. The argument that Congress could exclude Supreme Court appellate jurisdiction turns on the "exceptions" clause of Article III, which allows Congress to make exceptions to the Supreme Court's appellate jurisdiction.

There exist a number of arguments, however, that would preclude all or part of Congress' action. Most suspect is Congress' limitation of Supreme Court jurisdiction. The "exceptions" clause has never received a definitive interpretation, and certain commentators have argued that Congress may not make exceptions to the Court's jurisdiction which interfere with performance of its "essential functions". Though there is little linguistic or historical basis to support such a thesis, if accepted it would invalidate Congress' exclusion of Supreme Court appellate jurisdiction.

Other commentators have adopted a type of "floating" essential functions thesis—a theory that states that since Article III provides that the federal judicial power "shall be vested", the Article requires that *some* federal court (*either* the Supreme Court *or* a lower federal court) exercise the judicial power. Under this theory, the Act is invalid because it removes *both* lower court *and* Supreme Court jurisdiction. However, these theories have never received judicial acceptance.

In *Crowell v. Benson*, the Supreme Court did indicate that separation-of-powers principles dictate that the judiciary have the final say on the meaning of the Constitution, but it is not clear whether that requirement could not be satisfied by *state* court review. The issue of state court review is also relevant to the due process concern, and will be discussed under that heading.

Due Process

Due process has been construed to require the provision of an independent forum for the adjudication of constitutional rights. At least in regard to actions of the federal government, state courts—who are bound to enforce the Constitution through the Supremacy Clause—meet this independence requirement. However, under the doctrine of *Tarble's Case*, state courts may not be allowed to directly control the actions of federal officials.

If the rule of *Tarble* were held applicable even when the federal forum has been congressionally closed (which was not the case in *Tarble* itself), it is conceivable that the Act's exclusion of federal judicial review would be unconstitutional. The question would then come down to whether the newly created review board could satisfy due process. However, if the limit of *Tarble* on state court jurisdiction were to fall, then the requirements of due process and the separation-of-powers consideration of *Crowell* would be satisfied.

II.

1. *Lack of Subject Matter Jurisdiction:* The correctness of the court's ruling here turns on definition of "principal place of business" under 28 U.S.C. § 1332(c), because under that section a corporation is a citizen of *both* its state of incorporation *and* the state of its principal place of business. If Illinois is found to be the state of B Corporation's principal place of business, it will be deemed a citizen of both Illinois and New York, and therefore there would not exist complete diversity between A and B. If the test of "principal place of business" that is adopted is the place of operation, B Corporation will be deemed a citizen of Illinois. However, if the test chosen is the one that focuses on the place where policy is made, B would be deemed a citizen of only New York. Lower courts have split on which test to employ.

2. *Rulings on Claims of C and A:* The court correctly ruled on both motions, assuming C's claim against A arises out of the same transaction or occurrence as the suit between A and B. C is allowed to assert his claim against A, even though no diversity exists between them, under a theory of ancillary jurisdiction. However, A would not be allowed to sue C under a state law claim, because of the Supreme Court's holding in *Owen Equipment v. Kroger.*

III.

1. *Remand to State Court:* The district court correctly remanded to state court, because of the statutory rule that cases may be removed to federal court only when the case could have been brought in federal court originally. Since no federal issue appeared on the face of the plaintiff's well-pleaded complaint, the federal court would lack "federal question" jurisdiction, even though the defendant raised a federal issue in his answer.

2. *State Court Power to Adjudicate Patent Defense:* The state courts were incorrect and the Supreme Court correct on the issue of state court power to adjudicate the federal patent claim. While it is true that under 28 U.S.C.A. § 1338 federal jurisdiction for suits under the patent laws is exclusive, the Supreme Court held in *Lear, Inc. v. Adkins* that state courts much adjudicate defenses under the patent laws. This is because the opposite conclusion would threaten enforcement of federal patent law policy.

3. *Appealability:* 28 U.S.C.A. § 1257 allows Supreme Court review of only *final* decisions of the state's highest court. Since the state supreme court here reviewed a denial of a summary judgment motion, its decision could not be deemed "final" in any technical sense of the term.

Though the Court has recognized a number of exceptions to the strict finality requirement, particularly in *Cox Broadcasting Corp. v. Cohn,* none of those exceptions would apply to this case. Therefore the Supreme Court incorrectly agreed to review the state supreme court's decision.

*

APPENDIX C

GLOSSARY

A

Abstention A judge-made doctrine authorizing federal courts to relinquish jurisdiction over an action in favor of the state courts in order to further important interests of federalism. The doctrine is sub-divided into specific categories. *See Pullman* abstention, *Burford* abstention, *Thibodaux* abstention, and *Colorado River* abstention.

Adequate State Ground Doctrine A judge-made principle that prevents the Supreme Court from reviewing a state court decision when the decision is premised, at least in part, on grounds of state law, so that even if the Supreme Court were to alter the disposition of the federal issue in the case, the result would remain the same.

Ancillary Jurisdiction A judge-made doctrine allowing a federal district court to exercise jurisdiction of a case as an entirety and determine matters which are incidental to the exercise of its primary jurisdiction over a matter even though the court lacks jurisdiction to hear those incidental matters standing alone. This expansion of the federal courts' jurisdiction occurs primarily in cases involving impleadar, cross-claims, and interpleadar.

Anti-Injunction Act A federal statute providing that a federal court may not enjoin state proceedings unless expressly authorized by Congress, or where necessary in aid of its jurisdiction, or to protect or effectuate its judgment. 28 U.S.C.A. § 2283.

Appeal Review of the decision of a lower court by a higher court. An appeal to the Supreme Court is technically a matter of right, but the Court may decide to dispose of a case summarily rather than grant a full hearing upon appeal.

Article I Courts *See* legislative courts.

Article III Courts Federal courts whose judges receive the protections of salary and tenure provided by Article III of the Constitution. Matters heard by them include the following types of cases: those arising under the Constitution and the laws and treaties of the United States, those to which the U.S. is a party, and those between states and between citizens of different states.

B

Burford Abstention A form of judge-made abstention that authorizes a federal court to defer to a state's review system when the subject matter is better adjudicated under a complex regulatory scheme and concerns predominately local factors in sensitive areas of state concern.

C

Certification A procedure, authorized by state law, allowing a federal court to submit unsettled issues of state law to a state's highest court for determination while retaining jurisdiction over the action. This procedure can be used instead of abstention, but certification is not available in all states.

Certiorari A statutorily-provided means of obtaining Supreme Court review. The Supreme Court uses its discretion in choosing whether to review a lower court's proceedings. The votes of four Justices are required. A denial of certiorari by the Supreme Court is not a decision on the merits.

Civil Rights Removal A statute, 28 U.S.C.A. § 1443, authorizing the removal of a case from state to federal court in any of the following circumstances: 1. where a person has been "denied or cannot enforce" a civil right of equality in a state court; 2. where a person is being sued or prosecuted for performing "any act under color of authority derived from any law providing for equal rights;" or 3. where a person is the subject of suit for refusing to perform an act that would be inconsistent with a law providing for equal rights. The denial clause has been narrowly construed to permit removal only when a state statute or constitutional provision invades a federal civil right, or when a federal statute immunizes from prosecution the very conduct for which a person is being prosecuted.

Claim Preclusion *See res judicata.*

Collateral Estoppel A rule that provides that when an issue of fact or mixed law and fact has been decided in a previous action brought under a different cause of action between the same parties or their privies, it cannot be relitigated.

Colorado River Abstention A category of judge-made abstention under which a federal court may in extreme circumstances abstain due to concurrent state judicial proceedings in order to avoid harassment of the parties or duplication of effort.

Comity The notion that the federal system will operate best if the states are allowed to perform their legitimate functions without undue interference from federal courts. Federal judicial deference to state courts. This principle was used in part to justify the *Younger* doctrine.

Complete Diversity The requirement that the federal courts exercise the diversity jurisdiction only when *all* plaintiffs are citizens of different states from *all* defendants. Developed originally by Chief Justice Marshall in *Strawbridge v. Curtiss*, the rule was held in 1967 to derive from the diversity statute, rather than Article III, allowing Congress to modify the rule if it so desires. The Federal Interpleadar Act is an example of congressional provision for only "minimal" diversity (i.e., *at least* one plaintiff is a citizen of a state different from the state of *at least* one defendant).

Concurrent Jurisdiction A situation in which tribunals of more than one system have jurisdiction over a case. For example, the federal and state courts have concurrent jurisdiction in diversity of citizenship actions.

Constitutional Facts A constitutional doctrine, deriving from separation-of-powers principles, that provides that the Article III federal courts are not bound by an administrative agency's findings of facts when such findings have constitutional implications. Though today the federal court may not conduct a *de novo* proceeding to make its own findings regarding such facts, it still is supposed to make an independent inquiry on the basis of the preexisting record.

D

Declaratory Relief A procedure allowing a litigant to seek a binding decision to settle a controversy prior to engaging in conduct which may lead to legal liability. The procedure is authorized in federal court by federal statute. However, the procedure is limited by the constitutional requirement of case or controversy.

Diversity Jurisdiction The exercise of federal court jurisdiction over cases involving parties from different states. Under the present diversity statute, the requisite jurisdictional amount must also be present.

Domicile The permanent or ordinary place of residence of a person or corporation. A party has only one domicile, though he may have more than one "residence".

E

England Procedure A procedure, devised in *England v. Louisiana St. Bd. of Medical Examiners*, providing that after a federal court has referred issues of state law to a state court under *Pullman* abstention and the state court has adjudicated the state law issues, a litigant has the right to return to federal court to have his federal claims adjudicated.

Erie Doctrine A principle, derived from *Erie Railroad Co. v. Tompkins*, determining a federal court's choice between state and federal rules to be used in a case which is before the court under its diversity jurisdiction. In *Erie*, the Court held that the federal courts are bound by the constitutional limits of

Congress' power to prescribe statutory law for such suits and by the statutory limits prescribed for the courts by the Rules of Decision Act and the Rules Enabling Act.

Exceptions Clause A provision of Article III authorizing Congress to make exceptions and regulations to the Supreme Court's appellate jurisdiction.

Exhaustion of Remedies This doctrine requires that relief must be sought in one forum before entering another. Exhaustion of state administrative or judicial remedies may be required before a federal court will adjudicate a case. A state criminal defendant must exhaust his state judicial remedies before obtaining federal habeas corpus relief. However, the Supreme Court has held that a federal civil rights plaintiff, suing under 42 U.S.C.A. § 1983, need not first exhaust state administrative or judicial remedies.

Expressly Authorized Exception An exception to the bar of the Anti-Injunction Act providing that a federal court may issue an injunction to stay proceedings in a state court when such an injunction has been expressly authorized by an act of Congress. 28 U.S.C.A. § 2283. Courts have found such an authorization in such laws as the Securities Exchange Act and 42 U.S.C.A. § 1983, the Civil Rights Act.

F

Federal Common Law A body of decisional law developed by the federal courts. The application of this body of common law is limited by the *Erie* doctrine and by the Rules of Decision Act, which provides that except for cases governed by the Constitution, the treaties of the United States, or acts of Congress, federal courts are to apply state law. Areas in which federal common law have been developed include federal "proprietary" interests, admiralty and foreign relations.

Federal Question Jurisdiction The exercise of federal court power over those claims arising under the Constitution, acts of Congress, or the treaties of the United States.

Final Judgment A decision that terminates the action. An appeal to a higher court must ordinarily be from a final judgment.

Forum Non Conveniens The discretionary power of a court to decline jurisdiction when, in the interest of justice, the action should proceed in another forum. This power is usually used when another forum would be more convenient for the parties because the parties, witnesses, or evidence is located in that forum.

Full Faith and Credit The enforcement of one jurisdiction's law or decisions in the court of another forum. Under the Constitution, a state must give the judgment of a court of another state the authority that would be accorded it by the courts in the state in which the judgment was rendered. Under the Full Faith and Credit Act, the federal courts must recognize the judgments of state courts.

H

Habeas Corpus A writ used to test the legality of a prisoner's detention but not to determine his innocence or guilt. It is a Latin expression meaning "you have the body."

I

In Aid of Jurisdiction Exception An exception to the Anti-Injunction Statute authorizing a federal court to issue an injunction to stay proceedings in a federal court where such an injunction is necessary in aid of the federal court's jurisdiction. 28 U.S.C.A. § 2283. This exception has generally been limited to cases which are in rem when the federal court has acquired jurisdiction of the subject matter prior to the state court action.

Injunction An equitable remedy which prohibits a party from performing a particular act. Injunctions may be either temporary or permanent.

Issue Preclusion *See* collateral estoppel.

J

Johnson Act of 1934 A statute providing that federal district courts cannot enjoin an order issued by a state administrative body affecting rates charged by a public utility. 28 U.S.C.A. § 1342.

Judicial Review The principle that courts may examine the constitutionality of the actions of the executive and the legislature. Courts will decline to rule on those issues which are purely political questions. *See* political question.

Jurisdictional Amount Requirement The dictate that a case may be heard in federal court only if a specified monetary amount is in controversy. Presently, the requirement appears in the general diversity statute, 28 U.S.C.A. § 1332, which provides that the amount in controversy must exceed $10,000, exclusive of interests and costs.

L

Legal Certainty Test A means of determining whether the jurisdictional amount has been met. It provides that the amount claimed in the complaint will control unless it appears to a "legal certainty" that the claim is for less than the minimal amount necessary to establish jurisdiction.

Legislative Courts Federal courts whose judges lack constitutional protections of salary and tenure, under authority other than Article III, usually Article I and the "necessary and proper" clause. Congress has the power to make all laws necessary to execute such courts' functions, and it may require such courts to perform non-judicial activities. Examples are the territorial courts, the tax Court and the local courts of the District of Columbia.

M

Manufactured Diversity The improper or collusive creation of diversity of citizenship for the sole or primary purpose of obtaining federal court jurisdiction. Such a practice is prohibited by 28 U.S.C.A. § 1359.

Mootness Doctrine The principle that when the matter in dispute has already been resolved, there is no actual controversy that would be affected by a judicial decision, and federal courts will not exercise their jurisdiction. Although federal courts will not hear any case that has been mooted, they may exercise their jurisdiction when the behavior is likely to recur but to continually evade review.

O

Our Federalism *See* comity.

P

Pendent Jurisdiction The extension of federal court power to a dispute over which the court has no independent jurisdiction, when the dispute and one that does fall within the federal court's jurisdiction derive from a common nucleus of operative fact. However, though a federal court possesses *power* to exercise pendent jurisdiction, it may in its *discretion* decline to exercise it if to do so would unduly burden the court or cause undue confusion. Traditionally, the concept has applied only to suits between a single plaintiff and single defendant. *See also* "ancillary jurisdiction" and "pendent party" jurisdiction.

Pendent Party Jurisdiction Extension of federal jurisdiction in a case between parties properly in federal court to a claim by or against an additional litigant, over which the federal courts lacks independent subject matter jurisdiction. The Supreme Court held in *Aldinger v. Howard* that pendent party jurisdiction may not be employed to exercise jurisdiction over a state tort claim against a municipality as part of a civil rights suit under 42 U.S.C.A. § 1983 against a state officer, and expressed serious doubt concerning the use of the doctrine in most other contexts. However, the Court indicated that the principle may be used in cases of exclusive federal jurisdiction.

Political Question Doctrine The principle that a federal court will refuse to decide issues which it determines are committed to other branches of the government by the Constitution, or for which no judicially discoverable and manageable standards can be found, or where judicial determination may create enforcement difficulties or institutional conflicts.

Pullman Abstention The doctrine that a federal court may stay a case involving a federal constitutional question to give the state courts the opportunity to interpret an ambiguous state law which can be construed in a manner which will render it constitutional, although unconstitutional constructions are also possible. *See also* "England Procedure."

R

Removal The process authorizing a case to be transferred from state to federal court before a final decision occurs. *See also* "Civil Rights Removal".

Res Judicata The principle that a final judgment by a court of competent jurisdiction is an absolute bar to a subsequent action involving the same cause of action between the same parties or their privies.

Ripeness The principle that the federal courts require an actual, present controversy, and therefore will not act when the issue is only hypothetical or the existence of a controversy merely speculative.

Rules of Decision Act A statute that provides that state law shall be regarded as the rules of decision in a federal court unless the federal Constitution, a treaty of the United States, or an act of Congress otherwise requires or provides. 28 U.S.C.A. § 1652. Courts have used federal statutes which are indirectly implicated in a case as the basis of developing a federal common law in order to circumvent the act's apparent stringent prohibition of such common law.

S

Standing The principle that only a party with a tangible and legally protectible interest has the capacity to obtain judicial resolution of a controversy. The plaintiff must be able to show that he has suffered or will suffer actual injury and that there is a causal nexus between the injury suffered and the conduct complained of. A taxpayer who challenges the constitutionality of a federal action must establish a logical link between his status as a taxpayer and the type of federal action he is challenging. He must also prove that there is a nexus between his "status and the precise nature of the constitutional infringement alleged." *Flast v. Cohen*, 392 U.S. 83 (1968). Within the limits of the case-or-controversy requirement of Article III, Congress may grant an express right of action to those who would otherwise meet these requirements. *See also* "third party standing."

State Sovereign Immunity The principle that there can be no legal action against a state unless it has consented to the suit. The doctrine has a common law basis and, to an undefined extent, may have received some level of constitutional protection in the Eleventh Amendment. Additionally, certain Supreme Court decisions have held that a state may implicitly waive its sovereign immunity by participation in a federal program instituted by Congress under its Article I powers.

Supremacy Clause Article VI, clause 2 of the Constitution, providing that the Constitution, treaties and laws of the United States are the "supreme law of the land; and the Judges in every State shall be bound thereby, any thing in the Constitution or laws of any State to the contrary notwithstanding."

T

Tax Injunction Act of 1937 A statute that mandates that federal district courts not interfere with the assessment or collection of any state tax where a plain, speedy and efficient remedy is available in the state courts. 28 U.S.C.A. § 1341.

Taxpayer Standing *See* "Standing".

Thibodaux Abstention The judge-made principle that a federal court has the discretion to abstain in order to allow state courts to decide difficult issues of public importance that, if decided by the federal court, could result in unnecessary friction between state and federal authorities.

Third-Party Standing Assertion of one individual's right by another. Traditionally, third-party standing has not been allowed in federal court. However, on occasion the practice is allowed, in order to protect important interests that might otherwise be undermined. The classic example is the First Amendment overbreadth doctrine, which allows an individual who could constitutionally be prosecuted for his conduct to challenge a statute on its face because it reaches constitutionally protected, as well as unprotected conduct.

V

Venue The particular place within a jurisdiction in which a court may adjudicate a cause of action. In the federal courts, the term refers to the district in which suit is brought. Venue may be determined by where the action arose or where the parties reside or conduct their business. The venue statute for civil actions in federal district courts is 28 U.S.C.A. § 1391.

W

Well-Pleaded Complaint Rule The principle that the federal courts have federal question jurisdiction only when the plaintiff's complaint, properly drawn, establishes the presence of a controlling issue of federal law. Though the general federal question statute, 28 U.S.C.A. § 1331, makes no explicit reference to the requirement, the Supreme Court has construed the statute to impose the requirement.

Y

Younger Doctrine The principle, developed by the Supreme Court in *Younger v. Harris* and other cases, that federal courts should not interfere with an ongoing state criminal proceeding, either by injunction or declaratory relief, unless the prosecution has been brought in bad faith or as harassment. The *Younger* doctrine has also been applied in civil actions where the state is a party and important state substantive goals are implicated.

APPENDIX D

TEXT CORRELATION CHART

Federal Jurisdiction Black Letter Series	P. Bator, P. Mishkin, D. L. Shapiro, & H. Wechsler, The Federal Courts and the Federal System (2d ed. 1973)	D. Currie, Federal Courts: Cases and Materials (1982)	C. McCormack, J. Chadbourn, & C. Wright, Federal Courts: Cases and Materials (7th ed. 1982)	M. Redish, Federal Courts: Cases, Comments, and Questions (1983)	W. McCormack, Federal Courts (1984)	H. Fink, M. Tushnet, Federal Jurisdiction: Policy and Practice (1984)
I. Problems of Judicial Review	108–120, 140–241, 1047–1048	12–19, 33–110	11, 20–23, 39–61, 494–495, 506–511	1–137	143–150	275–397
II. Congressional Power to Regulate Federal Jurisdiction	309–356, 360–375, 400–415, 418–420	111–125, 148–159	6, 8n, 889–892	138–206	73–102	53–92
III. Legislative Courts	326, 375–385, 392–415	127–148	93–104	207–261	73–80	228–258
IV. Federal Question Jurisdiction	844–926	160–232	105–185	319–362	104–151, 424–425	459–481
V. Diversity Jurisdiction	1050–1102	252–368	186–233	424–461	80–83, 46–52, 217–223, 426, 154–191	401–458
VI. Pendent and Ancillary Jurisdiction	917–927, 1067–1076, 1078–1080	216–221, 227–228, 303–313	145, 146, 150, 189, 266, 783	462–509	193–194, 210, 212–216, 217–224, 226–227	476–481, 528–549
VII. Jurisdictional Amount	31, 33, 430–431, 951–955, 960–962, 1050–1051	349–368	234–271	510–533	185–191	452–458
VIII. Supreme Court Jurisdiction	242–308, 439–662, 1539–1629	767, 773–813, 819–829	889–980	279–318	1–2	817–874
IX. State Courts and Federal Power	431–438, 538–573	208–211, 523–529	386–390, 422–426	262–278	521–525, 105–106, 400–408	3–19

Federal Jurisdiction Black Letter Series	P. Bator, P. Mishkin, D. L. Shapiro, & H. Wechsler, The Federal Courts and the Federal System (2d ed. 1973)	D. Currie, Federal Courts: Cases and Materials (1982)	C. McCormack, J. Chadbourn, & C. Wright, Federal Courts: Cases and Materials (7th ed. 1982)	M. Redish. Federal Courts: Cases, Comments, and Questions (1983)	W. McCormack, Federal Courts (1984)	H. Fink, M. Tushnet, Federal Jurisdiction: Policy and Practice (1984)
X. State Sovereign Immunity and the Eleventh Amendment	926–947	530–613	427–459	534–585	423–479	117–161
XI. Abstention	233–241, 985–1009	614–772	463–535	586–622	484–486, 521–525	681–694
XII. The Anti-Injunction Statute	966, 1234–1238, 1245–1254	687–710, 737	391–437	623–658	400–422	638–645
XIII. "Our Federalism" The Doctrine of *Younger v. Harris*	1021–1029	710–741	494–545	659–727	400–408	615–638
XIV. Removal Jurisdiction	422, 833–840, 1195–1199	206–207	272–333	625–626, 634	95–101	480–506
XV. Civil Rights Removal Jurisdiction	423, 1218–1230	748–752	273–319	788–812		502–505
XVI. Habeas Corpus	1424–1538	833–904	546–579	728–787	499–510	716–816
XVII. The Law to be Applied in the Federal Courts: The *Erie* Doctrine	691–754	387–423	595–660	365, 422, 425	45–54, 60–63, 137–138	163–201
XVIII. Federal Common Law	756–832	168, 424–460, 495–509	661–703	362–423	137–142	30–33

APPENDIX E

TABLE OF CASES

Ableman v. Booth, 109
Adler v. Board of Education, 31
Aldinger v. Howard, 78, 79, 80, 101
Allegheny, County of v. Frank Mashuda Co., 129
Allen v. Baltimore & Ohio Railroad, 120
American Fire & Casualty Co. v. Finn, 154
American Insurance Co. v. Canter, 48
American Well Works Co. v. Layne and Bowler Co., 58, 59
Atlantic Coast Line R.R. v. Brotherhood of Locomotive Engineers, 134, 135

Baker v. Carr, 33, 34, 35
Banco Nacional de Cuba v. Sabbatino, 187
Bank of America National Trust & Savings Association v. Parnell, 186
Bank of the United States v. Deveaux, 64, 65
Barber v. Barber, 67
Battaglia v. General Motors Corp., 42
Bernhardt v. Polygraphic Co. of America, Inc., 174

Bivens v. Six Unknown Named Agents of Federal Bureau of Narcotics, 189, 190
Bosch, Estate of, Commissioner v., 182
Broadrick v. Oklahoma, 30
Brown v. Allen, 166
Burford v. Sun Oil Co., 13, 126, 129, 130, 192
Bush v. Lucas, 190
Byrd v. Blue Ridge Rural Electric Cooperative, Inc., 17, 18, 174, 175, 176, 178, 180

Carlson v. Green, 190
Chapman v. Barney, 66
Charles Dowd Box Co. v. Courtney, 108
Chisholm v. Georgia, 11, 116, 117
City of (see name of city)
Claflin v. Houseman, 107, 110
Clearfield Trust Co. v. United States, 185, 186
Cohen v. Beneficial Industrial Loan Corp., 94
Colorado River Water Conservation District v. United States, 126, 130
Commissioner v. _____ (see opposing party)
Construction & General Laborers' Union v. Curry, 95
Corabi v. Auto Racing, Inc., 70

County of (see name of county)
Cousins v. Wigoda, 34
Cox Broadcasting Corp. v. Cohn, 95, 96
Crowell v. Benson, 44, 45, 49

Dahnke-Walker Milling Co. v. Bondurant, 93
Daniels v. Allen, 168
Davis v. Passman, 189
DeFunis v. Odegaard, 31
Dice v. Akron, Canton & Youngstown R.R. Co., 112
Dick Meyers Towing Service, Inc. v. United States, 80
Dombrowski v. Pfister, 141, 142
Donovan v. City of Dallas, 138
Doran v. Salem Inn, Inc., 144
Douglas v. City of Jeannette, 141
Douglas v. New York, N.H. & H.R.R., 112
Duke Power Co. v. Carolina Environmental Study Group, Inc., 28

Edelman v. Jordan, 92, 121, 124
Employees of Department of Public Health & Welfare v. Department of Public Health & Welfare, 118, 123
England v. Louisiana State Board of Medical Examiners, 131

Erie Railroad Co. v. Tompkins, 17, 18, 172, 173, 174, 176, 178, 184
Estate of (see name of party)
Ex parte (see name of party)

Fair Assessment in Real Estate Association, Inc. v. McNary, 137
Fay v. Noia, 17, 168, 169
Federated Department Stores, Inc. v. Moitie, 152
Fenner v. Boykin, 141
Fiske v. Kansas, 100
Fitzpatrick v. Bitzer, 119, 124
Flast v. Cohen, 27
Forgay v. Conrad, 94
Franchise Tax Board v. Construction Laborers Vacation Trust for Southern California, 60
Francis v. Henderson, 169
Freeman v. Howe, 76
Frothingham v. Mellon, 27

Garcia v. San Antonio Metropolitan Transit Authority, 111
Georgia v. Rachel, 160, 161
Gerstein v. Pugh, 143
Gibbs v. United Mine Workers, 101
Gilligan v. Morgan, 34
Glidden Co. v. Zdanok, 49
Goldwater v. Carter, 34
Greenwood, City of v. Peacock, 161
Griffin v. McCoach, 181
Guaranty Trust Co. of New York v. York, 17, 173, 174, 175, 178
Gully v. First National Bank in Meridian, 59

Hanna v. Plumer, 18, 176, 177, 178, 179, 180
Hans v. Louisiana, 117, 118
Harman v. Forssenius, 127
Henry v. Mississippi, 98, 99
Herb v. Pitcairn, 97, 112
Hicks v. Miranda, 92, 144
Hinderlider v. La Plata River & Cherry Creek Ditch Co., 184, 189
Howard v. Lyons, 187
Huffman v. Pursue, Ltd., 145, 146
Hurn v. Oursler, 74
Hutto v. Finney, 121

Illinois v. City of Milwaukee, 90, 91, 189

Johnson v. Mississippi, 162
Juidice v. Vail, 146

Kermarec v. Compagnie Generale Transatlantique, 188
Kerotest Manufacturing Co. v. C-O-Two Fire Equipment Co., 138
Kimbell Foods, Inc., United States v., 186

Klaxon Co. v. Stentor Electric Manufacturing Co., 180
Klein, United States v., 43
Kline v. Burke Construction Co., 137
Kossick v. United Fruit Co., 189
Kramer v. Caribbean Mills, Inc., 69

Lear Inc. v. Adkins, 109
Lehman Brothers v. Schein, 132, 182
Leiter Minerals, Inc. v. United States, 134
Lockerty v. Phillips, 39
Los Angeles, County of v. Davis, 32
Louisiana Power & Light Co. v. City of Thibodaux, 13, 126, 128, 129
Louisville, Cincinnati & Charleston Railroad Co. v. Letson, 65
Louisville & Nashville Railroad v. Mottley Co., 60, 152
Luther v. Borden, 33

McCardle, Ex parte, 40, 41, 51
McClung v. Silliman, 110
McSparran v. Weist, 70
Marbury v. Madison, 90
Martin v. Hunter's Lessee, 111
Mason v. American Wheel Works, 182
Mercantile National Bank v. Langdeau, 95
Michigan v. Long, 100
Middlesex County Ethics Committee v. Garden State Bar Association, 147
Milwaukee, City of v. Illinois and Michigan, 189
Minneapolis & St. Louis R. Co. v. Bombolis, 113
Missouri ex rel. Southern Ry. v. Mayfield, 112
Mitchum v. Foster, 136, 140
Mondou v. New York, N.H. & H.R.R., 111
Monell v. Department of Social Services of the City of New York, 79
Monroe v. Pape, 79
Moore v. New York Cotton Exchange, 76
Moore v. Sims, 146
Moses H. Cone Memorial Hospital v. Mercury Construction Corp., 131
Murdock v. City of Memphis, 96

National League of Cities v. Usery, 111
National Mutual Insurance Co. v. Tidewater Transfer Co., 43
Navarro Savings Association v. Lee, 66
Nelson v. Keefer, 84

Nevada, United States v., 91
New York v. Ferber, 30, 77
NLRB v. Nash-Finch Co., 134
Northern Pipeline Construction Co. v. Marathon Pipe Line Co., 49, 50

Ohio v. Wyandotte Chemicals Corp., 91
Osborn v. Bank of the United States, 56, 73
Owen Equipment & Erection Co. v. Kroger, 77, 78, 79

Palmore v. United States, 49
Parden v. Terminal Railway, 122, 123
Pennhurst State School & Hospital v. Halderman, 121
Phillips, Nizer, Benjamin, Krim & Ballon v. Rosenstiel, 67
Powell v. McCormack, 35
Preiser v. Rodriguez, 165

Quern v. Jordan, 124

Radio Station WOW, Inc. v. Johnson, 94, 95
Railroad Commission of Texas v. Pullman, 12, 13, 126, 127, 128, 129, 192
Raines, United States v., 29
Reetz v. Bozanick, 128
Rizzo v. Goode, 146
Roe v. Wade, 31, 32
Rogers v. Alabama, 98
Rose v. Lundy, 166
Rose v. Mitchell, 167
Rosewell v. La Salle National Bank, 137
Royall, Ex parte, 165

St. Paul Mercury Indemnity Co. v. Red Cab Co., 83, 84
Samuels v. Mackell, 140, 144
SCRAP, United States v., 29
Sheldon v. Sill, 39
Shoshone Mining Co. v. Rutter, 59
Sibbach v. Wilson & Co., 179
Sierra Club v. Morton, 29
Simon v. Eastern Kentucky Welfare Rights Organization, 28
Skelly Oil Co. v. Phillips Petroleum Co., 60
Smith v. Kansas City Title & Trust Co., 59
Smith v. Sperling, 64
Snyder v. Harris, 87, 88
Sosna v. Iowa, 32
South Carolina v. Regan, 91
Southern Pacific Co. v. Jensen, 188
Southern Pacific Terminal Co. v. Interstate Commerce Commission, 31
Spock v. David, 82

TABLE OF CASES

Standard Dredging Corp. v. Murphy, 188
State Farm Fire & Casualty Co. v. Tashire, 63
Steffel v. Thompson, 144, 145
Stone v. Powell, 167
Strauder v. West Virginia, 159, 161
Strawbridge v. Curtuss, 62
Sullivan v. Little Hunting Park, Inc., 98
Supreme Tribe of Ben-Hur v. Cauble, 78
Swift v. Tyson, 17, 18, 172, 173, 180, 184

Tarble's Case, 109, 110, 111
Tennessee v. Davis, 110, 150
Testa v. Katt, 111
Texas v. White, 34
Textile Workers Union v. Lincoln Mills, 57
Toucey v. New York Life Insurane Co., 134, 135
Townsend v. Sain, 166, 167

Trafficante v. Metropolitan Life Insurance Co., 26
Trainor v. Hernandez, 143, 146

United Mine Workers of America v. Gibbs, 74, 76
United Public Workers of America v. Mitchell, 30
United States v. _____ (see opposing party)
United States Parole Commission v. Geraghty, 32
United Steelworkers of America, AFL–CIO v. R.H. Bouligny, Inc., 66

Valley Forge Christian College v. Americans United for Separation of Church and State Inc., 27
Vendo Co. v. Lektro-Vend Corp., 136
Virginia v. Rives, 159, 161

W.T. Grant Co., United States v., 32
Wainwright v. Sykes, 17, 99, 168, 169
Walker v. Armco Steel Corp., 179, 180
Warth v. Seldin, 28
Wilburn Boat Co. v. Fireman's Fund Insurance Co., 188
Will v. Calvert Fire Insurance Co., 130, 131
Williams v. United States, 49
Wolff v. McDonnell, 166
Wooley v. Maynard, 144, 145

Yakus v. United States, 43
Yazell, United States v., 186
Young, Ex parte, 120, 121, 122
Younger v. Harris, 14, 140, 142, 143, 144, 145, 146, 147, 190, 192

Zablocki v. Redhail, 144
Zahn v. International Peper Co., 87, 88
Zucht v. King, 92